W9-CRN-749

The Written Word III

The Written Word III

BASED ON
THE AMERICAN HERITAGE DICTIONARY

Houghton Mifflin Company · Boston

Editor for the revised edition, Karen Stray Nolting.

Library of Congress Cataloging-in-Publication Data

The Written word III : based on the American heritage dictionary.
   p.   cm.
  Includes bibliographical references.
  ISBN 0-395-53958-7
  1. English language—Usage. 2. English language—Grammar—1950– 3. Report writing. I. American Heritage dictionary. II. Title: Written word three. III.Title: Written word 3.
PE1460.W76   1990
428.2—dc20   90-4154
                                     CIP

Manufactured in the United States of America

Contents

Introduction

The Written Word III is the third edition of a widely respected guide to the skills necessary for using language effectively: grammar, spelling, usage, word formation, writing, and research. It has been revised and updated to reflect the best current advice on writing clearly.

The first part of *The Written Word III*, "The Mechanics of Writing," analyzes the overall structural aspects of writing. This section provides you with the basic tools for spelling, using, and styling English correctly. This section includes a "Usage Guide" based on the recommendations of *The American Heritage Dictionary*'s celebrated Usage Panel; rules for writing numbers and compound words; a list of commonly used prefixes and suffixes; the basic rules of standard English grammar and sentence structure; and a sound map to help you find a word in the dictionary if you are uncertain of its spelling.

"How it is Written," the second part of *The Written Word III*, provides samples of writing used in schools and offices, including resumes, business letters, minutes, and reports. This section also explains how to plan, research, write, and index a research paper, as well as how to document sources. *The Written Word III* includes both the traditional method of footnoting sources as well as the newer method of parenthetical documentation within the text. The material discussing the newer method is taken from Joseph F. Trimmer, *A Guide to MLA Documentation* (Houghton Mifflin Company, 1989). The section concludes with an expanded and updated guide to basic reference works.

The last section of *The Word Book III* consists of appendixes, including a list of abbreviations; a guide to the metric system; and tables of symbols and signs, Roman numerals, national holidays, and units of currency.

The Written Word III is intended to be a reference work for all who wish to develop the ability to write effectively and express themselves clearly.

The Mechanics
of Writing

Guide to Spelling

To write correctly you must have (or find) the word. You must also know how to syllabicate it, because it is often necessary to divide the word at the end of a line. Words are divided only at the end of a syllable, and there are rules covering division for different situations that may arise.

It is always preferable to avoid division, but often this is not possible. Certain divisions are even done purposely: for example, in legal documents words are sometimes divided at the end of one page and carried over to the beginning of the next page to show the authenticity and continuity of that document.

Words are often divided according to pronunciation. Words that look alike may be syllabicated differently, and in other cases the syllabication may change according to the context of the sentence in which the words are used: for example, the words *project, progress, refuse, present, re-collect* and *recollect*.

If you do not know the syllabication of a word, look it up in your *Word Book* (Houghton Mifflin Company) which lists most of the words you will need. If the word is not there, you should then turn to your *American Heritage Dictionary* (Houghton Mifflin).

Words must of necessity be divided in order to justify the right-hand margin of printed material: this prevents a ragged right margin and presents a pleasing and attractive appearance to a typewritten (business) letter. In the preparation of manuscript or copy for printing or publication and in transcription the following rules are generally followed and will aid you in this preparation.

Rules for dividing words, dates, and numbers

The rules that follow are intended to offer writers, editors, secretaries, and proofreaders a guide to traditional practice in word division. The general principles stated here reflect conservative practices followed by printers and publishers and not the comprehensive syllabication indicated in *The American Heritage Dictionary* and *The Word Book,* which reflects the phonetic structure of the word. However, word breaks indicated here will always coincide with one or more syllable divisions as shown in these other books.

1. Never divide a word of one syllable or a word that is pronounced as one syllable:

   | breadth | mashed | point | cough |
   | horde | yipes | fringe | vibes |

2. Words beginning or ending with a single-letter syllable should never be divided before or after the single letter:

   ane-mia, *not* a-nemia *or* anemi-a
   uto-pia, *not* u-topia *or* utopi-a

3. Words like *area, Ohio, ego, ogre* should not be divided at all, because no matter how the word is

divided there will be a single vowel either at the end of a line or the beginning of the next line:

abash	idea	oozy
abet	idler	open
abide	idyll	ozone
able	iota	unique
above	Iowa	unit
easy	ivy	unite
echo	oblige	Ural
Eden	oblique	usurp
ibis	ocean	uric
icy	oleo	yeasty

4. A word with an internal single-syllable vowel should be divided after the vowel:

> visi-tation, *not* vis-itation
> oxy-gen, *not* ox-ygen
> maxi-mum, *not* max-imum

5. The preceding rule does not apply to the suffixes *-able* and *-ible* or to words in which the vowel standing alone is the first syllable of a root word. Then the division is *before* that vowel, not *after* it.

> account-able
> answer-able
> prob-able
> collaps-ible
> divis-ible

However there are many words ending in *-able*

and *-ible* where the *a* and *i* do not stand alone as a single syllable. They are divided after the vowel:

> capa-ble
> horri-ble
> charita-ble
> ineligi-ble

When in doubt about any of the *-able, -ible* words, look them up (see p. 34).

6. The following final syllables are never divided in editing, proofreading, and transcription, although in poetry they are sometimes pronounced as if they had two syllables:

-ceous (herba-ceous)	*-gious* (egre-gious)
-cial (cru-cial)	*-sial* (controver-sial)
-cion (coer-cion)	*-sion* (tor-sion)
-cious (deli-cious)	*-tial* (bes-tial)
-geous (gor-geous)	*-tion* (ra-tion)
-gion (reli-gion)	*-tious* (adventi-tious)

7. When a final consonant of a word is doubled in the formation of inflected forms by the addition of a suffix, the division is between the consonants:

red-der	thin-nest	bar-ring
control-ling	dim-mer	regret-ted

But if the root word ends in a double or single

6

consonant, division is after the consonants or consonant:

fall-en	coerc-ing
confess-ing	confid-ing

When there are double interior consonants the division is between the first two consonants:

foun-tain	hin-drance
ter-res-trial	confes-sion
recom-mend	bat-tlement
expres-sive *but*	
express-way	

When *-ing, -ed,* or *-er* are added to a verb ending in *-le,* the division comes before one or more of the consonants, as in the preceding rule:

> gig-gled
> daw-dled
> whis-tler
> fiz-zling
> crum-bling

8. Hyphenated words are divided at the hyphen:

all-fired	window-dressing
self-control	public-spirited
strait-laced	wash-and-wear
make-believe	tam-o'-shanter *(divide at*
ready-made	*either hyphen)*

Compound words, if possible, are divided between their elements:

steel-worker	under-cover
barn-yard	over-estimate
wing-span	hail-fellow

Many words are made up of a prefix plus a word. Division is always after the whole prefix.

The most commonly used prefixes are:

all-	infra-	pro-
ante-	inter-	pseudo-
anti-	intra-	re-
bi-	micro-	self-
co-	mid-	semi-
contra-	neo-	sub-
counter-	non-	super-
de-	out-	trans-
extra-	over-	tri-
hyper-	post-	ultra-
hypo-	pre-	un-

9. Do not divide abbreviations or acronyms:

UNESCO	FAA
WAVES	Ph.D.
OCS	p.m.
D.A.R.	D.D.S.

10. Do not divide numbers of less than five numerals. If a number has five or more digits, divide after

a comma:

346,-422,898 *or* 346,422,-898   10,-000

In business correspondence numbers should never be divided.

11. Do not divide dates between the month and the day, but between the day and year in text.

October 12,   *not*   October
1984   12, 1984

In business correspondence these should never be divided.

12. The division of proper nouns follows the rules for division of common nouns. In business correspondence, however, the division of proper nouns should not be necessary and well might result in confusion or error.

13. If it is necessary to divide a proper name formed of initials and a last name, divide after the initials:

T. S.   *not*   T.
Eliot   S. Eliot

e. e.   *not*   e.
cummings   e. cummings

Try to avoid separating a name from a title:

Dr. Martin   Ms. Jones
John Martin, M.D.   Rev. Smythe

In business correspondence these should not be divided.

14. The division of contractions is to be avoided if possible. If it is necessary to divide a contraction, it should be done according to the syllabication:

> should-n't
> have-n't
> Hallow-e'en

In business correspondence these should never be divided.

15. Do not divide years, time, temperatures, latitudes, longitudes, compass directions, or similar units.

A.D. 19	4:30 p.m.	40°28′
NNW	28°C	

Commonly misspelled words

Some words are more difficult to spell than others and are often misspelled by many people. These commonly misspelled words, each followed by its correct syllabic division according to the preceding rules, are listed below.

Word	*Correct division*
abscess	ab-scess
absence	ab-sence
accede	ac-cede
accept	ac-cept
acceptance	ac-cep-tance
accessible	ac-ces-si-ble
accessory	ac-ces-so-ry
accidentally	ac-ci-den-tal-ly
accommodate	ac-com-mo-date
accordance	ac-cor-dance
according	ac-cord-ing
accrued	ac-crued
accumulate	ac-cu-mu-late
accuracy	ac-cu-ra-cy
accustomed	ac-cus-tomed
achievement	achieve-ment
acknowledgment	ac-knowl-edg-ment
acquaintance	ac-quain-tance
acquiesce	ac-qui-esce
acquire	ac-quire
across	*none*
adapt	*none*
address	ad-dress
adequate	ade-quate
adjourned	ad-journed
adjustment	ad-just-ment
admirable	ad-mi-ra-ble
advertisement	ad-ver-tise-ment
advice (*noun*)	ad-vice

11

Word	Correct division
advisable	ad-vis-able
advise (*verb*)	ad-vise
adviser	ad-vis-er
advisor	ad-vis-or
advisory	ad-vi-so-ry
affidavit	af-fi-da-vit
aggravate	ag-gra-vate
agreeable	agree-able
allotment	al-lot-ment
allotted	al-lot-ted
allowable	al-low-able
allowance	al-low-ance
all right	*none*
almost	al-most
already	al-ready
altogether	al-to-geth-er
amendment	amend-ment
among	*none*
analysis	analy-sis
analyze	ana-lyze
anesthetic	an-es-thet-ic
announcement	an-nounce-ment
annoyance	an-noy-ance
annual	an-nu-al
antarctic	ant-arc-tic
anticipate	an-tici-pate
anticipation	an-tici-pa-tion
anxiety	anxie-ty *or* anxi-ety
anxious	anx-ious
apologize	apolo-gize
appearance	ap-pear-ance
appetite	ap-pe-tite
appliance	ap-pli-ance
applicable	ap-pli-ca-ble
applicant	ap-pli-cant
appointment	ap-point-ment
appraisal	ap-prais-al
appreciable	ap-pre-cia-ble
appropriate	ap-pro-pri-ate
approximately	ap-proxi-mate-ly
architect	ar-chi-tect

Word	Correct division
arctic	arc-tic
argument	ar-gu-ment
arrangement	ar-range-ment
article	ar-ti-cle
artificial	ar-ti-fi-cial
ascertain	as-cer-tain
assassin	as-sas-sin
assess	as-sess
assessment	as-sess-ment
assessor	as-ses-sor
assignment	as-sign-ment
assistance	as-sis-tance
associate	as-so-ci-ate
assured	as-sured
athletics	ath-let-ics
attendance	at-ten-dance
attention	at-ten-tion
attorneys	at-tor-neys
authorize	au-thor-ize
auxiliary	aux-il-ia-ry
available	avail-able
bankruptcy	bank-rupt-cy
bargain	bar-gain
basis	ba-sis
beginning	be-gin-ning
believe	be-lieve
beneficial	bene-fi-cial
beneficiary	bene-fi-ci-ary
benefit	bene-fit
benefited	bene-fit-ed
bookkeeper	book-keep-er
bough	*none*
bouillon	bouil-lon
brief	*none*
brilliant	bril-liant
brochure	bro-chure
budget	budg-et
bulletin	bul-le-tin
bureau	bu-reau
business	busi-ness
businessman	busi-ness-man

Word	Correct division
businesswoman	busi-ness-wom-an
busy	*none*
cafeteria	cafe-te-ria
calendar	cal-en-dar
campaign	cam-paign
cancelable	can-cel-able
canceled	can-celed
cancellation	can-cel-la-tion
candidate	can-di-date
canister	can-is-ter
cannot	can-not
capacity	ca-paci-ty
capital (*city*)	capi-tal
capitol (*building*)	capi-tol
career	ca-reer
casserole	cas-se-role
casualty	casu-al-ty
catalogue	cata-logue
census	cen-sus
cessation	ces-sa-tion
challenge	chal-lenge
characteristic	char-ac-ter-is-tic
choice	*none*
choose	*none*
circuit	cir-cuit
circumstances	cir-cum-stances
civilized	civi-lized
client	cli-ent
clientele	cli-en-tele
collateral	col-lat-er-al
colloquial	col-lo-qui-al
colonel	colo-nel
column	col-umn
coming	com-ing
commission	com-mis-sion
commitment	com-mit-ment
committee	com-mit-tee
comparable	com-pa-ra-ble
comparatively	com-para-tive
comparison	com-pari-son
compelled	com-pelled

Word	*Correct division*
compelling	com-pel-ling
competent	com-pe-tent
competitor	com-peti-tor
complaint	com-plaint
compliment	com-pli-ment
compromise	com-pro-mise
concede	con-cede
conceivable	con-ceiv-able
concern	con-cern
concession	con-ces-sion
concurred	con-curred
concurrence	con-cur-rence
condemn	con-demn
condescend	con-de-scend
conference	con-fer-ence
confident	con-fi-dent
confidential	con-fi-den-tial
congratulate	con-gratu-late
conscience	con-science
conscientious	con-sci-en-tious
conscious	con-scious
consensus	con-sen-sus
consequence	con-se-quence
consequently	con-se-quent-ly
consignment	con-sign-ment
consistent	con-sis-tent
continuous	con-tinu-ous
controlling	con-trol-ling
controversy	con-tro-ver-sy
convenience	con-ven-ience
convenient	con-ven-ient
cordially	cor-dial-ly
corporation	cor-po-ra-tion
correlate	cor-re-late
correspondence	cor-re-spon-dence
correspondent	cor-re-spon-dent
corresponding	cor-re-spond-ing
council (*group*)	coun-cil
counsel (*advice*)	coun-sel
counterfeit	coun-ter-feit
courteous	cour-te-ous

Word	Correct division
courtesy	cour-te-sy
coverage	cov-er-age
creditor	credi-tor
crisis	cri-sis
criticism	criti-cism
criticize	criti-cize
curiosity	cu-ri-osi-ty
current	cur-rent
customer	cus-tom-er
cylinder	cy-lin-der
debtor	debt-or
deceive	de-ceive
decide	de-cide
decision	de-ci-sion
deductible	de-ducti-ble
defendant	de-fen-dant
defer	de-fer
deferred	de-ferred
deferring	de-fer-ring
deficit	defi-cit
definite	defi-nite
definitely	defi-nite-ly
delegate	dele-gate
dependent	de-pend-ent
depositors	de-posi-tors
descend	de-scend
description	de-scrip-tion
desirable	de-sir-able
despair	de-spair
deteriorate	de-te-rio-rate
develop	de-vel-op
development	de-vel-op-ment
device (*tool*)	de-vice
devise (*make, give*)	de-vise
diaphragm	dia-phragm
diarrhea	di-ar-rhea
difference	dif-fer-ence
dilemma	di-lem-ma
dining	din-ing
director	di-rec-tor
disappear	dis-ap-pear

Word	Correct division
disappoint	dis-ap-point
discipline	dis-ci-pline
discrepancy	dis-crep-an-cy
dissatisfied	dis-sat-is-fied
dissipate	dis-si-pate
distinguish	dis-tin-guish
dormitory	dor-mi-to-ry
eagerly	ea-ger-ly
economical	eco-nomi-cal
ecstasy	ec-sta-sy
edition	edi-tion
effect	ef-fect
effervescent	ef-fer-ves-cent
efficacy	ef-fi-ca-cy
efficiency	ef-fi-cien-cy
efficient	ef-fi-cient
eligible	eli-gi-ble
eliminate	elimi-nate
ellipse	el-lipse
embarrass	em-bar-rass
emergency	emer-gen-cy
emphasis	em-pha-sis
emphasize	em-pha-size
employee	em-ploy-ee
enclose	en-close
encouraging	en-cour-ag-ing
endeavor	en-deav-or
endorsement	en-dorse-ment
enterprise	en-ter-prise
enthusiasm	en-thu-si-asm
envelop (*surround*)	en-vel-op
envelope (*paper cover*)	en-ve-lope
environment	en-vi-ron-ment
equipment	equip-ment
equipped	*none*
especially	es-pe-cial-ly
essential	es-sen-tial
esteemed	es-teemed
etiquette	eti-quette
exaggerate	ex-ag-ger-ate
exaggerating	ex-ag-ger-at-ing

17

Word	Correct division
exaggeration	ex-ag-geration
exceed	ex-ceed
excellence	ex-cel-lence
excellent	ex-cel-lent
except	ex-cept
exceptionally	ex-cep-tion-al-ly
excessive	ex-ces-sive
executive	ex-ecu-tive
exercise	ex-er-cise
exhibition	ex-hi-bi-tion
exhilarate	ex-hila-rate
exhilaration	ex-hila-ra-tion
existence	ex-is-tence
expedite	ex-pe-dite
expenditure	ex-pen-di-ture
expense	ex-pense
experience	ex-pe-ri-ence
explanation	ex-pla-na-tion
extension	ex-ten-sion
extraordinary	ex-traor-di-nary
extremely	ex-treme-ly
facilities	fa-cili-ties
fallacy	fal-la-cy
fascinate	fas-ci-nate
fascinating	fas-ci-nat-ing
favorable	fa-vor-able
favorite	fa-vor-ite
feasible	fea-si-ble
February	Feb-ru-ary
fictitious	fic-ti-tious
finally	fi-nal-ly
financier	fin-an-cier
foliage	fo-li-age
forcible	for-ci-ble
forego (*precede*)	fore-go
foreign	for-eign
forfeit	for-feit
forgo (*relinquish*)	for-go
formerly	for-mer-ly
fortunately	for-tu-nate-ly
forty	for-ty

Word	Correct division
forward	for-ward
fourth	*none*
freight	*none*
friend	*none*
fulfill	ful-fill
fulfilling	ful-fill-ing
fulfillment	ful-fill-ment
furthermore	fur-ther-more
gauge	*none*
genuine	genu-ine
government	gov-ern-ment
governor	gov-er-nor
grateful	grate-ful
grievance	griev-ance
guarantee	guar-an-tee
guerrilla	guer-ril-la
gypsy	gyp-sy
handkerchief	hand-ker-chief
handled	han-dled
haphazard	hap-haz-ard
harass	har-ass
hardware	hard-ware
hazardous	haz-ard-ous
height	*none*
hemorrhage	hem-or-rhage
hesitant	hesi-tant
hoping (*expect*)	hop-ing
hopping (*jump*)	hop-ping
hydraulic	hy-drau-lic
hygiene	hy-giene
hypocrite	hypo-crite
hypocrisy	hy-poc-ri-sy
icicle	ici-cle
identical	iden-ti-cal
illegible	il-leg-ible
immediately	im-me-di-ate-ly
immense	im-mense
imperative	im-pera-tive
impossible	im-pos-si-ble
inalienable	in-al-ien-able
inasmuch as	in-as-much (as)

Word	Correct division
incidentally	in-ci-den-tal-ly
inconvenience	in-con-ven-ience
incurred	in-curred
indebtedness	in-debt-ed-ness
indelible	in-del-ible
independent	in-de-pend-ent
indictment	in-dict-ment
indispensable	in-dis-pen-sa-ble
individual	in-di-vidu-al
inducement	in-duce-ment
inevitable	in-evi-ta-ble
inferred	in-ferred
influential	in-flu-en-tial
initial	ini-tial
inoculate	in-ocu-late
inquiry	in-quiry
installation	in-stal-la-tion
intellectual	in-tel-lec-tu-al
intelligence	in-tel-li-gence
intention	in-ten-tion
interfere	in-ter-fere
intermittent	in-ter-mit-tent
interrupted	in-ter-rupt-ed
intimate	in-ti-mate
investor	in-ves-tor
iridescent	iri-des-cent
irrelevant	ir-rele-vant
irresistible	ir-re-sis-ti-ble
itemized	item-ized
itinerary	itin-er-ary
it's	*none*
jeopardize	jeop-ard-ize
journal	jour-nal
judgment	judg-ment
justifiable	jus-ti-fi-able
knowledge	knowl-edge
laboratory	labo-ra-to-ry
legible	leg-ible
legitimate	le-giti-mate
leisure	lei-sure
length	*none*

Word	Correct division
letterhead	letter-head
liaison	li-ai-son
library	li-brary
license	li-cense
lieutenant	lieu-ten-ant
lightning	light-ning
likable	lik-able
liquefy	liq-ue-fy
livelihood	live-li-hood
loose	*none*
lose	*none*
magazine	maga-zine
maintenance	main-te-nance
manageable	man-age-able
management	man-age-ment
manufacturer	manu-fac-tur-er
manuscript	manu-script
marshal	mar-shal
mathematics	mathe-mat-ics
maximum	maxi-mum
medical	medi-cal
memorandum	memo-ran-dum
menus	men-us
merchandise	mer-chan-dise
mileage	mile-age
miniature	minia-ture
minimum	mini-mum
minuscule	min-us-cule
miscellaneous	mis-cel-la-ne-ous
mischievous	mis-chie-vous
modernize	mod-ern-ize
molecule	mole-cule
monotonous	mo-noto-nous
mortgage	mort-gage
murmur	mur-mur
mutual	mu-tu-al
necessarily	nec-es-sari-ly
necessary	nec-es-sary
negligible	neg-li-gi-ble
negotiate	ne-go-ti-ate
neighborhood	neighbor-hood , neigh-bor-hood

Word	Correct division
nevertheless	never-the-less
	nev-er-the-less
nickel	nick-el
niece	*none*
noticeable	no-tice-able
oblige	*none*
occasion	oc-ca-sion
occasionally	oc-ca-sion-al-ly
occupant	oc-cu-pant
occurred	oc-curred
occurrence	oc-cur-rence
occurring	oc-cur-ring
offense	of-fense
offering	of-fer-ing
official	of-fi-cial
omission	omis-sion
omitted	omit-ted
opportunities	op-por-tu-ni-ties
opportunity	op-por-tu-ni-ty
ordinarily	or-di-nari-ly
ordinary	or-di-nary
organization	or-gani-za-tion
organize	or-gan-ize
original	origi-nal
overdue	over-due
paid	*none*
pamphlet	pam-phlet
paradise	para-dise
parallel	par-al-lel
paralleled	par-al-leled
parallelled	par-al-lelled
parentheses	pa-ren-the-ses
parenthesis	pa-ren-the-sis
partial	par-tial
participant	par-tici-pant
participate	par-tici-pate
particularly	par-ticu-lar-ly
patronage	pa-tron-age
peaceable	peace-able
peculiar	pe-cu-liar
perceive	per-ceive

Word	Correct division
peril	per-il
permanent	per-ma-nent
permissible	per-mis-si-ble
permitted	per-mit-ted
perpendicular	per-pen-dicu-lar
perseverance	per-se-ver-ance
personal	per-son-al
personnel	per-son-nel
persuade	per-suade
petition	pe-ti-tion
phase	*none*
Philippines	Phil-ip-pines
philosophical	philo-sophi-cal
philosophy	phi-loso-phy
physician	phy-si-cian
planning	plan-ning
plateau	pla-teau
plausible	plau-si-ble
pleasant	pleas-ant
pleasure	pleas-ure
pneumonia	pneu-mo-nia
politician	poli-ti-cian
Portuguese	Por-tu-guese
possess	pos-sess
possession	pos-ses-sion
practical	prac-ti-cal
practically	prac-ti-cal-ly
practice	prac-tice
precede	pre-cede
precisely	pre-cise-ly
precision	pre-ci-sion
predecessor	prede-ces-sor
preferable	pref-er-able
preference	pref-er-ence
preferred	pre-ferred
prejudice	preju-dice
preliminary	pre-limi-nary
premium	pre-mi-um
previous	pre-vi-ous
price list	*none*
principal (*main*)	prin-ci-pal

Word	Correct division
principle (*rule*)	prin-ci-ple
prior	pri-or
privilege	privi-lege
probability	proba-bili-ty
probably	proba-bly
procedure	pro-ce-dure
proceed	pro-ceed
professor	pro-fes-sor
prominent	promi-nent
prosecute	prose-cute
psychology	psy-cholo-gy
purchase	pur-chase
pursue	pur-sue
quantity	quan-ti-ty
questionnaire	ques-tion-naire
quiet	qui-et
quite	*none*
realize	re-al-ize
reasonable	rea-son-able
receipt	re-ceipt
receive	re-ceive
receiving	re-ceiv-ing
recipe	reci-pe
recognize	rec-og-nize
recognized	rec-og-nized
recommend	rec-om-mend
recurrence	re-cur-rence
reference	ref-er-ence
referred	re-ferred
referring	re-fer-ring
regrettable	re-gret-ta-ble
reign	*none*
reimburse	re-im-burse
relevant	rele-vant
remember	re-mem-ber
remembrance	re-mem-brance
reminisce	remi-nisce
remiss	re-miss
remittance	re-mit-tance
rendezvous	ren-dez-vous
renewal	re-new-al

Word	Correct division
repetition	repe-ti-tion
representative	rep-re-sen-ta-tive
requirement	re-quire-ment
requisition	req-ui-si-tion
resistance	re-sis-tance
respectfully	re-spect-ful-ly
respectively	re-spec-tive-ly
response	re-sponse
responsibility	re-spon-si-bili-ty
responsible	re-spon-si-ble
restaurant	res-tau-rant
restaurateur	res-tau-ra-teur
reticence	reti-cence
ridiculous	ri-dicu-lous
route	*none*
salable	sal-able
salary	sala-ry
saleable	sale-able
satisfactorily	sat-is-fac-to-ri-ly
schedule	sched-ule
scissors	scis-sors
scurrilous	scur-ri-lous
secretary	sec-re-tary
securities	secu-ri-ties
seize	*none*
seized	*none*
separate	sepa-rate
sergeant	ser-geant
serviceable	serv-ice-able
shepherd	shep-herd
sheriff	sher-iff
shipment	ship-ment
shipping	ship-ping
siege	*none*
significant	sig-nifi-cant
similar	simi-lar
simultaneous	si-mul-ta-ne-ous
sincerity	sin-ceri-ty
skiing	ski-ing
skillful	skill-ful
solemn	sol-emn

Word	Correct division
someone	some-one
somewhat	some-what
sorority	so-rori-ty
specialize	spe-cial-ize
specific	spe-cif-ic
spontaneity	spon-ta-nei-ty
spontaneous	spon-ta-ne-ous
stationary (*still*)	sta-tion-ary
stationery (*supplies*)	sta-tion-ery
statistics	sta-tis-tics
statutes	stat-utes
strength	*none*
strictly	strict-ly
submitted	sub-mit-ted
subscriber	sub-scrib-er
substantial	sub-stan-tial
succeed	suc-ceed
succeeded	suc-ceed-ed
successful	suc-cess-ful
succession	suc-ces-sion
sufficient	suf-fi-cient
superintendent	su-per-in-ten-dent
supersede	su-per-sede
supervisor	su-per-vi-sor
supplement	sup-ple-ment
surprise	sur-prise
surveillance	sur-veil-lance
survey	sur-vey
suspicion	sus-pi-cion
sustenance	sus-te-nance
sympathy	sym-pa-thy
synchronous	syn-chro-nous
tariff	tar-iff
temporarily	tem-po-rari-ly
temporary	tem-po-rary
tentative	ten-ta-tive
terrestrial	ter-res-tri-al
their	*none*
there	*none*
thoroughly	thor-ough-ly
through	*none*

Word	Correct division
throughout	through-out
too (*also*)	*none*
tournament	tour-na-ment
tourniquet	tour-ni-quet
tragedy	trage-dy
tranquillity	tran-quil-li-ty
tranquilizer	tran-quil-iz-er
transferred	trans-ferred
typing	typ-ing
ultimately	ul-ti-mate-ly
unanimous	unani-mous
undoubtedly	un-doubt-ed-ly
unfortunately	un-for-tu-nate-ly
unique	*none*
unison	uni-son
unmanageable	un-man-age-able
unnecessary	un-nec-es-sary
until	un-til
urgent	ur-gent
usable	us-able
usually	usu-al-ly
utilize	util-ize
vacancy	va-can-cy
vacuum	vacu-um
vague	*none*
valuable	valu-able
various	vari-ous
vehicle	ve-hi-cle
veil	*none*
vendor	ven-dor
vicinity	vi-cini-ty
vilify	vili-fy
visible	vis-ible
volume	vol-ume
voluntary	vol-un-tary
volunteer	vol-un-teer
warehouse	ware-house
warrant	war-rant
warranty	war-ran-ty
weather (*meteorology*)	weath-er
weird	*none*

Word	Correct division
whether *(if)*	wheth-er
wholesale	whole-sale
withhold	with-hold
worthwhile	worth-while
wretched	wretch-ed
writing	writ-ing
wrought	*none*
yield	*none*

Words with confusing endings

-ance

abeyance
abidance
acceptance
accordance
acquaintance
acquittance
admittance
affiance
alliance
allowance
ambulance
appearance
assistance
assurance
attendance
balance
brilliance
capacitance
circumstance
clearance
complaisance
compliance
concordance
connivance
contrivance
conveyance
countenance
counterbalance
deliverance
discontinuance
discordance
disturbance
encumbrance
endurance
enhance
entrance
expectance
extravagance
finance

forbearance
fragrance
furtherance
grievance
ignorance
importance
inheritance
instance
insurance
intemperance
intolerance
irrelevance
issuance
maintenance
nuisance
observance
ordinance
ordnance
performance
precipitance
preponderance
pursuance
quittance
radiance
reconnaissance
redundance
relevance
reliance
reluctance
remembrance
remittance
remonstrance
renaissance
repentance
resemblance
resistance
resonance
riddance
romance

-ance

significance
substance
surveillance
sustenance
temperance
tolerance
transmittance
variance
vigilance

-ence

absence
abstinence
adherence
adolescence
affluence
audience
belligerence
benevolence
coherence
commence
competence
complacence
concurrence
condolence
confidence
confluence
conscience
consistence
continence
contingence
convergence
correspondence
credence
deference
dependence
despondence
difference
diffidence
diligence
disobedience
divergence
excellence
experience
imminence
impatience
impertinence
impotence
improvidence
impudence
incidence
incompetence
inconsequence
incontinence
independence
indifference
indolence
indulgence
inexperience
inference
influence
inherence
innocence
insistence
insolence
insurgence
intelligence
interdependence
interference
intermittence
irreverence
luminescence
magnificence
negligence
obedience
occurrence
penitence

-ence

permanence
persistence
pertinence
precedence
presence
prevalence
prominence
providence
prudence
recurrence
reference
residence

resilience
reticence
reverence
science
silence
subsistence
transcendence
transference
translucence
transparence
valence
violence

-ant

abundant
acceptant
accountant
adjutant
applicant
arrogant
assailant
attendant
benignant
claimant
coadjutant
commandant
complainant
complaisant
compliant
concomitant
conversant
covenant
currant
defendant
deodorant
descendant
determinant
discordant
disinfectant
disputant

distant
dopant
equilibrant
exorbitant
extravagant
exultant
flagrant
flippant
fragrant
gallant
hesitant
hydrant
ignorant
immigrant
important
incessant
inconstant
indignant
intolerant
intoxicant
irrelevant
irritant
itinerant
lieutenant
malignant
militant

-ant

observant
occupant
pedant
pennant
petulant
pheasant
pleasant
poignant
precipitant
predominant
pregnant
preponderant
propellant
protestant
protuberant
pursuant
quadrant
recalcitrant
redundant

relevant
reliant
reluctant
repentant
repugnant
resistant
resonant
restaurant
servant
significant
stagnant
sycophant
tenant
tolerant
triumphant
truant
vagrant
vigilant
visitant

-ent

abhorrent
absorbent
accident
affluent
antecedent
astringent
beneficent
coherent
comment
competent
complacent
component
concurrent
confident
consistent
constituent
content
contingent
convergent

corespondent
correspondent
current
decedent
dependent
despondent
deterrent
different
diffident
diligent
discontent
effervescent
eminent
equivalent
evident
expedient
existent
immanent
imminent

-ent

impatient
impertinent
improvident
imprudent
impudent
incident
inclement
incompetent
incontinent
incumbent
indecent
independent
indigent
indifferent
indolent
indulgent
inexpedient
inherent
innocent
insistent
insolent
insolvent
insurgent
intelligent
intermittent
irreverent
magnificent
malevolent

negligent
obedient
omnipotent
opponent
patient
penitent
permanent
persistent
pertinent
preeminent
propellent
provident
prudent
recurrent
remittent
repellent
resplendent
respondent
reverent
stringent
subsequent
succulent
transcendent
translucent
transparent
urgent
vehement
violent

-ible & -able

The suffix -*able* is encountered far more frequently than its complement -*ible;* hence we are listing only words ending in the latter form. Both forms are entered for words that can take either suffix with an asterisk (*) next to the preferred form.

accessible
adducible
admissible
apprehensible
audible
avertible
coercible
cohesible
collapsible
collectible* *or*
  collectable
combustible
compatible
comprehensible
compressible
conductible
contemptible
contractible
convertible
corrigible
corruptible
credible
deducible
deductible
defensible
depressible
descendible
destructible
diffusible
digestible
dirigible
discernible

discussible
dismissible
distensible
divertible
divisible
edible
educible
eligible
exhaustible
expansible
expressible
extendible
extensible
fallible
feasible
flexible
forcible
gullible
ignitible *or*
  ignitable*
impassible
impressible
includible *or*
  includable*
incontrovertible
indefeasible
indefectible
indelible
inducible
intelligible
invertible
invincible

irascible
irresistible
legible
negligible
omissible
ostensible
perceptible
perfectible
permissible
persuasible
pervertible
plausible
preventible *or*
  preventable*
producible
reducible
remissible
reprehensible
repressible
responsible
reversible
sensible
suggestible
suppressible
susceptible
suspendible
tangible
terrible
transmissible
vendible
visible

34

A sound map for poor spellers

How can you look up a word in a dictionary to check its spelling when you have to know how to spell it in order to look it up? Most spelling difficulties are caused by speech sounds that can be spelled in more than one way (the standard alphabet has twenty-six characters to represent the forty or more sounds of the English language). The following chart, although far from comprehensive, will translate sounds into their most common spellings. If you look up a word and cannot find it check the sound map and try another combination of letters that represent the same sound.

Sound	Spelling	In These Sample Words
a (as in pat)	ai	plaid
	al	half
	au	laugh
a (as in mane)	ai	plain
	ao	gaol
	au	gauge
	ay	pay
	e	suede, bouquet
	ea	break
	ei	vein
	eig	feign
	eigh	eight, neighbor
	ey	prey
a (as in care)	ae	aerial
	ai	air

Sound	Spelling	In These Sample Words
	ay	prayer, Ayrshire
	e	there
	ea	pear
	ei	their
a (as in father)	ah	**ah**
	al	balm
	e	sergeant
	ea	heart
b (as in bib)	bb	blubber
	bh	**bhang**
	pb	cupboard, raspberry
ch (as in church)	c	cello
	Cz	**Czech**
	tch	latch
	ti	question
	tu	denture
d (as in deed)	dd	muddle
	ed	mailed
e (as in pet)	a	any
	ae	aesthetic
	ai	said
	ay	says
	ea	thread
	ei	heifer
	eo	leopard
	ie	friendly
	oe	**Oedipus**
	u	burial

Sound	Spelling	In These Sample Words
e (as in be)	ae	Caesar
	ay	quay
	ea	each, beach
	ee	beet
	ei	conceit
	eo	people
	ey	key
	i	piano
	ie	siege
	oe	phoenix
f (as in fife)	ff	stiff
	gh	enough
	lf	half
	ph	photo, graph
g (as in gag)	gg	bragged
	gh	ghost
	gu	guest
	gue	epilogue
h (as in hat)	wh	who
	g	Gila monster
	j	Jerez
i (as in pit)	a	village, climate, certificate
	e	enough
	ee	been
	ia	carriage
	ie	sieve
	o	women
	u	busy
	ui	built
	y	nymph

Sound	Spelling	In These Sample Words
i (as in pie)	ai	aisle
	ay	aye, bayou
	ei	height
	ey	eye
	ie	lie
	igh	sigh, right
	is	island
	uy	buy
	y	sky
	ye	rye
i (as in pier)	e	here
	ea	ear
	ee	beer
	ei	weird
j (as in jar)	d	gradual
	dg	lodging, dodge
	di	soldier
	dj	adjective
	g	register, gem
	ge	vengeance
	gg	exaggerate
k (as in kick)	c	call, ecstasy
	cc	account
	ch	chaos, schedule
	ck	crack
	cqu	lacquer
	cu	biscuit
	lk	talk
	q	Aqaba
	qu	quay
	que	claque, plaque

Sound	Spelling	In These Sample Words
kw (as in **qu**ick)	ch	**ch**oir
	cqu	ac**qu**ire
l (as in **l**id)	ll	ta**ll**, **ll**ama, **Ll**oyd
	lh	**Lh**asa
m (as in **m**u**m**)	chm	dra**chm**
	gm	paradi**gm**
	lm	ba**lm**
	mb	plu**mb**
	mm	ha**mm**er
	mn	sole**mn**
n (as in **n**o)	gn	**gn**at
	kn	**kn**ife
	mn	**mn**emonic
	nn	ca**nn**y, i**nn**
	pn	**pn**eumonia
ng (as in thi**ng**)	n	i**n**k, a**n**chor, co**n**gress, u**n**cle
	ngue	to**ngue**
o (as in p**o**t)	a	w**a**ffle, w**a**tch, w**a**ter, wh**a**t
	ho	**ho**nest
	ou	tr**ou**gh
o (as in n**o**)	au	h**au**tboy, m**au**ve
	eau	bur**eau**, b**eau**
	eo	y**eo**man
	ew	s**ew**
	oa	f**oa**m, f**oa**l
	oe	J**oe**
	oh	**oh**
	oo	br**oo**ch
	ou	sh**ou**lder
	ough	d**ough**, bor**ough**

Sound	Spelling	In These Sample Words
	ow	low, row
	owe	owe, Marlowe
o (as in paw or for)	a	all, water
	al	talk
	ah	Utah
	ar	warm
	as	Arkansas
	au	maudlin, gaunt, automobile
	augh	caught
	aw	awful, drawn, Choctaw
	oa	oar, broad
	ough	bought, thought
oi (as in noise)	oy	boy
ou (as in out)	au	sauerkraut
	hou	hour
	ough	bough
	ow	sow, scowl
oo (as in took)	o	woman, wolf
	ou	should
	u	full, cushion
oo (as in boot)	eu	maneuver
	ew	shrew
	ieu	lieutenant
	o	do, move, two
	oe	canoe
	ou	soup, group
	ough	through
	u	rude
	ue	blue, rue
	ui	fruit, bruise

Sound	Spelling	In These Sample Words
p (as in pop)	pp	happy
r (as in roar)	rh	rhythm
	rr	cherry
	wr	write
s (as in say)	c	cellar, cent
	ce	sauce
	ps	psalm
	sc	scene, abscess
	sch	schism
	ss	pass
sh (as in ship)	ce	ocean
	ch	chandelier
	ci	special, deficient, gracious, magician
	psh	pshaw
	s	sugar
	sch	schist
	sci	conscience
	se	nauseous
	si	pension
	ss	tissue, mission
	ti	election, nation, martial
t (as in tie)	ed	stopped
	pt	ptisan
	th	Thomas
	tt	letter
	tw	two
u (as in cut)	o	son, income
	oe	does
	oo	blood
	ou	couple, trouble

Sound	Spelling	In These Sample Words
yoo (as in use)	eau	beautiful
	eu	feud
	eue	queue
	ew	pew
	ieu	adieu
	iew	view
	ue	cue
	ui	suit
	you	you, youth
	yu	yule
u (as in fur)	ear	earn, learn
	er	herd, fern, term
	eur	restaurateur
	ir	bird, first
	or	work, word
	our	journey, journal, scourge
	yr	myrtle
v (as in valve)	f	of
	ph	Stephen
w (as in with)	o	one
y (as in yes)	i	onion
	j	hallelujah
z (as in zebra)	cz	czar
	s	rise, hers
	ss	dessert
	x	xylophone
	zz	fuzz
zh	ge	garage, mirage
	s	pleasure, vision

A, e, i, o, or *u*

These vowels are often represented in phonetic transcriptions by a symbol called the schwa (ə). The schwa is used to represent the indeterminate vowel sound in many unstressed syllables. It receives the weakest level of stress within a word and thus varies in sound from word to word. The **a** in about, the **e** in item, the **i** in edible, the **o** in gallop, and the **u** in circus are all pronounced with the schwa sound. Here are some frequently misspelled words that contain syllables with the schwa sound. If you look up such a word and fail to find it, try another vowel:

absence definite exaggerate **humorous** privilege
correspondence desperate grammar prejudice
separate

Note: The letter **x** spells six sounds in English: ks, as in box, exit; gz, as in exact, exist; sh, as in anxious; gzh, as in luxurious, luxury; ksh (a variant of gzh), also as in luxurious, luxury; and z, as in anxiety, xerography.

Punctuation

Apostrophe

1. Indicates the possessive case of nouns, proper nouns, and indefinite pronouns:

   > her aunt's house
   > the children's toys
   > Keats's "Ode to Psyche"
   > someone's bright idea
   > one's own home

2. Indicates the plurals of figures, letters, or words used as such:

   > 42's and 53's
   > in the 1700's
   > *x*'s, *y*'s, and *z*'s
   > an article with too many *however*'s

3. Indicates the omission of letters in contractions:

   > isn't   that's
   > couldn't   o'clock

4. Indicates the omission of figures:

   > the class of '12

Brackets

1. Enclose words or passages in quotations to indicate the insertion of material written by someone other than the original writer:

   > . . . On these two commandments hang [are based] all the Law and the Prophets.
   > And summer's lease [allotted time] hath all too short a date [duration]; . . .

2. Enclose material inserted within matter already in parentheses:

> (Washington [D.C.], January, 1972)

Colon

1. Introduces words, phrases, or clauses that explain, amplify, exemplify, or summarize what has preceded:

> Suddenly I knew where we were: Paris.
>
> The army was cut to pieces: more than fifty thousand were killed or captured.
>
> The lasting influence of Greece's dramatic tradition is indicated by words still in our vocabulary: *chorus, comedy,* and *drama.*
>
> She has three sources of income: stock dividends, interest from savings accounts, and salary.

2. Introduces a long quotation:

> In his Gettysburg Address, Lincoln said: "Four score and seven years ago our fathers brought forth on this continent, a new nation, conceived in Liberty, and dedicated to the proposition that all men are created equal. ..."

3. Introduces lists:

> Among the conjunctive adverbs are the following: *so, therefore, hence, however, nevertheless, moreover, accordingly,* and *besides.*

4. Separates chapter and verse numbers in references to biblical quotations:

> Esther 2:17

5. Separates hour and minute in time designations:

> 1:30 P.M.
>
> a 9:15 class

6. Follows the salutation in a formal letter:

> Dear Sir or Madam:
> Gentlemen:

Comma

1. Separates the clauses of a compound sentence connected by a coordinating conjunction:

> There is a difference between the musical works of Mozart and Haydn, and it is a difference worth discovering.
> He didn't know where she got such an idea, but he didn't disagree.

The comma may be omitted in short compound sentences in which the connection between the clauses is close:

> She understood the situation and she was furious.
> He got in the car and he drove and drove.

2. Separates *and* or *or* from the final item in a series of three or more:

> Lights of red, green, and blue wavelengths may be mixed to produce all colors.
> The radio, television set, and records were arranged on one shelf.
> Would you rather have ice cream, cake, or pie for dessert?

3. Separates two or more adjectives modifying the same noun if *and* could be used between them without changing the meaning:

> a stolid, heavy gait
> a large, high-ceilinged room
> a polished mahogany desk

4. Sets off a nonrestrictive clause or phrase (one that if eliminated would not change the meaning of the sentence):

> The thief, who had entered through the window, went straight to the safe.

The comma should not be used when the clause or phrase is restrictive (essential to the meaning of the sentence):

> The thief who had entered through the window went straight to the safe.

5. Sets off words or phrases in apposition to a noun or noun phrase:

> Plato, the famous Greek philosopher, was a pupil of Socrates.
>
> The composer of *Tristan und Isolde,* Richard Wagner, was a leading exponent of German romanticism.

The comma should not be used if such words or phrases further specify the noun that precedes:

> The Greek philosopher Plato was a pupil of Socrates.
>
> The composer Richard Wagner was a leading exponent of German romanticism.
>
> The Dostoyevsky novel *Crime and Punishment* was required reading.

6. Sets off transitional words and short expressions that require a pause in reading:

> Unfortunately, Mrs. Lattimer hadn't read many Russian novels.
>
> Did he, after all, look American?
>
> Peterson lives with his family, of course.
>
> Indeed, the sight of him gave me quite a jolt.

7. Sets off words used to introduce a sentence:

> No, I haven't seen Rowbotham.
> Well, why don't you do as I ask?

8. Sets off a subordinate clause or a long phrase that precedes the principal clause:

> By the time they finally found the restaurant, they were no longer hungry.
> After the army surrendered, the general was taken prisoner.
> Of all the illustrations in the book, the most striking are those that show the beauty of the mosaics.

9. Sets off short quotations, sayings, and the like:

> Jo told him, "Come tomorrow for dinner."
> The candidate said, "Actions speak louder than words."
> "I don't know if I can," he said, "but maybe I will."

10. Indicates the omission of a word or words:

> To err is human; to forgive, divine.

11. Sets off the year from the month in dates:

> September 6, 1976, was Labor Day.
> Louis XVI of France was guillotined on January 21, 1793.

12. Sets off the state from the city in geographical names:

> Boston, Massachusetts, is the largest city in New England.

13. Separates series of four or more figures into thousands, millions, etc.:

> 57,395   12,364,903

The comma is not used in dates or page numbers:

14. Sets off words used in direct address:

> Mr. Wadsworth, please submit your report as soon as possible.
>
> Thank you, Emma, for your help.
>
> The forum is open to questions, ladies and gentlemen.

15. Separates a phrase that transforms a statement into a question:

> You did say you had the book, didn't you?
>
> Beethoven's "Eroica" is on the program, isn't it?

16. Sets off any sentence elements that might be misread if the comma were not used:

> Some time after, the actual date was set.
>
> To Mary, Anne was just a nuisance.
>
> Whenever possible, friends provide moral support.

17. Follows the salutation and complimentary close of informal letters and the complimentary close of formal letters:

> Dear Patsy,   Sincerely,

Dash

1. Indicates a sudden break or abrupt change in continuity:

> Well, you see—I—I've—I'm just not sure.
>
> He seemed very upset about—I never knew what.
>
> And then the problem—if it is a problem—can be solved.

2. Sets apart an explanatory or defining phrase:

> Foods high in protein—meats, fish, eggs, and

49

cheese—should be a part of the daily diet.

He suddenly realized what the glittering gems were —emeralds.

3. Sets apart material that is parenthetical in nature:

He stares soulfully heavenward—to the great delight of the audience—while he plays Chopin.

Allen—who had a lean face, a long nose, and cold blue eyes—was a stern, authoritarian man.

4. Marks an unfinished sentence:

Well, then, I'll simply tell her that—

"But if the plane is late—" he began.

5. Sets off a summarizing phrase or clause:

Noam Chomsky, Morris Halle, Roman Jakobson —these are among America's most prominent linguists.

6. Sets off the name of an author or a source, as at the end of a quotation:

There never was a good war, or a bad peace.
—Benjamin Franklin

Ellipses

1. Indicate the omission of words or sentences in quoted material:

This ended the power of the council . . . and the former regents were put on trial.

Because the treaty has not been approved by the Senate . . . it is not embodied in law.

Nor have we been wanting in Attentions to our British Brethren. . . . They too have been deaf to the Voice of Justice. . . .

2. Indicate a pause in speech or an unfinished sentence:

> "Yes ... I mean ... what ..." she stammered.
> I thought I had better not ...

3. Indicate the omission of a line or lines of poetry:

> Come away, O human child!
>
> . . . .
> For the world's more full of weeping than you
> can understand.
>
> —William Butler Yeats

Exclamation point

Indicates a command, an expression of strong emotion, or an emphatic phrase or sentence:

Scram!	You can't be serious!
Go home immediately!	Bravo!
What a ball game that was!	

Hyphen

1. At the end of a line, indicates that part of a word of more than one syllable has been carried over to the following line:

> Anatole France's actual name was Jacques Anatole Thibault.

2. Joins the elements of some compounds:

> great-grandfather
> cure-all
> ne'er-do-well

3. Joins the elements of compound modifiers preceding a noun:

> a well-dressed woman
> built-in bookcases
> a happy-go-lucky fellow
> a fire-and-brimstone sermon

a four-hour seminar
ten high-school students
a two-thirds share

4. Indicates that two or more compounds share a single base:

three- and four-volume sets
six- and seven-year-olds

5. Separates the prefix and root in some combinations:

anti-Semite, pro-American (prefix + proper noun or adjective)
re-election, co-author (prefix ending with a vowel, root beginning with a vowel)
re-form, reform (to distinguish between
re-creation, recreation similar words of different meanings)

6. Substitutes for the word *to* between two figures or words:

pages 6-20
the years 1920-29
the Boston-New York shuttle

Parentheses

1. Enclose material that is not an essential part of the sentence and that if not included would not alter its meaning:

In an hour's time (some say less) the firemen had extinguished the flames.

It was a dream (although a hazy one) of an ideal state, one in which poverty did not exist.

Marion doesn't feel (and why should she?) that she should pay a higher rent.

2. Often enclose letters or numerals to indicate subdivisions of a series:

> A movement in sonata form consists of the following sections: (a) the exposition; (b) the development; and (c) the recapitulation, which is often followed by a coda.

Period

1. Indicates the end of a complete declarative or mild imperative sentence:

> The carved ornaments on the façade date back to the fourteenth century.
> Come home when you can.

2. Follows the abbreviation of a word or words:

Jan.	Ave.
Mr.	pp.
Ms.	Co.
Rev.	Inc.
St.	c.c.

Question mark

1. Indicates the end of a direct question:

> What kind of work would you like to do?
> Who was that odd-looking stranger?

but

> I wonder who said "Speak softly and carry a big stick."
> He asked when Harold would leave.

2. Indicates uncertainty:

> Ferdinand Magellan (1480?–1521)

Quotation marks

1. Enclose direct quotations:

> "What was Berlin like during the war?" she asked.
> "Gentlemen," the store manager said to the salesmen, "our first customer has arrived."
> Will Rogers said: "Things in our country run in spite of government. Not by aid of it."
> According to one critic, the conductor was "readier to persuade than to dictate."

2. Enclose words or phrases to clarify their meaning or use, or to indicate that they are being used in a special way:

> "Dey" is a title that was formerly given to governors of Algiers.
> By "brace" we mean the bracket and line joining two or more staves of music.
> "The Big Apple," a name for New York City, is a phrase that was originated by jazz musicians.
> Supervisors are urged to "prioritize" their responsibilities.

3. Set off the translation of a foreign word or phrase:

> *Hakenkreuz,* "hooked cross," "swastika"
> *déjà vu,* "already seen"
> The Latin word *reclāmāre* means "to exclaim against."

4. Set off the titles of series of books; of articles or chapters in publications; of essays; of short poems; of individual radio and television programs; of songs and short musical pieces:

"The Horizon Concise History" series
"Some Notes on Case Grammar in English"
Chapter 9, "Four in Freedom"
Shelley's "Ode to the West Wind"
"The Lucille Ball Special"
Schubert's "Death and the Maiden"

Single Quotation Marks

Enclose quoted material within a quotation:

> "To me, the key word for the American Indian is 'paradox,' " Hunter said. "The Indian's loyalty is to his heritage, but his problem is how to function in the dominant society."

Use With Other Punctuation Marks

Put commas and periods inside closing quotation marks; put semicolons and colons outside. Other punctuation (question marks and exclamation points) should be put inside the closing quotation marks only when it is actually part of the matter being quoted.

Semicolon

1. Separates the clauses of a compound sentence having no coordinating conjunction:

   > The questions are provided by the analyst; the answers come from the data.
   >
   > Many industries were paralyzed by the strike; factory owners left the district, taking their money with them.

2. Separates the clauses of a compound sentence in which the clauses contain internal punctuation, even when the clauses are joined by a conjunction:

   > Picnic baskets in hand, we walked to the beach, chose a sunny spot, and spread out the blankets;

and the rest of the group followed us in a station wagon.

3. Separates elements of a series in which items already contain commas:

> Among the guests were Katherine Ericson; her daughter, Alice; Henry Faulkner, formerly of the Redding Institute; and two couples whom I could not identify.

4. Separates clauses of a compound sentence joined by a conjunctive adverb (*nonetheless, therefore, hence,* etc.):

> The cities that had been bombed were in ruins; indeed, they looked like extinct craters.

> We demanded a refund; otherwise we would get in touch with the Better Business Bureau.

Virgule (also called *slant, slash,* and *solidus*)

1. Separates the numerator of a fraction from the denominator:

> *c/d*

2. Represents the word *per*:

> miles/hour

3. Means "or" between the words *and* and *or*:

> articles of linguistic and/or sociological importance.

> Take skates and/or skis.

4. Separates two or more lines of poetry quoted in text:

> The actor had a memory lapse when he came to the lines "Why? all delights are vain, but that most vain / Which, with pain purchas'd, doth inherit pain," and had to improvise.

Capitalization

The following should be capitalized:

1. The first word of a sentence:

   > Some diseases are acute; others are chronic.
   > Aren't you my new neighbor?
   > Great! Let's go!

2. The first word of each line in a poem:

   > Poets that lasting marble seek
   > Must carve in Latin or in Greek.
   > —Edmund Waller

3. The first word of a direct quotation unless it is closely woven into the sentence:

   > Helen asked, "Do you think Satie was a serious composer?"
   > "For me," I answered, "he was simply amusing."
   > G. B. Shaw said that "assassination is the extreme form of censorship."

4. The first word of the salutation and of the complimentary close of a letter:

   > My dear Joyce   Sincerely yours
   > Dear Mr. Atkins   Very cordially

5. All words except articles, prepositions, and conjunctions in the titles of books, articles, poems, plays, etc.:

   > *All Quiet on the Western Front*
   > "The Finiteness of Natural Language"
   > "When the Lamp Is Shattered"
   > *Cat on a Hot Tin Roof*

6. Proper nouns and adjectives:

Billie Jean King	China, Chinese
Bruno Walter	Bohemia, Bohemian
Clare Boothe Luce	Morocco, Moroccan
Albert Einstein	Hegel, Hegelian

Do not capitalize words derived from proper nouns and adjectives and having distinct special meanings:

china plates
chinese red
a bohemian lifestyle
moroccan leather

7. The standard names of geographic divisions, districts, regions, and localities:

Arctic Circle	Mountain States
Western Hemisphere	Gulf Coast
South Pole	the North
Torrid Zone	the South
Continental Divide	the East
Old World	the West
Middle East	the Midwest
Far West	the Southwest

Do not capitalize words designating points of the compass unless they refer to specific regions:

Holyoke, Massachusetts, is eight miles north of Springfield. Turn east on Route 495.

8. The popular names of districts, regions, and localities:

the Barbary Coast	the Windy City
the Promised Land	the Loop
the Bible Belt	the East Side

9. The names of rivers, lakes, mountains, oceans, etc.:

Connecticut River	Mount Shasta
Lake Maracaibo	Long Island Sound
Rocky Mountains	Pacific Ocean

10. Names for the Deity, for a supreme being, and for the Bible and other sacred books:

God	Allah
the Almighty	Jehovah
the Savior	the Messiah
the Holy Spirit	the Bible
the Virgin Mary	the Koran
the Blessed Mother	the Talmud

11. The names of religious denominations:

Catholicism
Judaism
Protestantism
Buddhism
the Roman Catholic Church
the Protestant Episcopal Church
the Society of Friends
the Church of Jesus Christ of Latter-day Saints

12. The names of historical periods, events, documents, etc.:

the Middle Ages
the Reformation
the American Revolution
World War II
the Battle of Shiloh
the Declaration of Independence
the Magna Carta
the Constitution

13. The names of political entities, divisions, parties, etc.:

>the Byzantine Empire
>the Holy Roman Empire
>the French Republic
>the Populist Party
>the Democratic Party
>the Republican Party
>Democrat
>Republican

14. The names of legislative and judicial bodies:

>Congress · Parliament
>the Senate · Diet
>the House of Representatives · Knesset
>the United States Supreme Court
>the Permanent Court of International Justice

15. The names of departments, bureaus, etc., of the federal government:

>the Department of Agriculture
>United States Department of State
>Central Intelligence Agency
>Tennessee Valley Authority

16. The names of treaties, acts, laws, etc.:

>the Versailles Treaty
>the Clayton-Bulwer Treaty
>the Volstead Act
>the Sherman Antitrust Law

17. Titles—civil, military, noble, honorary, etc.—when they precede a name:

>Justice Frankfurter

General MacArthur
Mayor White
Queen Elizabeth II
Pope John XXIII
Professor Kittredge

But all references to the President and Vice President of the United States should be capitalized:

President Truman	the President
Vice President Wallace	the Vice President

18. Epithets used as a substitute for a name:

Eric the Red	the Great Emancipator
Ivan the Terrible	the Iron Chancellor

19. The names of peoples, races, tribes, etc.:

Maori	Bantu
Caucasian	Ute

20. The names of languages and of periods in the history of languages:

German	English
Old High German	Middle English

21. The names of geological eras, periods, etc.:

the Paleozoic era
the Precambrian period
the Bronze Age

22. The names of the constellations, planets, and stars:

the Milky Way	Mars
the Southern Crown	Venus
Jupiter	Polaris

23. Genus—but not species—names in binomial nomenclature:

> *Chrysanthemum leucanthemum*
> *Macaca mulatta*
> *Rana pipiens*

24. The names of holidays, holy days, months of the year, and days of the month:

Independence Day	Passover
Labor Day	Yom Kippur
Thanksgiving	Ramadan
Christmas	January
Easter	Monday

25. Personifications:

> I met Murder in the way— / He had a mask like Castlereagh.
>
> —Percy Bysshe Shelley

26. Trademarks:

Coca-Cola	Polaroid
Formica	Pyrex
Kleenex	Xerox

27. The names of buildings, streets, parks, organizations, etc.:

> the State House
> Symphony Hall
> Fort Tryon Park
> Logan Airport
> Tremont Street
> Route 91
> the Free and Accepted Masons
> Veterans of Foreign Wars
> the New York Yankees

Italics

1. Indicate titles of books, plays, and poems of book length:

   > *For Whom the Bell Tolls*
   > *The Little Foxes*
   > *Paradise Lost*

2. Indicate words, letters, or numbers used as such:

   > The word *buzz* is onomatopoeic; that is, it sounds like what it stands for.
   > *Can't* often means *won't*.
   > She formed her *n*'s like *u*'s.
   > A *6* looks like an upside-down *9*.

3. Emphasize a word or phrase. This device should be used sparingly:

   > Whenever Jack made a fool of himself, he was his *mother's* son.

4. Indicate foreign words and phrases that have not been assimilated into English:

   > editors, machinists, *pâtissiers,* barbers, and hoboes
   > his *Sturm und Drang* period

5. Indicate the names of the plaintiff and defendant in legal citations:

   > *Marbury* v. *Madison*

6. Indicate the titles of long musical compositions:

   > *The Messiah*
   > *Die Götterdämmerung*
   > Bartok's *Concerto for Orchestra*
   > Elgar's *Enigma Variations*

7. Indicate the titles of magazines and newspapers:

> *American Heritage* magazine
> *The New Yorker*
> the New York *Daily News*
> *The New York Times*

8. Set off the titles of motion pictures and television series:

> *The Sting*
> *All the President's Men*
> *Masterpiece Theater*
> *Upstairs, Downstairs*

9. Distinguish the names of genera and species in scientific names:

> *Homo sapiens*
> *Sciurus carolinensis*

10. Set off the names of ships, planes, trains, and spacecraft:

> *Queen Elizabeth II*
> *The Spirit of St. Louis*
> *The Wolverine*
> *Viking 1*

11. Set off the names of paintings and sculpture:

> *Mona Lisa*
> *Guernica*
> *Pietà*
> *The Burghers of Calais*

Word Compounding

There are four types of compound words. An open compound consists of two or more words written separately. A hyphenated compound has words connected by a hyphen. A solid compound is two words that are written as one word and express a single idea. A temporary compound consists of two or more words joined by a hyphen, usually to modify another word or to avoid ambiguity.

In general, permanent compounds begin as separate words, evolve into hyphenated compounds, and later become solid compounds. Reference works do not always agree on the current evolutionary form of a compound. The best rule of thumb is that the compound—no matter its form—should be clear in both meaning and readability (e.g., *shell-like* rather than *shelllike*). The following general rules apply to forming compounds.

Rules for open, hyphenated, and solid compounds

1. Normally, prefixes and suffixes are joined with a second element without a hyphen, unless doing so would double a vowel or triple a consonant. A hyphen is also used when the element following a prefix is capitalized, or when the element preceding a suffix is a proper noun.

anti-American	American-like
anticlimax	bell-like
anti-intellectual	childlike

2. The hyphen is usually retained with *all-*, *ex-* (meaning "former"), *half-*, *quasi-* (in adjective constructions), and *self-*.

> all-around (*but* allseed, allspice)
> ex-governor
> half-life (*but* halfhearted, halfpenny, halftone, halfway)
> quasi-scientific (*but* a quasi success)
> self-defense (but selfhood, selfish, selfless, selfsame)

3. Certain homographs require a hyphen to prevent mistakes in pronunciation and meaning.

> recreation (enjoyment)   release (to let go)
> re-creation (new   re-lease (to rent again)
> creation)

4. Two nouns or an adjective and noun are written solid when they have combined to form a single specialized term with a single primary accent. Often the meaning of the solid compound is different from the individual meaning of each word.

> bookkeeper   mothball
> footnote   shoptalk

5. Nouns or adjectives consisting of a short verb combined with a preposition are either hyphenated or

written solid depending on current usage. The same words used as a verb are written separately.

a breakup	break up a fight
a line-up	line up the pencils
a pushup	push up the window
a sit-up	sit up in bed

6. Compound personal pronouns are solid.

herself	myself
himself	ourselves

7. *Any, every, no,* and *some* are written solid when combined with *body, thing,* or *where.*

anybody	nobody
everything	somewhere

8. Two nouns of equal value are hyphenated when the person or thing is considered to have the characteristics of both nouns.

secretary-treasurer	city-state

9. Numbers from twenty-one to ninety-nine and adjective compounds with a numerical first element (whether spelled out or written in figures) are hyphenated.

twenty-one	48-inch floorboard
thirty-first	6-sided polygon
second-rate movie	19th-century history

10. Spelled-out numbers used with *-fold* are not hyphenated; figures and *-fold* are hyphenated.

tenfold	20-fold

11. Compounds of a number and *-odd* are hyphenated.

four-odd 60-odd

12. Many numerical compounds have evolved into solid compounds. A dictionary or wordbook will help you distinguish the exceptions.

fourscore (adjective) threesome (noun and adjective)

foursquare (adjective or adverb) three-square (adjective)

13. A modifying compound consisting of a number and a possessive noun is not hyphenated.

one week's pay 35 hours' work

14. Fractions used as modifiers are hyphenated unless the numerator or denominator of the fraction contains a hyphen. Fractions used as nouns are usually not hyphenated.

three-eighths inch twenty-four hundredths part

He ate one half of the pie. The pie was one-half eaten.

15. Modifying compounds are normally hyphenated, whether made up of two nouns, an adjective and a noun, or an adverb and an adjective.

high-school teacher hot-water bottle
wind-chill factor labor-management talks

best-dressed woman well-kept secret

However, if both meaning and readability are clear, or if the introduction of a hyphen would be intrusive, it is best to omit the hyphen.

16. Modifying compounds formed of capitalized words should not be hyphenated.

    Iron Age manufacture   New World plants

17. Scientific compounds are usually not hyphenated.

    carbon monoxide poisoning   dichromic acid solution

18. When a solid compound noun is preceded by an adjective modifying the first part of the compound, the compound should be separated.

    schoolgirl   high-school girl
    classroom   fourth-class room

19. Compound color adjectives are hyphenated.

    a red-gold sunset   a blue-green sweater

    Color compounds whose first element ends in -ish are hyphenated when they precede the noun, but should not be hyphenated when they follow the noun.

    a reddish-gold sunset   The sky is reddish gold

20. Adverb-and-adjective compounds should not be hyphenated if they follow the noun they modify.

    a much-improved situation   The situation is much improved.

21. If the adverb ends in *-ly* in an adverb-adjective compound, omit the hyphen.

    a finely tuned   a carefully worked
      mechanism   canvas

22. Compounds consisting of two adverbs and an adjective should not be hyphenated.

    a very well done maneuver

23. A foreign phrase used as a modifier is not hyphenated.

    a bona fide offer   a per diem allowance

24. Phrases used as modifiers are normally hyphenated.

    a happy-go-lucky person
    a here-today-gone-tomorrow attitude

25. Compound forms must always reflect meaning. Consequently, some compounds may change in form depending on how they are used.

    Anyone may go.   Any one of these
                              will do.

    Everyone is here.   Every one of these
                              is good.

Commonly confused compounds

The following is a list of frequently used compounds, showing if they are open, hyphenated, or solid. If the compound you are looking for is not entered, look it up in a dictionary or wordbook. Compounds that can be written in more than one way have the preferred form entered first.

aforementioned
aforesaid
after-hours
aftertaste
afterthought
air base
air-condition
air conditioner
airline
airliner
airmail (*v.*)
air mail *or* airmail (*n.*)
air mass
airspace
airtight
all-around
all-purpose
all right (*adv.*)
all-round
all-time
also-ran
anybody
anyhow
anyone
anyplace
anything
audio frequency
audio-visual
audiovisuals
ball bearing

ballpark *or* ball park
ballplayer
ball-point
bank account
bankbook
bank note
bankroll
beforehand
billboard
billet-doux
birthplace
birthrate
black and white (*n.*)
black-and-white (*adj.*)
blood count
blood pressure
blood stream *or*
    bloodstream
blue book *or* bluebook
blue chip
blue-collar
blue jeans
blueprint
blue ribbon
boarding house *or*
    boardinghouse
bondholder
bond paper
bone-dry
bookbinding

bookcase
bookend or book end
book jacket
bookkeeping
bookkeeper
bookmaker
book review
bookseller
bookshop
bookstore
bottom line (n.)
bottom-line (adj.)
boxcar
box office
box score
box spring
brainpower
brainstorm
brain trust
brainwash
brainwashing
brand-new
bread and butter (n.)
bread-and-butter (adj.)
breadwinner
break-in
breakout
breakthrough
breakup
briefcase
broadcast
broad-spectrum
broken-down
build-up or buildup
built-in
built-up
burnout
buttonhole
by-and-by
by-election
bylaw
by-line or byline
by-pass or bypass

by-product
call money
call number
campground
capital gain
carbon copy
carbon paper
cardboard
card-carrying
car-pool
carryall
carry-over
case load
case study
casework
cashbook
cash flow
cash register
castoff (n.)
cast-off (adj.)
catchall
catchword
chain-react
chain reaction
chain-smoke
chain smoker
chain store
checkbook
check-out
checkpoint
checkup
circuit breaker
city-state
civil rights (n.)
civil-rights (adj.)
class-conscious
classmate
classroom
clean-cut
cleanup
clear-cut
clearing house or
   clearinghouse

clipboard
closed circuit
close-out
close-up
coaction
co-anchor
co-author
coed or co-ed
coeducation or
  co-education
coequal
coexist
coffee shop
cohabit
cold-blooded
coldshoulder
color-code
colorfast
comeback
commeasure
committeeman
common-law marriage
common sense
comparison-shop
consciousness-raising
co-op
co-opt
copy-edit
copy-editing
copy editor
copywriter
costar or co-star
cost-effective
countdown
court-martial
courtroom
crackdown
crackup
crash-land
cross-country
cross-examine
cross-index
crossover

cross-purpose
cross-reference
crossroad
cross section
dark horse
daybook
day care
day labor
day-to-day
deadline
deathbed
death rate
de luxe or deluxe
devil-may-care
die-hard or diehard
direct action (n.)
direct-action (adj.)
dive-bomb
double check (n.)
double-check (v.)
double-cross
double-digit
double entry
double-space
double time
downplay
downtime
down-to-earth
downtown
dry-clean
dry cleaner
dry goods
everybody
everything
everywhere
ex officio
extracurricular
eye opener
fairway
fair-weather
far-fetched
filmmaker
filmstrip

finger tip
firehouse
fireproof
fire station
first aid
first-rate
foolproof
free lance (n.)
free-lance (v.)
free-lancer
free trade
freewill (adj.)
free will (n.)
garden-variety
ghostwriter
good will or goodwill
groundwork
grown-up
half-hour
halfway
handmade
hand-pick
handyman or handy
  man
head-hunter
head-hunting
headline
high frequency
high-level
high-pressure
high-rise
high-risk
high tech
holdup
horsepower
ill-advised
ill-use
in-and-out
inasmuch as
insofar as
interrelate
jawbone
jet lag

job lot
journeyman
keepsake
key money
keypunch
keystroke
king-size
labor-intensive
labor saving
landholder
landowner
large-scale
last-minute
lawmaker
layoff
layout
lead-in
lead-time
leave-taking
left-hand
letterhead
line-up
loose-leaf
loudspeaker
lowdown (n.)
low-down (adj.)
lower-case
man-hour
manpower
markdown
marketplace or market
  place
market price
market value
matter-of-fact
moneylender
moneymaker
money order
moreover
nation-state
nationwide
native-born
nearby

network
nevertheless
newfound
newly-wed *or* newlywed
newscast
newsstand
newsworthy
nonetheless
no-nonsense
nonprofit
no one *or* no-one
noontime
notebook
noteworthy
notwithstanding
nowadays
no-win
odd lot
offhand
off-hour
office boy
officeholder
off-line
offset
once-over
one-piece
one-side
onetime
one-up
one-upsmanship
on-line
out-and-out
outbid
out-of-date
overall
overrate
overrule
paperwork *or* paper work
parcel post
passbook
passer-by *or* passerby
payroll

pay-TV
per annum
per cent *or* percent
pipeline
postmark
postmaster
post office
postwar
proofread
proof sheet
push button
put-down
putoff
put-on
rank and file
read-out
real estate
recap
rework
rewrite
right-hand
road show
rollback
round trip
roundup
run-down
sales check
salesclerk
sales tax
say-so
scratchpad
secondhand *(adj.)*
second hand *(n.)*
second-string
sendoff
send-up
series-wound
setback
setup
short circuit *(n.)*
short-circuit *(v.)*
short cut
short-handed

short-term
sideline *or* side line
standby
stand-in
standup *or* stand-up
statewide
stockbroker
stock exchange
stock market
stockpile
stopgap
subbasement
subcommittee
subdivision
takeoff
take-out
takeover *or* take-over
taxpayer
textbook
thereafter
tie-in
tie-up
timecard
time clock
time-lapse
timesaving

time-sharing
timetable
titleholder
title page
trade-in
trademark
trade name
transcontinental
turnover
under way
up-and-coming
vice president
vice-presidency
view finder
viewpoint
wage earner
waterpower
wavelength
waybill
way station
wildlife
wind-up
work force
wrist watch
yearbook
zero-growth

Numbers

When should a number be spelled out and when should it be written in figures? In cases in which the following rules do not apply the choice is determined by the kind of piece you are writing; numbers are customarily written out in formal writing and figures employed in informal writing (including all forms of business writing). As with many areas covered in this book, consistency of style is paramount. Whatever method you use, stick with it throughout.

1. Numbers from one to ten are spelled out and numbers over ten are written in figures:

   > There are five candidates for the position.
   > We received 17 letters inquiring about the job.

2. Indefinite and round numbers are spelled out:

   > received dozens of angry calls
   > drove five hundred miles yesterday
   > a sixty-forty split of the profits

3. Definite amounts and long numbers are written in figures:

   > They paid $83,000 for the house.
   > She won the election by 759,323 votes.
   > The pistachio nuts are $12.95 a pound.

   Numbers in the millions and above, however, are written in either figures or words and followed by *million* or *billion*:

17 million
at a cost of four and a half million dollars
a three-billion dollar spacecraft

4. Two or more related numbers in the same sentence should be expressed in the same style; if one is more than ten, all should be expressed in figures:

Today he typed 4 reports, 11 memos, and 7 letters.

There were 25 applicants for the 12 positions.

5. Spell out numbers at the beginning of a sentence. If the sentence also contains numbers that appear in figures, you can either break rule 4 or rewrite the sentence so that the number does not come first:

Three shipments arrived today.

Five people applied for the 12 positions.

We received 5 applications for the 12 positions.

In sentences beginning with a long definite number it is now generally acceptable to use figures. Many people, however, do not like the appearance of such a sentence and would prefer to see it rewritten.

4,500 acres were used for growing corn.

The farm used 4,500 acres for growing corn.

6. Unrelated numbers in the same sentence should be distinguished for clarity. Figures and words can be used to differentiate them:

In three days we sold 24 cars, 6 campers, and 11 trucks.

Unrelated numbers should not be placed next to each other. You can spell out one of the numbers, use a comma to separate them, or rewrite the sentence:

The show consisted of 3 one-act plays.
In 1982, 16 incumbent senators were defeated.
There were 16 incumbent senators defeated in 1982.

7. Specific amounts of money are written in figures. The dollar sign is placed before the figure and the decimal point and ciphers are usually omitted:

$10.95 $35 $357,928 $5 a pair

Remember that indefinite numbers are spelled out; it is only in such cases that the word "dollar(s)" is used after the number (rather than the dollar sign before):

spent about twenty dollars at the market.
a forty- to fifty-dollar repair job.

Sums under a dollar are usually expressed in figures, but it is not uncommon to see sums spelled out in formal writing. The word cents is used following the words or figures in printing and formal writing; the cents sign is used in informal writing:

35¢   35 cents   thirty-five cents

Remember, however, that consistency would demand:

One item cost $1.25 and the other is $.69.

In legal documents sums are given in both words and figures:

sold at a price of five hundred dollars ($500)

8. Fractions standing alone are spelled out; if used as adjectives they must be hyphenated, if used as nouns they are open compounds:

received a two-thirds share
bought one third of a pound

Fractions in mixed numbers are expressed in figures; a space separates the whole number from the fraction, and a diagonal line separates the parts of the fraction:

3 1/2   20 7/8   9 2/3

9. When writing dates in which the day precedes the month, the date should be expressed in ordinal numbers or spelled out:

I met with her on the 6th of May.
We will see them again on the twelfth of July.

When the date follows the month regular figures are used:

They are arriving on August 21.
She was born on January 14, 1950.

In formal writing numbers applying to years, decades, and centuries are spelled out:

nineteen hundred and eighty-three
growing up in the sixties
the seventeenth century

In informal writing figures are often used, and if the date is abbreviated an apostrophe is used to show the part that has been left out:

John Kennedy was elected President in 1960.
a novel first published in the 1920's.
I haven't seen him since '73.

10. Street names above ten are expressed in ordinal figures (in this case two numbers can be placed next to one another):

My address is 60 31st Street.

You only need to use *st, nd, rd,* or *th* if a numbered street is not preceded by either East or West:

Her office is at 105 West 12 Street.

11. In formal writing the time of day is spelled out and used with o'clock. In informal writing figures are used with a.m. and p.m. and occasionally with o'clock:

The wedding reception will be held from eight o'clock to twelve o'clock.
Business hours are from 9:30 a.m. to 5 p.m.
Orders will be taken beginning at 10 o'clock.

12. Figures are used to express exact dimensions, sizes, measurements, and temperatures:

The painting measures 2 by 4 feet.

(Note that × for by and ″ and ′ for inches and feet are used only in technical writing.)

A mile equals 1,760 yards or 5,280 feet.

At birth the baby weighed 6 pounds 7 ounces.

The high today was 82 degrees Fahrenheit.

13. Percentages are expressed in figures followed by the word percent:

received a 10 percent discount.

Basic Rules of Standard English Grammar

What is grammar?

Grammar is a system of basic rules by which the words in a language are structured and arranged in sentences. Grammar deals with rules for word order, verb forms, plural and singular noun forms, and parts of speech, among other topics.

Virtually everybody who has heard English spoken from birth has learned *basic* English grammar. But not everybody has learned *standard* English grammar: the set of rules that govern what is generally considered to be "good" or "correct" grammar.

Some specific points of grammar present problems for many people whose native language is English. This section deals in particular with those points. Areas of difficulty are examined, and the reasons for difficulty are cited.

Traditional and new grammar

The second half of the twentieth century has witnessed a change in the way grammarians discuss grammar. Grammarians have begun to use new terms for certain classes of words. At the same time, other people have retained the traditional terms for these classes of words. The difference in classifying words does not make a difference in the way words are actually used.

The ways words operate in sentences have not substantially changed.

Verbs

English verb forms are fairly simple when you compare them with verb forms in many other languages.

The *present tense* of most verbs has only two forms, as illustrated by the verb "walk":

	Singular	Plural
first person	I walk	we walk
second person	you walk	you walk
third person	he, she, it walks	they walk

The two forms are *walk* and *walks*. The form *walks* is used only for the third-person singular. *He, she,* or *it* may be replaced by the name of one person, one thing, one place, or one idea.

> John walks.
> The cat walks.
> The puppet walks.
> Happiness walks the earth.

One basic rule of English grammar is:

A verb must agree with its subject in person and number.

That means that a first-person singular verb is used with "I," a third-person singular verb is used with any singular noun or third-person singular pronoun, and so on.

Some reasons people have problems when trying to apply this rule are:

1. They fail to recognize that *and* makes more than one.

   > John and Jane walk out on the boardwalk. (John + Jane = third-person *plural.*)
   >
   > Jane and I walk out on the boardwalk. (Jane + I = we = first-person *plural.*)

2. They fail to recognize that *or* does not create a plural.

   > Either John or Jane gets a paper each day. (Only one of the two of them gets the paper—sometimes one, sometimes the other.)

3. They fail to recognize the true subject.

   > A deck of cards sits on the shelf. (The verb is third-person singular because *deck* is the subject, not *cards.*)

The *past tense* for most verbs has only one form.

I walked	we walked
you walked	you walked
he, she, it walked	they walked

Regular past tenses are formed by adding an *-ed* to the verb. Sometimes a final *e* is dropped before adding the *-ed* (save, saved), sometimes a final *y* is changed to *i* before the *-ed* is added (worry, worried), sometimes a final consonant is doubled before adding the *-ed* (nap, napped). Most of these past tenses do not offer too much difficulty.

Many past tenses, however, are irregular. Irregular past tenses must be learned one by one. Most of these are learned during childhood. When in doubt, one can learn the past tense of a verb by consulting a dictionary.

Difficulties with past tenses arise when a person:

1. does not realize that a verb has an irregular past tense.
2. knows that a verb has an irregular past tense, but does not know what it is.
3. confuses the past tense with the past participle.

The *past participle* is the form of the verb that follows *have, has, had,* or another auxiliary verb.

I have walked	we have walked
you have walked	you have walked
he, she, it has walked	they have walked

Notice that for *walk* the past participle, *walked,* is the same as the past tense. This is true for all regular verbs. It is even true for some irregular verbs. But it is not true for *all* verbs.

Past tenses and past participles for irregular verbs have to be learned verb by verb. Although there are some patterns that are followed in several verbs, mistakes are sometimes made because the pattern does not hold for all verbs that *appear* to fit a pattern. For example, "sing, sang, sung" has a pattern that is followed in "ring, rang, rung." But it is *not* followed in "bring, brought, brought." Mistakes are made because some people try to carry out a pattern in the wrong places.

Because past tenses and past participles present so many problems, it is worth noting some general patterns.

1. Some irregular verbs have the same irregular form for past tense and past participle:

hold	held	held
bring	brought	brought
feel	felt	felt
sit	sat	sat
make	made	made

2. Some irregular verbs have the same form for the present tense, the past tense, and the past participle.

hit	hit	hit
burst	burst	burst
put	put	put
spread	spread	spread
thrust	thrust	thrust

3. Some irregular verbs change their form for the past tense and again for the past participle.

give	gave	given
do	did	done
grow	grew	grown
go	went	gone
see	saw	seen

4. A few verbs change the form for the past tense, but have the same form as the present tense for the past participle.

come	came	come
run	ran	run

The English language has about two hundred irregular verbs. The faulty use of the forms of these verbs creates a great deal of the trouble people have with English grammar. The time spent looking them up in a dictionary until the irregular forms are mastered is valuably spent.

The differences between the past tense and past participle should also be mastered. Standard English grammar requires that the distinction be maintained when there is a distinction. For example,

nonstandard:	*should be corrected to:*
I done it.	I did it. *or* I have done it.
I seen it.	I saw it. *or* I have seen it.
I should have went.	I should have gone.
They have came.	They have come. *or* They came.

The *infinitive* form of the verb is the form that begins with *to* (to walk, to hit, to bring, to give). Most verbs have an infinitive form. The infinitive form has several uses.

It follows another verb.

> I want *to go*.
> He tried *to walk*.
> She likes *to laugh*.

The infinitive may serve as a subject of a sentence.

> *To travel* requires money.

Split infinitives are subjects of much grammatical discussion. An infinitive is said to be split when a word or a group of words is placed between "to" and the rest of the verb. Although many grammarians do not object to splitting an infinitive, a few do.

> He had *to* hastily *wrap* the package.

may be changed to:

> He had *to wrap* the package hastily.

But an infinitive split by one adverb (as in the example above) is not universally considered objectionable.

Even people who do not usually object to splitting infinitives do object to splitting the infinitive with a long string of words:

> We had *to* carefully and slowly, picking out weeds as we went, *make* our way through the woods.

That example is generally considered to be poor grammar, or at least poor style. It can easily be changed to:

> We had *to make* our way through the woods slowly and carefully, picking out weeds as we went.

Defective verbs are verbs that do not have a full range of tenses and participles. Some examples of defective verbs are:

can	shall
could	may
will	must
would	ought
should	might

Note that the defective verbs do not have a separate third-person singular form:

I can	we can
you can	you can
he, she, it can	they can

Most of them do not have a past tense. *Could* is considered to be the past tense of *can,* and *would* the past tense of *will.* They do not have past participles or present participles. They have no future tense.

Different verbs must replace defective verbs for the sense of the missing tenses. The verb *to be* is a special case. Some grammarians do not consider it a verb at all. It is unlike other verbs in the number of forms it has and in the ways it is used.

The present tense of *to be* has a separate form for the first-person singular as well as for the third-person singular:

I am	we are
you are	you are
he, she, it is	they are

It has two forms, not one, for the past tense. Note that the first-person singular and the third-person singular use the same past tense.

I was	we were
you were	you were
he, she, it was	they were

The misuse of forms of the past tense of *to be* is a common grammatical error. "You was" and "they was" are simply incorrect.

Greater confusion exists because there are correct uses of "I were" and "he, she, it were." These forms may be used in the *subjunctive* (or *conditional*) mood. For example, the word "if," or anything that suggests "if," in the present or future may be followed correctly by "I were" or "he, she, it were."

If I were President
Suppose it were true.

The past participle for *to be* is *been*. Little difficulty arises out of the use of *been*. The most frequent grammatical lapse is the omission of the auxiliary verb.

incorrect:	*correct:*
I been gone.	I have been gone.
He been thinking.	He has been thinking.

A common error made with the forms of *to be* is to omit it entirely.

incorrect:	*correct:*
I cold.	I am cold. I was cold.
He big.	He is big.
They strong.	They are strong.

Forms of *to be* may be followed by an adjective.

> I am cold.
> You are calm.
> It is weak.
> We were frightened.
> The rabbit was furry.

There are a few other verbs that may be followed by an adjective. The verbs that may be are sometimes called *linking verbs*. The adjective modifies the noun or pronoun. Some linking verbs are: *appear, seem, feel, look.*

I seem cold.
You appear calm.
We looked frightened.

Verbs may be *transitive* or *intransitive*. A transitive verb has to have an object. An intransitive verb does not have an object. Some verbs are only transitive, some are only intransitive, some are both.

Examples of transitive verbs:

He stole a pig.
She meets me every Saturday.
They towed the boat.

Examples of intransitive verbs:

He steals for a living.
Let us meet soon.
The baby teethed.

Nouns

Nouns are either *proper* or *common*. Proper nouns are usually capitalized. In general, proper nouns are names of people, places, or certain categories of things. Trademarks are also capitalized. Common nouns are usually preceded by a definite article and represent one or all members of a class.

In English the form of the noun is the same whether it is the subject or the object of a verb.

subject	verb	object
The dog	bit	John.
John	bit	the dog.

Noun plurals are usually formed by adding -s (book, books) or -es (dish, dishes) to the singular or by dropping a -y and adding -ies (spy, spies). Nouns that form their plurals in these ways are considered to be regular.

But many nouns have irregular plurals. Some plurals are irregular because they are the same as the singular (sheep, sheep). Some are irregular because they have distinctly different forms that go back to Old English (mouse, mice). Some are irregular because they form their plurals as in the languages from which they come (locus, loci). Many foreign words in the plural are now acceptable following the English rules. For example, both *cortices* and *cortexes* are now considered to be acceptable English for the plurals of *cortex*.

Irregular plurals do not necessarily follow logical patterns. We have mouse/mice, louse/lice, but house/houses. Irregular plurals must be learned individually.

Whether the plural is regular or irregular, it takes the plural form of the verb. And the form is the same whether the noun is the object or subject of a verb.

> The boys hit the girls.
> The girls hit the boys.

Collective nouns and *nouns that are plural in construction* often confuse people. Which form of the verb is used with "the committee," "clothes," "clothing," "army," etc.?

To some extent, the logic of the meaning has to be considered. For collective nouns like *committee, army, flock,* or *congress,* one must consider whether the members are behaving as a single unit or as a set of individual units.

> Congress votes today.
> The committee argue frequently about their opinions.
> The cattle run off in different directions.
> The jury is sequestered in the hotel.
> The jury are fighting about their verdict.

Some nouns are constructed so that the form is by nature singular or plural.

> The clothing is on the bed where I left it.
> The clothes are on the bed where I left them.

It is not only necessary to have agreement with the verb; it is also necessary for any pronouns to agree in number with the noun.

Possessive forms of the noun are generally formed by adding *'s* to the singular and *'* to plurals that end in *s*. If the plural is irregular and does not end in *s*, then *'s* is added to the plural form.

singular	*plural*
the dog's bones	the dogs' bones
the lady's clothes	the ladies' clothes
the man's ties	the men's ties

The same possessive forms are used when the possessives are in the predicate position:

> These are the dog's.
> These are the dogs'.
> These are the lady's.
> These are the ladies'.
> These are the man's.
> These are the men's.

Pronouns

Personal pronouns present some of the greatest grammatical problems for speakers and writers of English. Unlike nouns, pronouns have different forms when they are used as subjects and objects. They also have two possessive forms and a reflexive form.

As *subjects* of verbs, the pronouns are:

singular	*plural*
I	we
you	you
he, she, it	they

Notice that "you" is both singular and plural; the same form is used whether one is addressing one person or several.

Most people tend to choose the correct form of the pronoun when there is only one pronoun required. (I went, he went, we went, they went.) Some people have problems when there is more than one pronoun.

	incorrect	*correct*
	Him and me went.	He and I went.
	Us and them went.	We and they went.

A good rule is to try each pronoun separately and see if it sounds correct. That will help you select the correct form in combinations.

	incorrect	*correct*
	Him went.	He went.
	Us went.	We went.

As *objects* of verbs or prepositions, the pronouns are:

singular	*plural*
me	us
you	you
him, her, it	them

Examples:

> John hit him.
> Mary fired her.
> Sally kissed us.
> James tried them.
> Phil looked at you.
> Henry gave the book to me.
> Sue sent for it.

Once again, people tend to choose the correct form of the pronoun when there is only one object. Some people have problems when there is more than one object.

	incorrect	*correct*
	John hit him and I.	John hit him and me.
	Sue sent for her and they.	Sue sent for her and them.

When in doubt, try each pronoun alone. You will probably select the correct form.

Possessive pronouns that occur before the noun are sometimes termed *determiners* or *determinatives*. Whatever grammarians call them, they have these forms:

singular	*plural*
my	our
your	your
his, her, its	their

Notice that there is no apostrophe in *its*.

These pronouns are generally placed before any adjectives that precede the noun:

my dog   my big dog   my big, red, ugly dog

Possessive pronouns in predicate position or in absolute form are:

singular	*plural*
mine	ours
yours	yours
his, hers, its	theirs

Examples of the use of these pronouns:

The book is mine.
Mine is the glory.
One room is ours, the other theirs.
Yours is not to reason why.
Is it his or hers?

In modern usage, these pronouns do not precede the noun. "Mine eyes have seen wonders" is archaic usage.

Reflexive pronouns end in *self* or *selves*.

myself	ourselves
yourself	yourselves
himself, herself, itself	themselves

They are used for emphasis or as an object (direct or indirect) of a verb or pronoun.

I hurt myself.
I did it myself.
Feed yourself.
You yourselves are to blame.
He talks to himself.
She gives herself airs.
It grew by itself.
They themselves saw it.

Notice that the reflexive pronouns have different forms for the second person singular and plural: yourself and yourselves.

There are other pronouns as well. For example,

either	each	all
few	somebody	anything
anyone	nobody	one
neither	both	some
something	someone	anybody
nothing	no one	many

People often have difficulty matching a pronoun to an antecedent. The pronoun must agree with its antecedent in person and number. But sometimes it is not clear what that person or number is.

> John lost his hat.
> One of the boys lost his hat.
> Somebody lost his hat.

The last example is acceptable if the hat was clearly a man's hat. For many years, *his* would have been acceptable whether the somebody were male or female— as long as it was not clear whether male or female. Grammatically, "somebody lost his hat" is still acceptable. But social forces have overtaken grammatical neatness on this issue.

Until recently, *his* was the correct pronoun to use if it were unclear whether the antecedent was male or female. But with greater insistence on women's equality, people are beginning to recognize a male bias in the universal use of *his* in such situations. A good alternative has not yet been discovered.

What are the possible solutions? Substitute "his or her" for "his." Rewrite the sentence entirely. Use the grammatically improper "their."

> Each is entitled to his own opinion.
> Each is entitled to his or her own opinion.
> Each is entitled to their own opinion.
> One is entitled to one's own opinion.
> People are entitled to their own opinions.

None of the solutions satisfies all the objections. But "his or her," although awkward, is gaining wide use. The sentences that avoid "each" may solve the problem, but such solutions may drive out the use of the word "each." And the meaning of the sentences are subtly altered. For the present, "his or her" may be the best of several unsatisfactory solutions.

Unclear antecedents occur when more than one noun or pronoun can logically be the antecedent.

> Marie told Lucy that she had won a prize.

Who won the prize, Marie or Lucy? The word "she" could refer to either. Technically, "she" is supposed to refer to the nearest antecedent, but in practice that rule does not work well. Sentences of this kind cannot be corrected by a simple repositioning of words. The sentences must be rewritten.

> Marie had won a prize, and she told Lucy about it.
> Lucy had won a prize, and Marie told her about it.

Adjectives

Adjectives modify nouns. They normally are placed before the noun. Several may be grouped together.

> the *blue* sky
> the *clear blue* sky
> the *clear, blue, cloudless* sky

Adjectives may also be placed after the verb *to be* or a linking verb.

> The sky is blue.
> The sky looks blue and clear.
> The sky appears blue, clear, and cloudless.

Adjectives may be grouped together, or some may be placed before the noun and others after *to be*.

> The blue sky is clear.
> The clear blue sky is sunny and cloudless.

Most adjectives may have a comparative or superlative form.

> blue, bluer, bluest
> clear, clearer, clearest

Those that do not may form comparatives or superlatives by adding *more* and *most*.

> beautiful, more beautiful, most beautiful

Adverbs

Adverbs modify verbs, adjectives, or the predicate parts of sentences. Many adverbs end in *-ly,* but many do not. And not all words that end in *-ly* are adverbs.

An adverb may be placed in various parts of a sentence. Sometimes the placement of an adverb affects the emphasis. If there is a customary location for an adverb, it is at the end of a sentence or clause.

> The moon rose *slowly.*
> *Slowly* the moon rose.
> The moon *slowly* rose.

Trouble occurs when people confuse adjectives and adverbs. Adverbs are used to modify verbs or adjectives. Adjectives modify nouns and pronouns.

incorrect	*correct*
She sings good.	She sings well. (*Well* modifies *sings.*)
He is real handsome.	He is really handsome. (*Really* modifies *handsome*).
The tie does not look well on you.	The tie does not look good on you. (*Look* is a linking verb and requires an adjective.)

Prepositions

Prepositions are words that show relationships, often between verbs and nouns or nouns and nouns.

Let's go *to* the movies.
the window *over* the door
I'll wait *for* you.

Prepositions take objects. That means that pronouns that follow prepositions should be in the objective form:

wait for *him*
talk to *her*
rule over *us*
write on *them*

The selection of the correct preposition is often a matter of custom. For example, you wait *for* somebody, if you are expecting him or her. You wait *on* somebody if you are a waiter or waitress. Many people say *wait on* when they mean *wait for*.

An old rule of grammar stated that a sentence should never end with a preposition. This rule is rarely observed. Often a sentence is made more stiff or awkward when a correction is made to avoid a preposition at the end.

Some words that are prepositions are also adverbs. The distinction between the two sometimes escapes people. Fortunately, there are few situations in which people must discern the difference. Unfortunately, some people who try to eliminate prepositions at the ends of sentences occasionally eliminate adverbs as well.

Conjunctions

Conjunctions are words that connect other words, phrases, or clauses.

Coordinating conjunctions connect equally constructed grammatical elements. These elements may be individual words, phrases, or independent clauses. For example, *and, or,* and *but* are coordinating conjunctions in the following:

> I like vanilla *and* chocolate.
> I do not like going to school *or* staying at home.
> Father works at home; *but* mother goes to an office.

The main concern when using coordinating conjunctions is to make sure the elements are equally constructed.

Correlative conjunctions come in pairs: *neither . . . nor, either . . . or, not only . . . but also.*

> He has *neither* the time *nor* the money for that scheme.
> We can *either* go to the zoo *or* visit grandma.
> *Not only* do I have to clean the mess, *but* I *also* have to pay damages.

Subordinating conjunctions introduce dependent clauses.

> We heard *that* you were sick.
> The man *who* came to dinner is my uncle.

Words into Sentences

What is a sentence?

A sentence is a separate grammatical unit that conveys an idea. A sentence usually has at least one subject and one verb. A written sentence ends in a period, question mark, or exclamation point.

Declarative sentences

Most sentences end in periods. They are declarative sentences. The simplest standard sentence has a noun or pronoun and a verb.

subject	verb
I	sleep.
He	eats.
Kittens	play.
We	tried.
You	fell.
Henry	swam.

These simple two-word expressions are complete sentences. Each has a subject and a verb; each ends in a period. In actual speech and writing, very few sentences follow this simple sentence pattern. Details are added to each part. A written passage that contained nothing but two-word sentences would be choppy, dull, and immature. But such simple sentences are useful as starting points from which to examine form and structure in longer sentences. In a long and complicated sentence it is often important to be able to pick out the subject and the verb.

Whenever I have an exam the following morning, *I sleep* fitfully all night.

_{subject} | _{verb}

Despite heavy rains and rough weather, *Henry swam,* across the lake to rescue the children.

_{subject} | _{verb}

Our pet *kittens,* those fluffy delights, *play* incessantly with balls of yarn.

_{subject} | _{verb}

Direct object

A simple *subject + verb* sentence, such as any of the preceding, must have an *intransitive verb,* a verb that does not take an object. If the verb is *transitive,* it must take a direct object.

The basic sentence pattern for a transitive verb is:

subject	verb	direct object
I	like	you.
He	eats	strawberries.
We	played	checkers.
Henry	hit	Charlie.
You	saw	something.

The verb, the object, and any words that modify the verb and object all belong to the *predicate* part of a sentence. A sentence has two parts: a *subject* and a *predicate*.

The direct object is part of the predicate of a sentence. Notice that in most cases the word order indicates which is the subject and which is the object. The form of the word does not change. Only the position changes.

subject	verb	direct object
Henry	hit	Charlie.
Charlie	hit	Henry.
Lisa	likes	someone.
Someone	likes	Lisa.

But for certain pronouns, there is a different form whether the pronoun is the subject or the object.

subject	verb	direct object
I	greeted	him.
He	greeted	me.
She	likes	us.
We	like	her.

It is important to remember to use the correct form for subject and object when dealing with these pronouns.

Even these sentences are unusually short. There are various ways to lengthen sentences. In general sentences are made longer by adding details. Each detail makes a sentence more specific. Both the subject and the predicate of a sentence can be modified by adding details.

Modifying the subject

The subject of a sentence is usually modified by adding articles, pronouns, demonstrative pronouns (all of which are sometimes called determiners), adjectives, and noun-modifiers. Adjectives can themselves be modified by adverbs.

Notice the way the subject of the simple sentence "The cat eats fish" can be given greater detail.

subject	predicate
The cat	eats fish.
The *striped tawny* cat	eats fish.
My striped tawny alley cat	eats fish.
That horribly fat alley cat	eats fish.

Modifying the predicate

The predicate of a sentence can also be modified. The verb may be modified or the direct object may be modified. Articles, pronouns, and adjectives may modify the direct object. Adverbs may modify the verb itself. Adverbs may also modify the adjectives that modify direct objects. In the simple sentence "The cat eats fish" the predicate can be also given greater detail.

subject	predicate
The cat	eats *raw* fish.
The cat	eats *raw smelly* fish.
The cat	eats *that* fish *quickly*.
The cat	eats *horribly smelly* fish.
The cat	eats *the raw, horribly smelly* fish *quickly*.

Notice the different functions of the adverbs, "horribly" and "quickly." The adverb "horribly" modifies "smelly"—an adjective. The adverb "quickly" modifies "eats"—the verb.

Indirect object

An indirect object is a noun or pronoun that names the person *to* whom or *for* whom or the thing *to* which or *for* which an action is done. The indirect object follows an action verb in the active voice and precedes the direct object. The best way to identify an indirect object is to imagine that the word "to" or "for" precedes it as you read the sentence.

subject	verb	indirect object	direct object
Tom	gave	Jenny	a gift.
They	built	themselves	a house.
He	told	Sarah	the news.
Ellen	cooked	the family	a meal.

If, however, the word "to" or "for" is actually part of the sentence, the noun or pronoun which follows it will be the object of the preposition "to" or "for," rather than an indirect object. The examples above could be rewritten to make the indirect object in each the object of a prepositional phrase, as follows:

subject	verb	direct object	prepositional phrase
Tom	gave	a gift	to Jenny.
They	built	a house	for themselves.
He	told	the news	to Sarah.
Ellen	cooked	a meal	for the family.

In each case, use of the word "to" or "for" has changed the distinctive order of the words in the sentence, which also identifies an indirect object.

"To be" and other linking verbs

A few verbs do not take any objects. These verbs are called *linking verbs* and form the predicate by linking the subject to a following noun or adjective. The most common linking verb is the verb "to be" and all its forms. Certain other verbs such as "appear," "seem," "look," "taste," or "smell" may follow the same pattern when they function as linking verbs.

The chief point to note is that *the adjective* that occurs in the predicate part of the sentence *modifies the subject.*

subject	verb	predicate adjective
Joan	is	*pretty.*
John	appears	*tall.*
The cat	seems	*frightened.*
The dress	looks	*good.*
The soup	tastes	*delicious.*
The rose	smells	*sweet.*

The words in italics are all adjectives that modify the subjects of the sentences. They are known as *predicate adjectives* or *predicate complements.* It is important to recognize this group. Failure to recognize a linking verb causes some people mistakenly to use an adverb instead of an adjective.

Sometimes the verb "to be" links two nouns. Then "to be" or any of its forms acts almost like an equal sign. The noun that follows "to be" is not an object. It is known as a *predicate nominative*.

subject	verb	predicate nominative
I	am	*a person.* (I = a person.)
Eddie	was	*a giant.*
Claudia	is	*a soprano.*
The sign	had been	*a beacon.*
They	were	*the leaders.*
Allan	was	*chairman.*

The predicate nominative in each sentence has been italicized to help identify it.

Sentences beginning with "there"

Many sentences begin with "There."

There are ten *people* in the room.
There is *hope.*
There are no *ghosts.*
There does not seem to be any *chance.*
There may be *some* left.
There was *one* left.

In such sentences, "There" is *not* the subject. The verb must agree with the noun or pronoun that follows it. When "There" begins a sentence, it usually signals that the verb comes before the subject.

There + verb + subject.

Because this is not normal English word order, writers often fall into the trap of failing to make the verb agree with the subject. In the examples above, the subject has been italicized.

Passive voice sentences

All the sentences so far have been in the *active voice*. In the active voice, the subject acts on the verb and the verb acts on the direct object, when there is one.

In the *passive voice,* the subject of the sentence *is acted upon by the verb*. What would have been the direct object in an active voice sentence becomes the subject of a passive voice sentence. To illustrate the difference:

active

subject	verb	direct object
Amy	found	the treasure.
Paul	hears	the bells.

passive

subject	verb	
The treasure	was found	by Amy.
The bells	are heard	by Paul.

Notice that the verb agrees with the subject. Notice also that an auxiliary verb is needed in the passive.

subject	+ auxiliary verb	
Phil	*was*	*seen* leaving the building.
Strawberries	*are*	*eaten* in early summer.

Unkind rumors	*have been*	*spread* about Gail.
The soldiers	*were*	*killed* instantly.
The fish	*was*	*eaten* quickly.
Linda	*was*	*interviewed* at home.

The use of the passive places the emphasis on the receiver of the action. That kind of emphasis is important in many kinds of writing. It is useful when the agents performing the action are unknown, unimportant, or unidentified. The passive voice is very important in scientific and technical writing; in fact, the passive is often the preferred style. The passive voice is often important in news reporting when sources may not be named. It is also important when the writer wants to focus attention on the object of the verb's action.

Although many composition books warn people against excessive use of the passive, writers should not avoid it completely. Instead its use should be applied wisely. Even in writing about movement, the passive has its place:

The ball *was caught* as Slugger slid home.

If instead, the writer said:

Lefty caught the ball as Slugger slid home.

the attention would be shifted to Lefty. That is not what the writer intended to do.

Interrogative sentences

An interrogative sentence is a sentence that asks a question. A spoken question is generally signaled by a raised tone at the end of the sentence. A written question is signaled by a *question mark* at the end of the sentence.

There are a limited number of words that can begin a question. Some questions begin with auxiliary verbs such as *is, do, are, can, may, have,* or *has.* The auxiliary comes before the subject. Often this means splitting the verb, with the auxiliary before and the rest of the verb after the subject.

auxiliary	subject	remaining verb
Did	he	*give* her the book?
Will	John	*go* home?
Is	she	*singing* tonight?
Has	the mail	*arrived?*
Were	the dogs	*barking?*
May	Jason	*visit* us?

Occasionally *have* or *is* may be used without a second verb to form a question. The verb comes before the subject in these sentences.

Are they at home?
Is she a singer?
Have you any wool?
Has he a home?

Questions may also begin with one of a small group of words that are used to begin questions: *who, what, where, when, how, why, which, whose.*

Who is coming to dinner?	*How* did they learn of it?
What did he do?	*Why* hasn't John written?
Where are my socks?	*Which* house is yours?
When will you leave?	*Whose* mess is that?

A question may be a single word. One-word questions begin with capitals. When a single word does form the entire question, a previous question or statement is understood.

(Somebody told the secret.)	Who?
(Will he announce the winner?)	When?
(I discovered the treasure.)	How? Where?
(He is not going.)	Why?

Occasionally a question may be phrased in the word order that normally is reserved for declarative sentences. Such questions end with a question mark in written matter. Questions in this form often indicate surprise.

He went to the ball game?
They have been invited to dinner?
She discovered the treasure?

Indirect questions are not interrogative sentences. They are declarative sentences and they end in periods. An indirect question is a sentence that mentions or suggests a question. To understand the difference, look below.

direct questions
Where do they live?
How much does it cost?
Where did he find it?

indirect questions
Ask them where they live.
Find out how much it costs.
She wondered where he found it.

An indirect question should not be worded the same way as a direct question. For example, "Ask them where do they live" is not good wording for an indirect question.

Exclamations

Exclamations are punctuated with exclamation points. An exclamation may express surprise, anger, or other strong emotion. Some words—interjections—are used chiefly in exclamations.

Wow!   Stop!
Phooey!   You rat!
You did it!   How good you are!
Don't hit me!   What a change!

Note that exclamations need not have subjects and verbs. The word order may be the same as or different from that of a declarative sentence.

Commands

Commands are always addressed to "you." In a command the word "you" is generally left out. It is usually understood without being said. A command is considered a full sentence even though the subject ("you") is not indicated.

> Bring me the book.   Tell me a story.
> Go to sleep.   Count to ten.

Sentence fragments

Sentence fragments are groups of words that *do not make a grammatical sentence*. Often they do not have a subject and a verb. They are incomplete.

There are many acceptable uses for sentence fragments. Sentence fragments are acceptable as exclamations:

> What fun!
> How lovely!

Sentence fragments are acceptable as questions, provided that a previous statement or question establishes the nature of the question:

	fragment
"Mr. Smith is away on vacation."	"For how long?"
"He will be back soon."	"When?"

Sentence fragments are also acceptable as answers to questions.

question	fragment answer
Where did he go?	Upstairs to his room.
Do you like him?	No.
When will he return?	Next week.

Many good writers may use sentence fragments effectively to accomplish a purpose, to establish a certain pace, or to suggest a disjointed quality.

> Into the alley he went. Up the fire escape. Over the wall. Around a corner. Into a bar.

Except for the first sentence, the passage above contains only sentence fragments. Such a passage may or may not work well in a given context.

The chief danger of using sentence fragments lies in not knowing that they are fragments, but thinking they are sentences. The writer of the following passage may or may not have known that the last two "sentences" are fragments:

> Strolling the ancient city's streets, I seemed to hear the ghosts of history telling of its founding centuries ago. *Of its trade with the Scythians and with tribes up and down the Danube. Telling of Alexander the Great.*

Why is neither a sentence? Let us examine them:

Of its trade with the Scythians, and with the tribes up and down the Danube.

The sentence has no verb. None of the nouns (trade, Scythians, tribes, or Danube) is the subject of the sentence. All are objects of prepositions.

Telling of Alexander the Great.

The only suggestion of a verb is *telling* — the present participle of *tell*. And the only noun is *Alexander the Great*, and that is not the subject of the sentence.

How could this paragraph be corrected to turn all the fragments into sentences? There are several ways.

The entire paragraph can be rewritten as one sentence.

> Strolling the ancient city's streets, I seemed to hear the ghosts of history telling of its founding centuries ago, of its trade with the Scythians and with tribes up and down the Danube, and also of Alexander the Great.

Or it can be rewritten by adding a subject to the two fragment sentences.

> Strolling the ancient city's streets, I seemed to hear the ghosts of history telling of its founding centuries ago. The ghosts seemed to tell of trade with the Scythians and with tribes up and down the Danube. The ghosts also told of Alexander The Great.

Sentence fragments may be long or short. But unless they are recognized, they cannot be avoided when avoidance is desired. People who are just beginning to master the elements of grammar and composition should try to avoid sentence fragments.

Sentence Structure and Patterns

Most of the sentences examined so far were fairly simple in structure. Each had a subject and verb. Some had a direct object and an indirect object. The subject, verb, or object may have been modified. But in each example there was generally only one subject, one verb, and one of each kind of object. It was fairly easy to identify the subject, verb, and objects in each.

Sentences can grow far more complicated than the examples we have seen. A sentence may have several subjects, verbs, or objects. Some sentences may have many *phrases* and *clauses*. The more complicated a sentence becomes, the more difficult it may be to identify the subject and predicate.

Coordinate elements

One of the simplest ways to enlarge a simple sentence is to use more than one subject, verb, or object. When there are multiple elements, it is important to keep them parallel in form. The multiple elements may be subjects.

multiple subjects:

Avoid such ill-matched combinations as "Wisdom, learning, and to know are not the same." "To know" is an infinitive and does not fit the pattern established by "wisdom, learning...". "Wisdom, learning, and knowledge..." would be better.

The multiple subject may be a series of phrases instead of individual words.

_____ subjects_____
Going to school, keeping house, and *maintaining a job* complicate her life. _____ subjects_____
Antique tapestries from France, handwoven Navaho blankets, ___ subjects___
and *Early American samplers* cover the walls.

There should be no comma between the last subject and the verb. And, of course, the verb must agree with the subject.

Sometimes one preposition will work for all elements of a series: Dreams *of* wealth, fame, and happiness kept her going.

It is acceptable either to repeat the preposition or to allow the one preposition to govern the various elements: Dreams *of* wealth, *of* fame, and *of* happiness kept her going. (Wealth, fame, and happiness are all understood to be objects of the preposition "of.") It is not good style to repeat it once and not again. For example, "Dreams of wealth, fame, and of happiness kept her going."

The same preposition may not work for all the elements in a series. It is then necessary to give the appropriate preposition for each element.

The multiple elements may be verbs:

multiple verbs:

He *cut, fit, and sewed* the clothes in one day.

She *tried, failed, and tried* again.

The children *dried* their tears and *began* to sing.

Note that two or more verbs may accompany a single subject. Sometimes the verbs are simple. Sometimes, as in the third example, the entire predicate may be multiple.

It is possible to have more than one verb, each with its objects or modifiers. A comma should not separate the subject from either verb.

> We *ate* our sandwiches and *drank* our milk.
> Jimmy *waved* good-by to his friends and *drove* home slowly.

When using auxiliaries with verbs, it is important to make sure that the tenses are maintained correctly. It is easy to forget that the auxiliary verb governs all the verbs in the series.

> He has *come* and *gone*. "Gone" is correct, not "went" because "has" governs both past participles.

The time machine *has not been*, perhaps never *will be*, invented.

Two different auxiliaries are needed: "has been" for the present perfect tense and "will be" for the future. The past participle goes with both.

The multiple elements may be objects:

multiple objects:

(direct objects):

   ⌜— objects ⌝
We ate *fish* and *chips*.

     ⌜— objects —⌝
Felicia bought *books, clothes,* and *records.*

    ⌜— objects ——————⌝
I enjoy *going to movies, riding a bicycle,* and *building birdhouses.*

(indirect objects):

    ⌜— indirect objects —⌝
Give the tickets to *Tom, Dick,* and *Harry.*

       ⌜——⌝ indirect objects
Did you throw the ball to *him* or at *him?*

In all the examples given so far there has been either one subject and several verbs, one verb and several subjects, or one verb and several objects. The verbs, the subjects and the objects may be multiple.

   ⌜two subjects⌝ ⌜— two verbs —⌝
a. Dick and Jane ran and skipped all the way.

Note that both subjects govern both verbs.

  ⌜—— two subjects ——⌝ ⌜— two verbs —⌝
b. The cat and the kitten sniffed and ate the fish
⌜two direct objects⌝
and chicken.

Both subjects may govern both verbs, *and* both verbs may govern both objects.

two subjects ⟶ 1st verb 1st object 2nd verb

c. The cat and the kitten ate the fish and drank

2nd object

the milk.

Example **c** differs from example **b**. In **c**, both subjects govern both verbs. But each verb has its own direct object.

Clauses

A clause is a group of words that has a subject and predicate. A clause may be *independent* or it may be *subordinate.*

An *independent clause* can be a sentence in itself. It can also be the main clause of a larger sentence. The main clause is sometimes called the "basic sentence."

A *subordinate clause* has a subject and a predicate, too. But it cannot stand by itself as a complete sentence. It depends on the main clause. The subordinate clause is sometimes called a "dependent clause."

subordinate clause ⟶ Independent clause

If it rains, we'll go home.

"We'll go home" can be a separate sentence. It is an independent clause.

"If it rains" cannot stand alone as a separate sentence. It is a subordinate clause.

Compound sentences

Compound sentences are made up of two or more *coordinate* independent clauses. *Coordinate* in this sense means of equal importance. A compound sentence is made up of clauses that could each be separate sentences if the writer wanted to write them as separate sentences.

> We tried and we failed.
>
> I tried to buy sugar, but the store was out of it.
>
> He will pick up the package tomorrow, or you will have to mail it.
>
> We climbed up the trail, and the snow nearly trapped us.
>
> John didn't win the trophy; he didn't even try.
>
> Henry will prepare the dessert, Molly will make the salad, and I'll cook the main course.
>
> People are born, people die, but the earth spins on.

Notice that the last two examples have more than two independent clauses. They are said to be in series. A series of three or more independent clauses may eliminate the coordinating conjunction after the comma in all but the last of the series.

Each of the above sentences can be rewritten as two or more separate sentences.

> We tried. And we failed.
>
> I tried to buy sugar. But the store was out of it.

He will pick up the package tomorrow. Or you will have to mail it.

We climbed up the trail. And the snow nearly trapped us.

John didn't win the trophy. He didn't even try.

Henry will prepare the dessert. Molly will make the salad. And I'll cook the main course.

People are born. People die. But the earth spins on.

The independent clauses of a compound sentence may be separated by:

- a comma and a coordinate conjunction *(and, and so, but, or, nor, for, yet, so): I tried to buy sugar, but the store was out of it.*
- a semicolon if there is no coordinate conjunction: *John didn't win the trophy; he didn't even try.*
- a coordinating conjunction alone only if the two clauses are very short: *We tried and we failed.*
- a comma may replace a semicolon only in very short sentences: *Sometimes you win, sometimes you lose.*

The subjects of the independent clauses in a sentence may be identical, or they may be different. But the subject must be stated in each clause. If it is not, the sentence is not a compound sentence.

Notice the difference between these two sentences.

> He ran, and he jumped.
> He ran and jumped.

The first sentence is a compound sentence. It can be separated into two sentences: *He ran. And he jumped.* The second sentence is not a compound sentence. Its subject is stated only once, and it is a simple sentence with coordinate verbs.

It is important to recognize the difference between the two kinds of sentences. The second sentence should not have a comma before "and." The first sentence should have a comma before "and."

Because independent clauses can be combined into a single sentence, some people have a tendency to overdo the combining or to punctuate incorrectly. Some common errors that arise from this tendency are:

Run-on sentences

Run-on sentences are sentences in which too many independent clauses have been combined. They are difficult to read. Run-on sentences can usually be corrected by separating the clauses into individual sentences. The conjunctions that connect the clauses of run-on sentences can then be eliminated.

run-on sentence	corrected to
The wicked witch cast a spell *so* the prince fell	The wicked witch cast a spell. The prince fell

asleep, *and* the princess didn't know what to do, *but* the king sent the knight to fight the dragon, *then* the prince awoke.

asleep, and the princess didn't know what to do. The king sent the knight to fight the dragon. Then the prince awoke.

Comma splice

A comma splice occurs when a comma without a coordinating conjunction separates the main clauses of a compound sentence. A comma splice can easily be repaired in one of four ways.

- insert a coordinating conjunction
- replace the comma with a semicolon
- rewrite the clauses to make separate sentences
- turn one clause into a subordinate clause

comma splice

The moon hid behind a cloud, all the world turned dark.

corrected to

The moon hid behind a cloud, and all the world turned dark.

or

The moon hid behind a cloud; all the world turned dark.

or

The moon hid behind a cloud. All the world turned dark.

or

Because the moon hid
behind a cloud, all the
world turned dark.

Fused sentences

Fused sentences are two or more sentences joined
without punctuation. Often the writer is under the
mistaken notion that a compound sentence has been
created. Fused sentences can be separated into individual sentences.

fused sentence	corrected to
He didn't ask me he just did it.	He didn't ask me. He just did it.
John said he was going to enter the big race then his mother said that she would not allow it.	John said he was going to enter the big race. Then his mother said that she would not allow it.

Complex sentences

A complex sentence has an independent clause and
a subordinate clause. The subordinate clause is usually
introduced by a subordinate conjunction *(if, because,
although, when, as soon as, whenever, even though,
before, since, unless, until,* etc.).

The subordinate clause may come before or after
the main clause. When it comes before the main clause,
a comma usually separates the clauses. (The subordinate clauses are in italics.)

I'll go to the dance *if mother lets me.*

(subordinate clause)

If mother lets me, I'll go to the dance.

(subordinate clause)

Because I laughed, the teacher asked me to leave the room.

The teacher asked me to leave the room *because I laughed.*

(subordinate clause)

When the rains fall, the river overflows.

He will return *as soon as he has train fare.*

Do you know the man *who sat next to you?*

We enjoyed the party *that you gave.*

Because the subordinate clause of a complex sentence has a subject and a verb, some people make the mistake of trying to set it up as a separate sentence. This results in sentence fragments. In this case, these sentence fragments can be corrected in two ways.

- The fragment can be woven into the main sentence.
- The subordinating conjunction can be eliminated, and the subordinate clause can become a main clause.

fragment	**corrected to**
He left the scene very quickly. Because the police were pursuing him for the theft.	He left the scene very quickly because the police were pursuing him for the theft.

or

He left the scene very quickly. The police were pursuing him for the theft.

Compound-complex sentences

Compound-complex sentences are sentences that have two or more independent clauses and at least one subordinate clause.

```
   ┌── subordinate clause ──┐   ┌── independent clause ──┐
```
After the war ended, prices continued to rise,

```
   ┌── independent clause ──┐
```
and the black market thrived.

```
   ┌────── independent clause ──────┐   independent clause
```
Everybody stopped speaking, and the ticking

```
                                                    sub-
```
clock was all that could be heard when the

```
ordinate clause
```
maharishi took the stage.

```
   ┌────── independent clause ──────┐  ┌ subordinate
```
The children filed out of the school as soon as

```
── clause ──┐  ┌── independent clause ──┐
```
the bell rang, and the janitors checked the class-

```
──┐  ┌── subordinate clause ──┐
```
rooms because they wanted to clean them.

Subordinate clauses as subjects, objects, modifiers

When subordinate clauses occur in sentences, they often fill the job of a particular part of speech. The entire clause may serve as a noun, an adjective, or an adverb.

When a subordinate clause fills the role of a noun, it may serve as a subject or an object.

as subject:

How the pyramids were built remains a mystery. [subject]

That she is an impostor cannot be proven. [subject]

What he found out is a secret. [subject]

as object of a verb:

The architect discovered *how the pyramids were built*. [object]

Can you prove *that she is an impostor?* [object]

We know *that he found the secret*. [object]

as object of a preposition:

John learned about *what had been said*. [object]

She will go to *whatever school she chooses*. [object]

as a predicate nominative:

The story is *that he disappeared*. [predicate nominative]

It seems *that he did run away*. [predicate nominative]

When a subordinate clause fills the role of an adverb, it modifies a verb, adjective, or another adverb.

modifying a verb:

He will return *as soon as he has train fare*. [verb] [subordinate clause]

Sally will dance *if you ask her*. [verb] [subordinate clause]

modifying an adjective:

The movie was funnier *than I expected*. [adjective] [subordinate clause]

Simon is as tall *as I am*. [adjective] [subordinate clause]

133

modifying an adverb:

    adverb ⌐

She ran quickly *as a gazelle might.*

    ⌐ adverb

He gossiped more indiscreetly *than I imagined possible.*

When a subordinate clause fills the role of an adjective, it generally modifies a noun.

modifying a noun:

    noun ⌐

I like the dress *that you bought.*

    ⌐ noun

I find myself on the street *where you live.*

noun ⌐

The man *who is wise* avoids trouble.

To summarize: A *noun clause* is a clause that functions as a noun in a sentence. An *adverbial clause* functions as an adverb in a sentence. An *adjectival clause* functions as an adjective in a sentence.

A noun clause *is not* a clause that begins with a noun. An adverbial clause *is not* a clause that begins with an adverb. An adjectival clause *is not* a clause that begins with an adjective.

Each of the clauses is so labeled because of its function in a sentence.

Periodic sentences

A periodic sentence is one in which the main clause comes at the end. Two or more clauses or phrases — often parallel in construction — lead up to the main clause. A periodic sentence can be very dramatic in effect if it is used well and infrequently. In a periodic sentence, it is important that the main clause justify the lead-up.

periodic sentence with subordinate clauses:

> Because he had burned their villages, because he had ignored
>
> their pleas for mercy, because his cruelty increased with his
>
> successes, *they attacked him* with unexpected savagery.
>   ⌐— main clause —⌐

periodic sentence with phrases:

> In winter, in summer, in good times and bad, in health and
> ⌐——— main clause ————⌐
> sickness, *he always had time for others.*

> Working long hours, saving every penny she could, denying
>
> herself luxuries. using every resource she had, *she man-*
> ⌐————— main clause —————⌐
> *aged to save enough for an education.*

> By the light of the moon, in out-of-the-way places, unseen
>   ⌐— main clause —⌐
> by mortals, *the wee folk gather.*

Phrases and verb forms

A phrase is a group of words that together have some
meaning. A phrase does not have to have a subject
and a verb, but it may. A clause or a short sentence
may be called a phrase, but most phrases would not
be called clauses. Clauses must have subjects and verbs.

Phrases may be used to modify nouns, adjectives,
verbs, and even complete sentences. The phrases may
be used in the same way that single words may be
used in a sentence.

Apposition

A noun or pronoun may have a noun or a phrase
in *apposition*. That is, a noun or phrase may stand next
to the noun or pronoun and extend its meaning.

Miss Grimsby, *our teacher,* is very strict.

We, *the committee,* are responsible for the decision.

My sister *Rosalie* has red hair.

You, *the organizer of the event,* deserve our thanks.

The girl *over there* is shy.

The book *under the counter* is rare.

The man *drinking coffee* is the spy.

We thanked our teacher, *Miss Grimsby.*

He winked at my sister *Rosalie.*

Notice that either the subject or the object may have a word or phrase in apposition. It is the first noun or pronoun—not the one in apposition—that determines the form of the verb. (We, the committee, *are,* not *is;* You—deserve, not "the organizer . . . deserves," etc.)

Object complement

Some verbs seem to have two objects. The second object is not really in apposition to the first. The second is an *object complement.*

The council elected John *president.*

We appointed Sara *leader.*

They named him *king of the jungle.*

An adjective can also be an object complement.

The heat made the plant *brown*.
Opposition turned the deal *sour*.

Verb forms in noun positions

The subject of a sentence need not be a noun. It may be a clause. It may also be an infinitive of a verb.

> *To travel* requires money.
> *To speak* honestly is difficult.

Even though the infinitive *(to speak)* may take the place of a noun, its verbal nature is maintained. It is modified by an adverb *(honestly)* as a verb would be modified. A noun would be modified by an adjective.

The infinitive can also serve as an object.

> He likes *to sit*.
> He wants *to play* hockey.

The object *(to play)* is still basically a verb. It has its own object *(hockey)*.

A *gerund* is the *-ing* form of a verb when used as a noun while conveying the meaning of a verb. A gerund may serve as a subject or an object. Many gerunds have become nouns in their own right.

> *Traveling* requires money.
> His *going* relieves us of a problem.
> We enjoy *singing*.
> Good *singing* gives us pleasure.
> *Singing* well gives us pleasure.

Note that a gerund *(singing)* may be modified by an adjective *(good)* or an adverb *(well)*. When the gerund has more of a noun sense, an adjective modifies it; when it has more of a verbal sense, an adverb modifies it.

Gerunds have more nounlike functions than infinitives. Gerunds may be used in apposition, as object complements, and as objects of prepositions.

Participles and other modifiers

A modifier may modify a word, a phrase, a clause, or a whole sentence. A modifier may be a word, a phrase, a clause, or a whole sentence.

As you know, a clause or a phrase may function as an adjective, an adverb, or a noun. The phrase or clause that modifies must be placed in the correct relationship to the word it modifies.

> *Having seen the house,* she left.
> *Though sick,* he went to work.

These examples are grammatically acceptable. The sentences could also be rewritten.

> She left *having seen the house.*
> He went to work *though sick.*

They still make sense. That is because the modifying phrase logically belongs with the pronouns (*she* and *he*).

Dangling modifiers

These occur when a modifier does not modify the subject of the main clause. Dangling modifiers usually occur at the beginnings of sentences.

Sentences have to be rewritten to correct the dangling modifier.

|——————— dangling modifier ———————|

Though sick, I saw him at work.   *After running the race,* we saw him faint.

corrected to

Though he was sick, I saw him at work.   We saw him faint after running the race.

Notice that the problem with the dangling modifier occurs because it has no subject of its own. The subject of the main clause is usually taken to be the subject of the modifier. That creates some ridiculous images. Once a writer learns to recognize the silliness of what was said unintentionally, that writer will make fewer and fewer such errors.

dangling modifier

On returning home, the door slammed shut. (The door was not returning home.)

Falling from the tree, the girl caught the apple. (In this case, the apple was falling from the tree, not the girl.)

Absolute construction

To complicate matters, there are some modifiers that modify the whole sentence. This kind of modifier is said to be an absolute construction.

The moment having arrived, we went inside the church. **absolute construction**

The cause lost, we abandoned our headquarters.

Apparently, the city was blacked out.
absolute construction

Such clauses, phrases, and individual words are acceptable English. They should not be confused with dangling modifiers. Sentence modifiers modify the whole sentence. Dangling modifiers unintentionally modify the wrong elements in a sentence.

Parenthetical remarks

Occasionally a writer wants to insert a comment or explanation within a sentence. That comment or explanation may not be a part of the actual sentence construction. The insertions are known as *parenthetical remarks*.

There are several kinds of parenthetical remarks and several different ways of punctuating them:

with commas;
with parentheses;
with brackets;
with dashes.

Commas are used only when the parenthetical remark is very short and flows well within the sentence.

My friend, *the one who moved to Chicago,* just got married.

John, *old and infirm though he is,* walked all the way home.

Commas are used in these sentences only for *nonrestrictive* phrases or clauses.

nonrestrictive	**restrictive**
My son, *the doctor,* sent me a letter. (The writer has one son who happens to be a doctor.)	My son *the doctor* sent me a letter. (The writer has more than one son. The one who is a doctor sent her the letter.)

Parentheses are used for longer material, further explanation, and side comments.

> The whole group (except for those who had resigned) agreed to settle the debt.

> The warriors had not really left town (as their letter seemed to indicate) but were waiting in ambush.

> The article on cryogenics (see page 38) suggests that the future may hold great appeal for some sufferers.

> He said he woodn't (*sic*) go. (*Sic* means that the word was originally written that way.)

Note that parentheses may be used for whole sentences as well as words or phrases.

Brackets are usually reserved for more formal situations than parentheses. But they may be used also in place of parentheses.

> . . . life, liberty, and the *pursuit* [italics added] of happiness.

> The women live in purdah [veils as required by religion and custom] and few men ever see their faces.

Dashes are used in the same way as parentheses are, to set off a parenthetical remark.

> The medium spoke of spirits—poltergeists, ghosts, ghouls—as if she thought we all believed in them.

> A two-week camping trip—whenever the weather allows us to leave—is the high point of our planned vacation.

Whether a writer uses parentheses, brackets, or dashes is often a matter of personal choice. Some writers tend to use parentheses; others use dashes. The important point is to be sure that the sentence that goes around the parenthetical remark makes sense in its own right. If you remove the parenthetical remark, the sentence should be grammatically correct.

Sentences into Paragraphs

Almost everything we write—letters, essays, stories, memoranda, term papers—is divided into paragraphs. Why do we make the divisions? How do we know what goes into a paragraph and when to stop and begin the next one?

A paragraph is a unit of thought. A writer tries to organize each paragraph around one theme or idea, and groups sentences that deal with each theme in one paragraph. Then the next theme is explored in the next paragraph. The theme may be highly structured with a main idea and subdivisions of that main idea. Or the theme may be loose enough so that the only organizing theme is the writer's perception of connected thoughts.

Often a theme is stated in the paragraph's topic sentence. The remaining sentences in the paragraph expand on the topic sentence by giving specifics. Often, but not always, the topic sentence is the first sentence of the paragraph.

Within a paragraph, the ideas should move easily from one sentence to the next. There should be a logic in the progression from sentence to sentence. The logic should be clear to the reader as well as to the writer.

What is true for each paragraph is also true for groups of paragraphs. There should be a clear logic in the progression from paragraph to paragraph. Often the progression of ideas can be seen just by reading the topic sentences in each paragraph.

These are some general rules for developing paragraphs:

1. Each paragraph should present a *unit*. It must be a grouping of sentences that are related to each other and to the main thought.
2. Each paragraph should present a complete thought and expand on it fully before ending the paragraph and beginning the next.
3. Within the paragraph, there should be a logic of movement: from general statement to specifics; from specific statements to general ones; from the beginning of an action to the end of the action; from a statement to a refutation to a re-examination of the original statement. The possibilities are numerous.
4. There should be a good balance of kinds of sentences. At times it is very effective to repeat the same structure in sentence after sentence within a paragraph. But this stylistic device can be over-used. It is more effective to vary the rhythm, length, and construction of sentences.
5. It is important to maintain the same person throughout a paragraph. Switching from "you" to "one" to "they" can be very disconcerting to a reader.
6. It is important to maintain the same tense for the

same subject within a paragraph. Events in the past should not be described in the present and also in the past. At times, some of the events in a paragraph may have taken place in the far past, others over a period of time. The sequence of tenses should make the time relationship clear.

7. The introduction of a new topic requires the beginning of a new paragraph.

Some paragraphs require special attention. They have special places within a written work and serve special functions.

The opening paragraph

The opening paragraph is the first paragraph of a written work. A major function of the opening paragraph is to engage the reader's attention. There are several customary ways of doing this.

1. Ask a question. The question should go to the heart of the material you deal with. The question may be asked as a direct question ("Are sharks monogamous?") or as an indirect question ("We wanted to know if sharks are monogamous").

2. Make a statement. The statement should be clearly worded. No qualifying phrases should offset the force of the statement. The statement may be the basic theme of the work or it may be the reason for writing the work ("There is no good published material on the breeding life of the shark").

3. Begin with a quotation. You may then proceed to agree or disagree with the quotation. In either case, the quotation should be directly related to the theme of the work.
4. Present a short anecdote. The anecdote may be directly or obliquely related to the rest of the piece.
5. Cite an opinion by an authority, or offer a common view with which you agree or disagree.

Transitional paragraphs

In a sense, every paragraph makes a transition from the paragraph before to the paragraph after. Some paragraphs, however, must make a major transition from one block of ideas to another block of ideas. There are several devices that make transitions flow more smoothly.

1. Summarize what has gone before, and lead in to the next theme with a transitional word or phrase such as "on the other hand," "but," "however," etc.
2. Find a link for the ideas before and the ideas after, and lead from one to the other.
3. Use a short paragraph that picks up a word or phrase from the preceding paragraph. Then introduce a main idea for what will follow.

Concluding paragraphs

A concluding paragraph is the finishing touch to a piece of writing. When a reader encounters a good concluding paragraph, there is no temptation to turn the page to see what comes next. How is this accomplished?

1. By summarizing the ideas that have gone before. This technique is effective only with long pieces of writing.
2. By drawing conclusions about what has been said.
3. By stating further questions to be explored at another time.

Usage Glossary

The material in this section, arranged alphabetically by topics, attempts to provide guidance in problems that are basic and therefore recurrent, especially in usage of the written word with its more exacting standards.

This glossary has also striven for wide-ranging coverage in concise form with a minimum of technical terms. *Formal usage,* as employed here, refers to that which conforms to established educated usage. *Informal* (colloquial) is applied to that which belongs to the usage of natural spoken language but which is considered usually inappropriate to careful writing, especially in certain cultural contexts, as in the standard written prose of ceremonial and official communications.

a, an Use *an* before words beginning with vowels (*a, e, i, o,* and *u*) and before words beginning with an unpronounced *h.* For example: *an athlete; an enormous cake; an umbrella; an heir; an honor.* Use *a* before all other words—those beginning with a consonant sound: *a doctor; a good decision.*

A is used before words beginning with a vowel that forms a consonant sound: *a union; a university; a usage glossary; a European.*

Both *a* and *an* are possible before words beginning with *h* in an unaccented syllable: *historic, historical, historian, hotel,* and *hypothesis,* for example. In modern usage, *a* is preferred in such examples, but *an* is also acceptable, especially in combinations such as *an historic occasion* and *an historical novel.*

When numbers are used in a sentence, treat them as corresponding words and make your choice of *a* or *an* according to the rules above: *a 40-hour week* (*a* before *forty*); *an 8-hour day* (*an* before *eight*).

able This adjective is often followed by an infinitive in the active voice (*able to see*), but not in the passive (not *able to be seen*).

(not) about to This construction, or variant also in the negative, is used to emphasize intention or express determination by means of understatement: *troops not about to surrender.* Though based on a legitimate meaning of *about* (ready or prepared), the expression is informal, often found in regional speech and writing reproducing that.

above With reference to something stated earlier in a piece of writing, *above* is better used as an adjective or adverb: *the above* (aforementioned) *statement; the material quoted above.* The noun usage is undesirable outside legal or commercial writing: *consult the above* (preferably *the above material, the figures cited above,* or the like).

accept, except Of these verbs, only *accept* means to receive or admit, to regard as right or true, or to bear up under. *Except,* often misused in the preceding senses because of similar pronunciation, means to leave out, exclude, or excuse.

acceptance, acceptation To denote the act of accepting or state of being accepted, use *acceptance. Acceptation* is employed, much less often, to denote the usual or accepted meaning of a word or expression.

acquiesce This verb usually takes the prepositions *to* (*acquiesced to their wishes*) or *in* (*acquiesced in the ruling*).

act, action As nouns these are sometimes interchangeable. But *act* is usually applied to a specific brief deed of a person, and *action* to a performance complex or long-range. *Act* stresses what is done rather than the process of doing; *action* emphasizes such process or function: *an act of mercy; one's actions* (acts considered collectively or as a chain of events); *the action of a drug.*

A.D. This abbreviation precedes the date, which is always a specific year rather than a century: *died A.D. 405* (not *in the fifth century A.D.*).

adapt, adopt Both refer to taking something or someone. *Adapt* adds the idea of changing or adjusting to a different use, need, or situation; *adopt* does not imply such change: *adapt machinery; a novel adapted for stage presentation; adapt to new surroundings;*

adopt a child; adopted the costume and customs of her new homeland.

admission, admittance Use *admittance* for physical entry to a specific place: *no admittance to the jury room.* Use *admission* for figurative entry (*admission of evidence*) or, when physical entry is involved, in the further sense of right or privilege of participation: *admission to a society; the price of admission to a theater.*

admit When it means to confess or acknowledge, *admit* is followed by a direct object, not by *to: admit a mistake; admit having made an error.* See the section headed "Picking a Preposition" for correct use of prepositions with *admit.*

adopt See **adapt, adopt.**

adopted, adoptive One refers to *adopted* children and *adoptive* parents.

advance, advanced, advancement The noun *advance* is applied to both actual forward movement and figurative progress; *advancement,* to figurative progress: *advances in science; the advancement of science; an advancement in rank.* The adjective *advance* implies actual precedence in position (*advance guard*) or time (*advance word*); *advanced* implies figuratively forward position with respect to a norm: *advanced mathematics; advanced thought.*

adverse, averse Both words express opposition, but from different points of view. Something *adverse* to a person or thing reflects opposition contrary to the subject's interest or will: *adverse decisions.* To be *averse* to something indicates opposition on the subject's part: *a perfectionist averse to overlooking any shortcoming.*

advice, advise The noun *advice* is the equivalent of counsel or guidance. The verb *advise* means to offer such guidance.

affect, effect Each is a verb and a noun. In practice, however, *affect* is almost always a verb and *effect* most often a noun. As verbs, *affect* is used principally in senses relating to influencing or causing a change in, and to simulating or imitating so as to make a desired impression (*drugs that affect the nervous system; affected poor health to gain sympathy*); *effect* means to bring about or make: *layoffs designed to effect savings.* As nouns, *affect* is now confined to psychology as a technical term; *effect* is used chiefly in the senses of result or influence: *a plea to no effect; the effect of drugs on the nervous system.*

afterward, afterwards Both are acceptable, but *afterward* is preferred in American written usage.

agenda Though plural in form, this noun is used with a singular verb: *The agenda is complete.* It is construed in a collective sense: a list of things to be done, especially the program for a meeting. *Agendum* (singular) is an item on an agenda. *Agenda* has developed its own plural: *agendas*.

aggravate Strictly, the verb means to make worse or more of a burden: *Smoking aggravates a sore throat.* Only informally does *aggravate* mean to annoy, provoke, irritate, or vex.

ago Use *ago* alone or followed by *that* or *when: I saw her last a week ago. It was a week ago that* (or *when*) *I saw her last. Ago* is redundant in combination with *since,* which stands alone: *It has been a week since I saw her last.*

ain't This contraction of *am not* is appropriate only to deliberately informal usage, chiefly to record uneducated speech, or as a device for providing humor, shock, or other special effect. Like all such devices, this one leaves the writer open to the risk of having his or her intention misunderstood. The interrogative form *ain't I?* has the virtue of agreement between pronoun and verb (unlike *ain't* used with other pronouns such as *it, he,* or *they,* or with nouns); but even this form has only slightly more acceptance than the others.

alibi In formal usage, employ *alibi* only as a noun: a form of defense whereby a defendant seeks to prove he or she was elsewhere when a crime was committed. When it means, in effect, an excuse, the noun is used informally. The verb (to make excuses) is used only for informal writing or speech.

all When *all* is the equivalent of *everything, the whole,* it takes a singular verb: *All is not in vain.* When the meaning is *each one of a group,* a plural verb follows: *All are now accounted for.* When a noun follows the expression *all but one,* it is singular and so is a verb after the noun: *All but one ship is accounted for. All of* invariably precedes a pronoun: *all of us;* it can precede a noun, but *all* is sufficient: *all* (*of*) *the buildings.* An informal usage couples *all* (adverb) with *that* in negative and interrogative sentences implying comparison: *She's not all that good. Is she all that good?*

all-around, all-round The second form, *all-round,* is preferable. Both forms are hyphenated, and each is used only as an adjective before a noun: *all-round* (comprehensive) *capability; an all-round* (versatile) *athlete.* These should not be confused with *all round* (or *all around*), written without hyphens and used adverbially (*a plan better all round*) and prepositionally: *went all round the town.*

all ready, already *All ready* expresses complete readiness; *already* expresses time adverbially: *He was now all ready, but the carriage had already departed.*

all right, alright   The form *alright* is a misspelling. These forms differ not in meaning but in acceptability. Use *all right*.

all together, altogether   *All together* is always applied collectively in the sense of closeness or unity, physical or figurative: *cattle huddled all together; democracies standing all together. Altogether* has the collective sense of *in all; all told: four choices altogether.* Or it can mean *entirely* (*altogether satisfactory*) or *on the whole: Altogether, I'm satisfied.*

allude, elude   They resemble each other in sound and appearance but not in meaning. To *allude* is to make an indirect reference to something. To *elude* someone or something is to avoid, evade, or escape from the person or thing.

allusion, illusion   These unrelated nouns are confused because they look and sound alike. An *allusion* is an indirect mention or reference. (Both *allude* and *allusion* are sometimes misused when a direct, explicit reference is indicated.) An *illusion* is an erroneous perception or impression. See also **delusion.**

along with   When these words introduce an addition, following the subject of a sentence or clause, the addition does not alter the number of the verb, which is governed by the subject: *The prime minister, along* *with the secretary, is expected in an hour*. The rule also applies to phrases introduced by *as well as, besides, in addition to, like, together with,* and *with*.

also   This is an adverb, not a connective. It cannot replace *and* in an example such as *fumes that pollute the air also damage building exteriors*. Make it: *and also damage*.

alternative, alternate   As a noun or an adjective *alternative* carries the meaning of one or the other: *annihilation, the alternative to surrender*. Or it can be used acceptably for more than two courses or choices: *four alternative game plans*. On the other hand, *alternate* carries the meaning of one coming after the other: *alternate periods of prosperity and recession; worked on alternate weekends*.

although, though   These are often interchangeable. *Although* is most often the first word of a concessive clause: *Although she was tired, she accepted. Though* does not always come first: *Tired though she was, she accepted. Though* is the more common in linking single words or phrases: *wiser though poorer*.

alumnus   This is the masculine form for a graduate or former student; the plural is *alumni*. The feminine terms are *alumna* and *alumnae*. The plural *alumni* is often used to denote all graduates or former students of co-educational schools.

A.M., P.M. Although *12 A.M.* denotes noon and *12 P.M.* denotes midnight, it is advisable to use *12 noon* and *12 midnight* to avoid confusion.

ambivalent This very special word is increasingly used, and misused. It describes the simultaneous existence of conflicting emotions or ideas (love and hate, for example) about a single person or thing. It is misused when the prevailing sense is that of *ambiguous* (unclear and thus open to several interpretations) or *equivocal* (evasive).

amend, emend Both verbs refer to improving by revising or editing. *Emend* is limited to that sense; *amend* most often refers to changing a document, such as a constitution, by formal addition.

American Indian See **Native American.**

among See **between, among.**

an See **a, an.**

anachorism, anachronism The first of these nouns denotes something out of place geographically (unsuited to its location), and the second something out of its proper time.

and etc. Make this just *etc.* The word *and* is part of et cetera (abbreviated etc.), which means *and other unspecified things of the same class.*

anticipate In constructions in the passive voice, *anticipate,* unlike *expect,* is not followed by an infinitive: *Trouble is expected* (or *expected to occur*). *Trouble is anticipated* (but not *anticipated to occur*). *A severe storm was anticipated* (but not *The storm was anticipated to be severe*).

anxious, eager These terms overlap to some extent when *anxious* has the sense of eagerly or earnestly desirous. In such instances, however, *anxious* should be used only when anxiety is present in some degree. Otherwise, *eager* is usually a much better choice: *anxious to hear that you arrived safely; anxious to see the new quarters* (where there is ground for concern); *eager to see your new apartment, your new car,* or the like.

any The pronoun *any* takes either a singular or plural verb, depending on how *any* is construed: *Any of these gifts* (any one among three or more) *is appropriate. Are any* (some; more than one) *of them within our means?*

In comparisons of like things, *any other* is preferable to *any* in an example such as: *The house seemed finer than any other he had known.*

An even less desirable use of *any* (adjective) with a singular noun is illustrated by *the most famous of any Spanish composer.* Make it *most famous Spanish composer; most famous of Spanish composers,* or *of all Spanish composers.*

Any (adverb) is chiefly appropriate to informal usage in interrogative and negative constructions such as: *Did the new part help any? At least it didn't hurt any.*

anymore, any more *Anymore* is an adverb of time, used in negative and interrogative constructions: *He doesn't go anymore* (at present). *Will they be away anymore* (from now on)? The two-word form is used in referring to a given thing, specified or understood: *The lamps were reasonable, but we don't need any more.*

anyone Especially in written usage, *anyone* should not be used in a construction such as *the most conscientious person of anyone I know.* Delete *of anyone* or make it *of all I know.*

anyone, any one *Anyone* is equivalent to *anybody;* it refers only to persons (indefinitely to any person whatsoever), and stresses *any.* In contrast, *any one* refers to any person or thing of a specified group and stresses *one: Anyone could foresee what might happen. There are five candidates; select any one. She recognized five possible courses, any one of which would present difficulty.*

anyone (anybody) These are singular terms that are used with singular verbs. Accompanying pronouns and pronominal adjectives within such constructions are also singular, especially in formal writing: *In such cir-*

cumstances anyone is liable to lose his (or *her* or *his or her,* but not *their*) *head occasionally.*

anyplace, any place *Anyplace* is an adverb equivalent to *anywhere.* In formal writing *anywhere* is the better choice. Only *any place,* the two-word form consisting of adjective and noun, is possible in an example such as *free to take any place that is not occupied.*

anyway, any way These are interchangeable only in the sense of *in any manner whatever: Handle it anyway,* or *in any way you choose.* When the sense is *nevertheless; at any rate; anyhow,* only *anyway* is possible: *The cost was exorbitant but we proceeded anyway.* When the sense is *any course or direction,* only *any way* is possible: *Try any way that seems appropriate. Any way they turned, danger was present. Anyways,* for *anyway,* is not acceptable on any level of usage.

anywhere The spelling as indicated is the only acceptable one. *Anywheres* is characteristic of uneducated speech.

apt, liable, likely Each of these is employed with an infinitive to express likelihood or probability. *Likely* is always appropriate when mere probability is involved: *It is likely to snow. Apt* implies probability based on a natural or known tendency: *storms apt to occur during the rainy season; apt to stammer when* *she becomes excited.* The idea of the possibility or probability of risk or disadvantage is inherent in *liable,* in careful usage: *liable to injure himself by scratching the wound.* In many examples, more than one of these adjectives is possible, but *liable* is misused in expressing only probability: *liable* (preferably *likely*) *to leave tomorrow.*

aren't I?   As a variant of *ain't I?,* this phrase has more acceptance than *ain't I?* especially in speech. In American usage, contrasted with British, however, *aren't I?* is often considered a self-conscious evasion, a genteelism, or an affectation.

as   When *as* is a preposition, meaning in the role, capacity, or function of, it is always followed by a noun or pronoun in the objective case. Otherwise the case of pronouns following *as,* or *as to,* may be nominative or objective, depending on the function of the pronouns and the desired sense: *You need her as much as I* (that is, *as much as I need her*). *You need her as much as me* (that is, *as much as you need me*).

When *as* is a conjunction equivalent to since or because, ambiguity sometimes results; *as* may be misconstrued as a reference to time: *She did not hear the bell as she was on the terrace.* Use of *since* or *because* makes the desired sense clearer. Omissions occur in the clauses introduced by the phrases: *As far as money, we haven't a great deal. There is no problem so far as time.* In both examples an addition is needed to complete the reference, such as: *as far as money is concerned; so far as time is involved.*

The conjunctive use of *as* for *that, whether,* or *if* is informal only: *I don't know as I can.*

Another conjunctive sense of *as* is *though*: *Strong as he was, he was unable to make headway.* Note that in such an example, *strong* (or another adjective) is not preceded by another *as*.

Asiatic, Asian *Asiatic* is interchangeable with *Asian* in referring to places, animals, etc.: *the Asiatic part of Turkey.* However, *Asian* is the preferred term in referring to the people of Asia because in this sense *Asiatic* is sometimes considered offensive.

as if, as though These are both acceptable and generally interchangeable: *It seemed as if* (or *as though*) *the day would never end.*

as ... as, so ... as In positive comparisons, *as ... as* is the construction employed: *as strong as an ox.* In negative comparisons, either *as ... as* or *so ... as* may be used: *not as* (or *so*) *bright as his sister.*

In positive comparisons, a common error is omission of the first *as* of a pair: *The sound was clear as a bell.* Make it *as clear as.*

as far as, so far as Errors of omission are common in sentences employing either of these phrases.

assume, presume   Both verbs indicate an act of taking something for granted. *Assume* is more appropriate to setting forth a hypothesis; *presume* is stronger in implying belief in the truth of the matter involved, in the absence of proof to the contrary. *Presume* may also imply an unwarranted conclusion. In senses not directly related to these, *presume* means to act overconfidently or to take unwarranted advantage of something.

assure, ensure, insure   All mean to make secure or certain, and all may be applied to the act of making something certain: *Success is assured* (or *ensured* or *insured*). Only *assure* means to make secure in the sense of setting a person's mind at rest: *assured her of our interest. Ensure* and *insure* also mean to make secure from harm: *ensure* (or *insure*) *a country against invasion.* In American usage, only *insure* is now in wide use in the sense of guaranteeing life or property against risk.

as well as   See **along with.**

at   The word is not expressed in indicating a location or position of rest in sentences such as *Where is he now? This is where he is.* In neither example is *at* used, following *he* (in the first) or *is* (in the second).

author   Its use as a transitive verb (*authored two books on astronomy*) has the sanction of earlier practice and of present-day definitions of the word. But many writers and editors now regard this usage as an unnecessarily graceless and pretentious device for expressing a simple idea.

avenge, revenge *Avenge* is only a verb; *revenge* is both noun and verb, though more common as a noun. Here they are compared as verbs. *Avenge* generally connotes the achieving of justice, whereas *revenge* stresses retaliation. *Avenge* usually has for its subject someone other than the person wronged; the latter, or the wrong itself, often serves as the direct object: *Hamlet avenged his father* (or *his father's murder*). *Revenge* usually has for its subject the person wronged, and is often used reflexively: *He revenged himself* (*of the wrong done him*).

averse See **adverse, averse.**

avert, avoid To *avert* something is to ward off or prevent it. *Avoid* is often loosely used for *avert* in that sense, but properly refers to staying clear of something. An organization such as the United Nations seeks to *avert* (not *avoid*) wars, to keep them from coming about. One *avoids* something in existence; a nation desiring to maintain neutrality tries to *avoid* a war in progress.

awake, awaken, wake, waken Though alike in meaning, these verbs are differentiated in usage. Each can be employed transitively and intransitively (that is, with a direct object and without one). But *awake* is principally intransitive (*awoke early*) and *waken* is transitive (*avoided wakening them*). In the passive voice, *awaken* and *waken* are the more common: *They were awakened* (or *wakened*) *by the sound of gunfire.* In figurative usage (distinguished from actual rousing from sleep), *awake* and *awaken* are the more prevalent: *awoke to the peril; when her fears were awakened.* Only *wake* is used with a preposition (*up*). The preferred past participle of *wake* is *waked*, not *woke* or *woken: after she had waked him.* The preferred past participle of *awake* is *awaked*, not *awoke: He had awaked once earlier during the storm.*

awhile, a while   *Awhile* is an adverb and modifies a verb: *rest awhile.* In the combination *a while, while* is a noun. *Awhile* is not preceded by *for*, whereas *while* can be. All the following are acceptable ways of expressing the same idea: *Stay awhile. Stay for a while. Stay a while.* But *stay for awhile* is a common misuse of *awhile.*

back of, in back of   These equivalents of *behind* are found on all levels, including formal: *a mile back of* (or *in back of*) *the front lines.* The principal objections to them are stylistic—that they are wordy and unattractive.

backward, backwards   Only *backward* is an adjective: *a backward glance; backward nations* (behind others in development). The corresponding adverb may be spelled either *backward* or *backwards,* and the forms are applicable interchangeably in all examples: *directed a glance backward; a mirror facing backward; going steadily backwards* (toward a worse condition).

bad, badly   In formal writing, the adjective *bad* is the only acceptable word of these two following linking verbs such as *feel* and *look: She felt bad* (ill). *He felt very bad* (regretful) *about his part in the unfortunate affair.* The adverb *bad* is informal (for *badly*); to qualify verbs such as act, dance, and write, *badly* is required, as it is in the example *His arm pained so badly* (or *severely*) *that he was unable to sleep.* In the corresponding sense of very much or greatly, *badly* is appropriate to all levels of usage in examples such as *badly in need of renovation.*

baited, bated   The first of the two participles is often misused for the second in the expression *bated breath,* which is proper as given. Traps and fishhooks are *baited;* animals and persons are *baited* when lured, attacked, or tormented.

balance   In bookkeeping this noun means remainder: the difference between the totals of the debit and credit sides of an account. By extension the same meaning (remainder or rest) is conveyed by *balance* in general usage: *The morning session runs until ten-thirty, and* *the balance of the time is your own*. In such examples *balance* is employed informally.

baleful, baneful Both adjectives describe what is harmful. *Baleful* is applied especially to what menaces, exerts evil influence, or foreshadows evil: *baleful surroundings; a baleful look*. *Baneful* is more often used in the sense of being directly destructive: *baneful treatment; a baneful influence*.

barbarian, barbaric, barbarous The adjectives are applied to primitive peoples, usually with distinctions that follow. *Barbarian,* the most general, means rough and uncivilized: *a barbarian society; barbarian culture*. *Barbaric* stresses crudeness or wildness of taste or style: *barbaric modes of expression; barbaric splendor*. *Barbarous* describes what is savage, cruel, or coarse: *barbarous customs; barbarous treatment*.

barbarism, barbarity *Barbarism* is applied to an uncivilized condition in general, with special emphasis on crudity of expression. A *barbarism,* in one sense of the term, is a word or form of language considered incorrect or nonstandard. *Barbarity* primarily denotes harsh or cruel conduct or an act that exemplifies such conduct.

barracks This noun is plural in form, used with either a singular or a plural verb. It can denote a single building: *Our barracks is well maintained*. Or it can be applied to a group of military buildings: *The barracks are situated in the south part of the base.*

bated   See **baited, bated.**

B.C.   This abbreviation always follows the date (unlike A.D.), and may be applied to any specified period (year, century, or era): *95 B.C.; first century B.C.* When neither A.D. nor B.C. appears, the time is assumed to be after Christ.

bear   The past participle of this verb is always *borne* for all senses except that which applies to the act of giving birth: *They had borne the load for generations. He has borne up well. She had borne the scar since childhood. The soil has borne abundant crops.* In the sense related to giving birth, the past particle *borne* is the usual form for all active-voice constructions and for passive constructions when followed by *by.* The alternate past participle *born* is employed for all other passive constructions indicating the fact of birth: *She has borne three children. Three children were borne by her, one of whom was born deaf.*

because   *Because* is sometimes used in informal speech to mean just because, as in *Because he works hard he thinks he should be promoted.* This use of *because* should be avoided in formal writing. See also **reason.**

befit   The past tense is *befitted,* not *befit.* The past participle also is *befitted.*

behalf This word presents more than the usual problem involved in selecting a preposition. Two related but different senses are conveyed by *behalf* when preceded by *in* and *on*—but the distinction has become blurred by the widespread practice of using *on* with *behalf* to convey both senses. In careful usage, however, *in behalf of Smith* (or *in Smith's behalf*) means in the interest of or for the benefit of Smith. *On behalf of Smith* (or *on Smith's behalf*) means as the agent of or on the part of Smith. If you speak *in behalf of* another, you may be acting quite independently and without the knowledge of the other person; if you speak *on behalf of another,* you are presumably the other person's agent or representative. In some examples either preposition might be defensible, for the two senses are not mutually exclusive.

being as, being as how As variants of *since, because,* or *inasmuch as,* these expressions occur principally in the speech of certain regions and are not acceptable in written usage except in reproducing the speech as dialogue: *We proceeded leisurely, being as* (or *being as how*) *the bus was not due for another hour.* Make it *since, because,* or *inasmuch as the bus was not due.* The expression *seeing as how* is used in approximately the same sense, and it too is not appropriate outside dialogue.

beside, besides In modern usage *beside* is usually a preposition: *a hut beside* (next to) *the road; a small* *contribution beside* (in comparison with) *yours. Besides* is also a preposition: *contributed a great deal besides* (in addition to) *that; had few friends besides* (except for) *us. Besides* is an adverb in these examples: *He wants to do this besides* (in addition; also). *I was tired; besides* (moreover; furthermore) *I had done my share. She cleaned her room but did very little besides* (otherwise; else). See also **along with.**

best, better   As adjectives and adverbs, these are the comparative (*better*) and superlative (*best*) forms of *good* and *well. Better* is the proper word to indicate superiority of one with respect to another (where only two are present): *The house is better* (adjective) *than ours. She dances better* (adverb) *than Sue. Best* is used to indicate pre-eminence in a group of three or more: *the best house on the block; dances best of all the chorus members. Best* is sometimes used in the sense of foremost to indicate not necessarily the position of one person or thing but of those in the front rank: *the ten best films of the year.* A less acceptable usage is that of *better* adverbially in the sense of more: *a distance better than a mile; spoke for better than a half-hour.* This is not confined to informal, but is less appropriate than *more* to formal writing.

between, among   Of this pair of prepositions, *between* is always the choice when only two persons or things serve as objects: *distinguish between right and* *wrong. Among* precedes three or more when they are considered collectively and no close relationship is indicated: *distribute food among the poor; a custom among the rich; life among the lowly.* When more than two are involved, some authorities invariably prescribe *among,* but even more recommend the use of *between* in certain of such examples. *Between* is also the choice when the objects number more than two and when they are considered individually and in a close working relationship: *a treaty between four nations.* Thus *between* is appropriate to terms such as treaty, pact, agreement, and discussion.

between . . . and   When *between* is used with two objects to indicate choice, *and* is the proper connective of the objects: *choose between luxury and integrity* (not *luxury or integrity*).

between each, between every   A usage common in speech but better avoided in writing is that employing *between* before *each* or *every* and a singular noun: *a rest between each class; cheese with paper between every slice.* Make it *after each class;* or *between classes, between the slices;* or *between each class (slice) and the next.*

between you and me   In this construction, the second pronoun is invariably *me,* not *I.* Both pronouns must be in the objective case. *Between you and I* is a very common error, sometimes a genteelism resorted to by those who think that *I* is somehow a finer or "more correct" word than *me*. But *between you and I* is still an error, and the attempt at refinement is misguided.

biannual, biennial *Biannual* is the equivalent of semiannual (happening twice each year). The three meanings of the adjective *biennial* are: lasting or living for two years; happening every second year; having a normal life cycle of two years.

bid The noun is well established on all levels of usage in a sense popularized by journalism: an effort or a striving. Thus, *a bid to restore harmony in a political party; a bid for the nomination.*
The following examples illustrate the past tense and past participle of the verb in various senses: (to direct; command) *bade him leave* and *had bidden,* or *bid, him leave;* (to utter) *bade her good-by* and *has bidden,* or *bid, her good-by;* (to summon) *bade him to the court* and *has bidden* or *bid him;* (card games) *bid four clubs* and *has bid four clubs;* (to offer) *bid $500 for the vase* and *had bid $500;* (to seek to win something; strive) *bid for the governorship* and *has bid for it.*

bimonthly The only acceptable sense is that signifying every two months—once every two months.

Semimonthly describes what occurs or is issued twice a month.

bite The past participle of the verb is *bitten* or *bit,* but only *bitten* is now standard in the passive voice: *She was bitten* (not *bit*) *by a snake.*

biweekly The word describes what happens every two weeks. *Semiweekly* has the sense of twice a week.

biyearly This term is applied to something occurring or issued every two years. *Semiyearly:* happening twice a year.

black The term *black* is preferred instead of *Negro,* and it is usually, but not always, written without an initial capital letter.

blame for, blame on See "Picking a Preposition."

blanch, blench *Blanch* refers to whitening or becoming pale; *blench,* to drawing back or flinching.

blatant, flagrant Applied to what is offensive or evil, both adjectives stress conspicuousness. *Blatant* often implies loudness, bluster, or conduct that calls attention to itself through its force and crudity. Something *flagrant* calls attention to itself through its shocking violation of what is right and proper. *Blatant* stresses the mode of commission, and *flagrant* the nature or effect of the deed: *a blatant appeal to prejudice; blatant huckstering of a candidate; a flagrant miscarriage of justice.*

blink See "Picking a Preposition."

bloc, block The first of these nouns is limited to the political sense of a group or coalition united by a common purpose. *Block* less often expresses that sense and has many others as well.

blond, brunet As adjectives, these may be applied to both sexes. As nouns they are usually restricted to males. *Blonde* and *brunette,* as nouns and adjectives, are applied only to females.

boast The verb, in its transitive sense, to take pride in possessing, is well established but distasteful to some through its association with the primary sense of *boast: boasted one of the best-equipped laboratories.*

born, borne See **bear.**

both In all its usages, *both* is limited to two. In the following example it should be deleted: *famous in both America, Europe, and the Far East. Both* is loosely used for *each* in the following: *Both criticized the other. An image was projected on both halves of the screen* (make it *on each half* or *images on both halves*).

The phrase *the both* should be avoided. In the following, delete *the: congratulated (the) both of us.*

Possessive constructions with *both* are illustrated by *the parents of both* and *the fault of both* (preferable to *both their parents, both their fault,* or *both's fault*).

bourgeois, bourgeoise, bourgeoisie The last of these terms is the collective noun signifying the middle class. *Bourgeois* is applied to a single member of that class; it is also the adjective that describes someone or something considered typically middle-class. *Bourgeoise* is the noun denoting a female member of the middle class, and the corresponding adjective applied to females.

brief, short The adjective *brief* is generally restricted to time (duration), whereas *short* is applied to both time and extent (physical measurement): *a short,* or *brief, visit; short hair; short pants; a short,* or *brief, introduction.*

bring, take *Bring* indicates movement toward the writer or speaker or person named, or toward a place usually occupied by him or her. *Take* expresses movement away from the writer, speaker, or person named, or from such a place. *Bring* implies *come here with* (to my place); *take* implies *go there with* (to another's place): *Bring proof of identity when you come. I took checks to the bank and brought back cash. She* *brought a friend to her house for dinner, and later took the friend home.*

The past tense and past participle of *bring* is *brought* —never *brung*.

Britain, Briton   *Britain* is the country, the island comprising England, Scotland, and Wales. A *Briton* is a native of Britain.

broad, wide   *Broad* is the usual choice when the noun it modifies is a surface or expanse considered as such: *broad shoulders; broad river. Wide* is used when the desired sense stresses space (distance across a surface) considered specifically (*a table five feet wide*) or indefinitely but emphatically: *The river is wide here.* Often the terms are interchangeable. In more figurative senses, the choice is governed solely by established idiom: *broad smile; wide mouth.*

broadcast   The past tense and past participle is either *broadcast* or *broadcasted.*

broke, broken   *Broke* is acceptable only as the past tense of *break.* The past participle is *broken: She broke her toe yesterday. She has broken her toe. The bone is broken.*

brunet, brunette   See **blond, brunet**

bug   The noun meaning a device for electronic eavesdropping has established itself on all levels of usage.

The same is true of the verb, to install such a device in (a room).

bureaucrat, bureaucratic Though the noun and adjective are usually defined in neutral terms, these words are generally employed derogatorily with the implication of excessive rigidity, self-importance, or pettiness.

burgle The word is the informal variant of the verb *burglarize.*

bus The verb meaning to transport (schoolchildren) in a bus has established itself on all levels. The past tense and past participle is usually *bused* and the present participle *busing.* The practice of such transporting of children is also expressed by *busing.*

but One of the senses of *but,* both as a preposition and as a conjunction, is except. When an inflected word such as a pronoun follows *but* in such usage, the choice of a pronoun depends on the part of speech one assigns *but.* When *but* and the word that follows it occur at the end of a sentence, *but* is generally construed as a preposition, and the word that follows is in the objective case: *No one saw it but me.* In a typical variant of that example, *but* is construed as a conjunction, and the pronoun agrees in case with the word that precedes *but: No one* (subject) *but I* (nominative) *saw it.*

The adverb *but,* meaning *no more than* or *only,* should not be used in a sentence containing another related negative: *It will last but a week* (not *won't last but a week*).

but that, but what These expressions, containing a redundant *but* and meaning *that* (conjunction), are typified by *There is no doubt but that* (or *but what*) *they will try.* They usually occur in sentences that begin with a negative and follow with the words *doubt* or *question.* The example with *but that* is found on all levels of usage, including formal; the variant employing *but what* is not acceptable on any level. Even the *but that* construction is objected to by many writers and editors on the ground that it is unnecessarily wordy. *There is no doubt that they will try* expresses the identical meaning.

cacao, coco, cocoa *Cacao* is the tree whose seed, cacao bean, is the source of chocolate, cocoa (the powder and beverage), and cocoa butter. *Coco* is the tree whose fruit is the coconut.

callous, callus Only *callus* is the noun denoting thickened skin (and the noun is one of the most frequently misspelled words in the language). *Callous* is an adjective describing hands and feet having calluses, and something showing emotional hardness and insensitivity. *Callous* (verb) means to make or become callous. *Callus* (verb) means to develop a callus.

Thus *callous hands; hands calloused* (or *callused*) *by hard work; callous disregard for others' rights.*

can, may Although the distinction is not often observed in everyday speech, these auxiliary verbs have different functions, especially in formal writing. *Can* is used to indicate ability to do something; *may,* to ask, grant, or deny permission to do it.

cannot but Though it is a form of double negative, this expression is acceptable in examples such as *We cannot but regret this action.* The same sense is expressed by *can but regret, can only regret, must regret,* and *cannot help regretting.*

canvas, canvass The material associated with sails, tents, and paintings is *canvas. Canvass* (noun and verb) has reference to the acts of examining, soliciting sales orders or votes, and surveying public opinion by polling.

capital, capitol Congress and state legislatures meet in the building called *capitol.* The town or city that is the seat of a government is a *capital.* The latter term also is the noun used in finance and accounting and in architecture; it is the adjective meaning chief and first-rate. *Capital letter* and *capital punishment* are written thus.

careen The verb expresses two senses: that of moving rapidly in an uncontrolled manner, lurching or swerving; and that of leaning and tilting, in nautical usage. In the first sense, a synonym is *career* (to move or run at full speed; go headlong).

casual, causal   The adjective describing chance occurrence and informal or relaxed dress or behavior is *casual*. The adjective referring to a cause is *causal*.

celebrant, celebrator   The second of these nouns denotes a participant in any celebration, more often non-religious festivities: *New Year's Eve celebrators. Celebrant* is now widely found in that general sense, but the usage is disputed by some who would confine the word to a priest or other person participating in a religious ceremony or rite.

center   See "Picking a Preposition."

ceremonial, ceremonious   The first of these adjectives is applied principally to things, and the second to persons and things. In addition, *ceremonial* is essentially a general, categorizing term pertaining to ceremony: *ceremonial garb; ceremonial occasion. Ceremonious* stresses formality and display, often in the unfavorable sense of pompousness.

certain   The word is frequently qualified by *more* and *most: Nothing could be more certain than that.* This despite the fact that in most of its senses, *certain* seems to be an absolute term, not capable of comparison. In short, in usage there are degrees of certainty.

certainty, certitude   Both nouns imply the absence of doubt. *Certainty* is applied to a clearly established fact or to the condition of being certain when one's belief is based on careful examination of evidence. *Certitude* is complete assurance which may be based more on faith than on objective grounds.

chafe, chaff   Chafe is principally a verb meaning to wear away or irritate by rubbing, or to annoy or become annoyed. As a noun, *chaff* denotes grain, hay or straw, and trivial or worthless matter. As a verb, *chaff* means to make fun of good-naturedly.

chain reaction   Use this term in the sense of events each of which induces or otherwise influences a successor. A chain reaction is more than a series of similar occurrences which have no such relationship as described.

chair, chairman, chairperson   These three nouns are interchangeably used to refer to one who presides over a group. The terms *chair* and *chairman* can also be used as verbs.

chaperon   The noun is also spelled *chaperone*. The principal verb forms are illustrated by: *She chaperons her niece. She chaperoned; has* or *had chaperoned; is chaperoning; used to chaperon.*

childish, childlike   When applied to adults, *childish* is almost invariably a derogatory term; applied to children, the word lacks that connotation. *Childlike* is generally favorable on all age levels, suggesting endearing traits characteristic of children.

Chinaman   This is considered an offensive term used in place of the preferred a *Chinese* or *a Chinese man.*

chord, cord   *Chord* is the noun used in music and geometry and to denote emotional response. *Cord* is the term for string, electric wire, a raised rib on fabric, and a unit of measure for cut wood. Common terms in anatomy are *spinal cord* (or *chord*) and *vocal cord.*

cite, quote   Both verbs apply to making reference to something. To *cite* is to make mention, not necessarily by reproducing exact wording, which is the sense inherent in *quote.*

claim   The verb is established on all levels in the sense of asserting or maintaining, a usage once disputed: *The air force claims that the battleship is obsolete. Claim,* meaning to demand as one's due, has always been good usage.

classic, classical   These adjectives are interchangeable in some senses, including those dealing with ancient Greek and Roman culture, though *classical* is more frequent in that respect. *Classic* is invariably the choice to indicate, in a general way, highest rank.

clean, cleanse   These are distinguished in usage when employed as verbs. *Clean* is applied literally to express the action of removing dirt, stain, or the like. *Cleanse* can be employed in that way, but more often means to free from sin or guilt.

clench, clinch Both mean to secure or hold. Transitively (employing a direct object), either can be used to indicate the fastening of nails or the like (though *clinch* is the more common) and in nautical usage (to fasten by knotting). One *clenches* an object held, the fingers or fists, and the jaws or teeth. One *clinches* (secures) a bargain, argument, or verdict. *Clinch* is also used, intransitively, in boxing in referring to the act of holding an opponent.

climactic, climatic *Climactic:* pertaining to or constituting a climax. *Climatic:* pertaining to climate (meteorological conditions).

close, near Both describe proximity in time or space, but *close* is the better choice when immediate proximity is meant.

clue This is the preferred spelling for the noun that denotes an aid in the solution of a problem or mystery, and also for the corresponding verb. The variant form, *clew,* also has other senses that are not in as widespread use.

coco, cocoa See **cacao.**

cohort Only in informal usage does the word mean a companion or associate. The well-established senses are a division of a Roman legion, and a group united in a struggle. Note that both refer to collectives, not to an individual.

collide, collision   In their literal (physical) senses, the words often refer to the coming together of persons and things that are both in motion. But the words are also acceptably applied to situations in which one person or thing is in motion and the other stationary.

company   Use it with a singular verb when the word means any of the following: a business association, companionship or society (*company that is congenial*), a military or naval unit, a theatrical troupe. When *company* denotes any group or assemblage or a group of guests, it may take a singular verb, with reference to a unified body, or a plural one, when the members are considered individually.

compare   See "Picking a Preposition."

compare, contrast   To *compare* is to examine in order to note similarities or differences, or to liken. To *contrast* is to set in opposition in order to show or emphasize differences. Like or unlike things can be *compared;* only essentially unlike things are *contrasted.*

complacent, complaisant   *Complacent* most often describes one who is self-satisfied. It can also be applied to one who shows a desire to please, but that sense is more often expressed by *complaisant.* The corresponding nouns are *complacency* (less often *complacence*) and *complaisance.*

complected In formal usage, make it *complexioned: dark-complexioned. Complected* is a regional term, one identified with a geographic area and having identifiable differences from the standard form of a language.

complement, compliment *Complement* is something that completes; *compliment,* an act of expressing praise or courtesy. *Compliments* is the term for a greeting or remembrance. *Complimentary* is the term that describes something given free: *a complimentary ticket.*

complete In certain of the adjective's senses (having all necessary or normal parts, and concluded or ended), *complete* is an absolute term and therefore not capable of qualification by the words *more* or *most.* When *complete* refers to comprehensiveness of scope or thoroughness of treatment, however, the word is not considered absolute and is acceptably used in examples such as *the most complete book on American judo.*

compose, comprise *Compose* means to make up the constituent parts of something, and therefore to constitute or form it. *Comprise* means to consist of or be composed of. The whole comprises the parts; the parts do not comprise the whole, nor is the whole comprised of its parts: *The Union comprises fifty states. Fifty states compose* (or *constitute*) *the Union. The Union is composed of fifty states.*

comprehensible, comprehensive Something *comprehensible* is capable of being understood. Something *comprehensive* is large in scope or content. In a lesser-used sense, *comprehensive* refers to one capable of understanding or perceiving easily or well.

comprise See **compose, comprise.**

condition In the sense of disease or ailment, the noun is acceptable on all levels of general usage: *a heart condition.* It is not a scientific term, however, and is better avoided in scientific writing.

confidant, confidante, confident A *confidant* is a male person to whom secrets or private matters are confided. *Confidante* is the corresponding feminine term. *Confident* is an adjective describing one who has confidence, self-assurance, or lack of doubt in a more general sense.

congenial, congenital These are wholly unrelated adjectives. *Congenial* describes a person having one's tastes, habits, or temperament. Or the term is applicable to something agreeable. *Congenital* means existing at birth but not hereditary (*congenital deformity*) or having a specified character as if by nature: *a congenital liar.*

connote See **denote, connote.**

consequential In the sense of being important or significant (that is, having consequence), this adjective is disputed by some modern usage authorities. The word is still used to mean self-important, pompous, or conceited, and, in its primary sense, to mean resultant (following as an effect, result, or conclusion). In that last-named sense, the word is synonymous with the adjective *consequent. Consequent* is the more common term and is the choice when resultant is meant: *Theft was charged, and the consequent investigation led to his dismissal. Consequential* sometimes implies an indirect or secondary result.

consider When the verb means *to regard as* or *think to be* or *to believe,* it is followed by a direct object without *as: She considered him a fool.* The construction *consider . . . as* is used when the verb means to study or examine: *The documentary considers him as statesman and as writer.*

considerable, considerably *Considerable* is principally an adjective meaning fairly large in amount, extent, or degree (*a man of considerable means*), or worthy of consideration. *Considerably* is the corresponding adverb, and only this word can qualify a verb, as in *aided him considerably* (to a fairly great extent). Only *considerably* can qualify an adjective, as in *acted considerably strange.*

consist of, consist in   See "Picking a Preposition."

consul, council, councilor, counsel, counselor   *Consul* denotes an officer in the foreign service of a country. *Council* and *councilor* refer principally to a deliberative assembly (a city council or student council, for example), its work, and its membership. *Counsel* and *counselor* pertain chiefly to advice and guidance in general and to a person who provides it (a lawyer or camp counselor, for example).

contact   As a verb meaning to get in touch with, *contact* is informal. On the level of formal writing, preferable alternatives include more specific verbs: write, telephone, and call, for example. As a noun meaning an acquaintance (who might be of use) or connection, *contact* is better established and appropriate to all levels.

contemporary   As an adjective, the word sometimes causes confusion over the period meant. When it is used in a context having no other reference to time, it indicates the period of the writer or speaker. When it appears in a context with persons or things of the past, the logical assumption may be that it pertains to the same past period, though often the intended meaning is otherwise. As a result, *modern* may be a better choice in some examples: *a Restoration play in modern dress.* Such wording is more explicit than *a Restoration play in contemporary dress.*

contemporaneous, contemporary Both adjectives refer to persons or things that exist or occur at the same time, but *contemporaneous* applies more often to things: *volcanic eruptions contemporaneous with earthquakes; contemporary poets and artists.*

contemptible, contemptuous *Contemptible* is applied to what deserves contempt. *Contemptuous* describes someone who manifests or feels contempt or scorn for another person or for a thing.

continual, continuous *Continual* can refer to uninterrupted action but is now largely restricted to what is intermittent or repeated at intervals: *the baby's continual crying. Continuous* implies either action without interruption in time or unbroken extent in space: *a continuous vigil; a continuous slope of terrain.*

continuance, continuation, continuity In law, *continuance* refers to postponement or adjournment to a future date. In other senses of the word, it is sometimes interchangeable with *continuation.* But *continuance* is the choice when reference is being made to duration of a condition: *the governor's continuance in office; a machine's continuance in service. Continuation* has special reference to prolongation or resumption of action and to physical extension: *the continuation of a welfare program; continuation of the hallway to the rear of the house. Continuity* has the more special sense of that which is uninterrupted: *the continuity of bipartisan foreign policy preceding a change of administrations.*

contrast See **compare, contrast.**

convince, persuade The verbs, though related, are not identical in meaning. *Convince* means to persuade one decisively of a truth or a necessity. *Persuade* suggests winning over by reasoning, argument, or inducement. The words differ also in structural application. *Convince* is followed by *of* or a clause introduced by *that,* but not by an infinitive with *to. Persuade* is used with all three constructions: *He convinced her* (or *she was convinced*) *of his sincerity. He convinced her* (or *she was convinced*) *that she should leave. He persuaded* (not *convinced*) *her to leave.* The use of an infinitive following *convince* is an especially common error.

cope In formal usage, the verb is used with *with* to indicate the act of contending or striving, especially on even terms or with success. The object of the preposition *with* specifies the person or thing contended against: *cope with unhealthy living conditions.* Recently the verb has been used increasingly, on an informal level, without the preposition *with;* no adversary is stated, and the sense is the general one of getting along well by overcoming obstacles: *To survive in business, one must be able to cope.*

cord See **chord, cord.**

corespondent, correspondent *Corespondent* denotes the partner of the defendant in a divorce suit; *correspondent,* one who communicates by means of letters or who writes for newspapers or periodicals.

council, counsel See **consul.**

couple When the noun denotes a man and woman united, it may be used with either a singular or plural verb, but the plural construction is more common. Whatever the choice, it should be expressed consistently within the context: *The couple are changing their voting residence* (or *is changing its*).

In the sense of *a few* or *several,* the noun is employed, informally, with *of: a couple of years.*

credible, creditable, credulous Someone or something *credible* is believable or worthy of confidence. A *creditable* person or thing deserves commendation. A *credulous* person is given to believing too readily and is therefore gullible; or the term can describe something arising from or characterized by too ready belief, such as an act or manner.

criteria This is the most common plural form of the noun *criterion.* It may not be used in any of these expressions: *a criteria; one criteria; the only* (sole) *criteria.* Use *criterion* in all these.

czar This is the form commonly found in American usage to denote a king or emperor, a tyrant or autocrat, and (informally) a chief or leader: *the energy czar. Tsar,* considered a more accurate transliteration of the Russian, is found in scholarly writing in reference to one of the Russian emperors.

dare A peculiarity of this verb is that it has two forms in the third-person singular, present tense indicative. The regular form is inflected, *dares: He dares to disagree.* The other is uninflected, *dare,* which occurs mainly in interrogative and negative constructions employing an infinitive without *to* or an unstated but understood infinitive: *Dare he disagree* (or *Does he dare disagree*)? *He dare not.*

The form *dare say* (or *daresay*) is usually followed by a clause without an introductory conjunction: *I dare say she regretted it.*

dastardly The adjective stresses the idea of cowardice, and is loosely used when it is applied to any reprehensible act that is not cowardly.

data The noun is plural in form. The singular is *datum,* denoting a fact or proposition. In its most common meaning, the collective *data* refers to information, especially that organized for analysis or used as the basis for decision-making. As a collective, *data* is capable of being construed as both a singular and a plural term; it is followed by both plural and singular verbs in modern usage: *These data are inconclusive. This data is inconclusive.* The example with a plural verb is more appropriate to a formal level.

deadly, deathly   As adjectives, these are distinguished in usage. *Deadly* is now largely confined to what causes death or extreme distress: *a deadly disease; deadly boredom.* *Deathly* is applied to what resembles or suggests death: *deathly silence; deathly pallor.* As adverbs, *deadly* means to an extreme (*deadly earnest*) and *deathly* means extremely or very: *deathly afraid.* Idiom governs the choice in these related adverbial senses.

debut   Use it as a noun only. The verb usage (*a company that debuts its new models; a television series that debuts tonight*) is not well established.

defective, deficient   *Defective* describes that which has a discernible fault, and is therefore primarily concerned with quality. *Deficient,* followed by *in,* is applied to what has insufficiency or incompleteness, and is therefore a quantitative term associated with *deficit.*

definite, definitive   Both refer to the condition of being defined precisely or set forth explicitly. *Definitive,* moreover, is applied to what is unalterably final, a sense that *definite* does not have. A *definite* decision is precise and unequivocal; a *definitive* decision is, in addition, usually beyond change or appeal.

delusion, illusion A *delusion* is a false belief, held without reservation, that comes from self-deception, the imposition of another person, or mental disorder. An *illusion* is a false impression that may result from faulty observation, wishful thinking, or false perception that one eventually recognizes as false—or that one knows all along is false, as in the case of a magician's tricks (also called *illusions*) or the images in a carnival fun-house mirror (*optical illusions*). *Illusion* suggests what is transitory; *delusion* more often portends disadvantage or harm.

denote, connote *Denote* means to signify directly. *Connote* means to suggest to the mind what is not explicit. In speaking of words, *denote* is used to indicate the thing a word names, and *connote* to indicate our associations with that thing: *The word* bachelor *denotes an unmarried man and connotes a life of pleasure and carefree amusements.*

depend When the word indicates condition or contingency, it is always followed by *on* or *upon*: *The incumbent is the favorite, but it depends on how heavy the vote is.* Especially in written usage, *on* must not be omitted in such an example.

deprecate, depreciate The primary sense of *deprecate* is to express disapproval of; to protest or plead against. In one sense, *depreciate* means to make (someone or something) seem less; to belittle. No doubt because the words look so much alike, they have been subject to confusion, and *deprecate* is now often found in examples expressing the approximate meaning of *depreciate,* often with reference to mild self-belittlement or self-effacement: *deprecated her own contribution; a self-deprecating* (or *self-deprecatory*) *manner.* Such use of *deprecate* is disputed, though common, and a safer course is to write *played down,* or *depreciated, her contribution; a self-effacing* or *self-depreciatory manner.*

dessert, desert *Dessert* has only the sense of last course of a meal. *Desert* denotes an arid region and that which is deserved, as in *just deserts.* As such, these are nouns. *Desert* is also a verb synonymous with forsake, leave, and abandon.

die In assigning a cause of death, the usual construction is *die of* or *as a result of: died of* (not *from*) *heart disease.*

different from, different than See "Picking a Preposition."

dilemma In careful usage the word should be applied only to a situation that permits choice between two equally balanced alternatives. Usually the choices are equally undesirable; less often *dilemma* refers to a hard choice between attractive courses. The word denotes a predicament that seemingly defies a satisfactory solution, not just any predicament or difficult problem.

direct, directly   The two adverbs are interchangeable when they mean *in a straight line,* or *not deviating from a course* (*went direct,* or *directly, to my home*) and when the sense is that of *without anyone or anything intervening* (*direct,* or *directly, from wholesaler to buyer*). When the meaning is either *exactly* or *at once,* only *directly* is possible.

discomfit, discomfiture   The verb and corresponding noun were originally confined to the senses of defeat and frustration. In modern usage they are more often applied to examples in which the prevailing sense is merely that of discomfort, disconcert, uneasiness, or confusion.

discover, invent   Something that is *discovered* was in existence before a person became the first to find or learn of it. Examples of discovered things are countries, bodies of water and other geographic features, deposits of precious metals, the elements studied in chemistry and physics, and scientific laws and truths. Something that is *invented,* like the typewriter and Braille system, did not have prior existence. *Invent,* therefore, may be equated with *create.*

disinterested, uninterested   *Disinterested* means lacking self-interest and bias: *approached the problem as* *a disinterested observer, desirous only of determining facts.* One who has no concern with a subject and is therefore indifferent to it is *uninterested,* not *disinterested.* The distinction, still valued by most usage authorities despite the blunting of it by common practice, is that between impartiality (*disinterested*) and indifference (*uninterested*).

dissociate, dissociation These are the usual forms, used interchangeably with *disassociate* and *disassociation.*

distinct, distinctive *Distinct* applies to what is clearcut, and *distinctive* to what sets a person or thing apart from others. A *distinct* sound is readily heard, whereas a *distinctive* sound is both that and unlike others. *Distinct* speech is clear; *distinctive* speech calls attention to the style of delivery. *Distinct* organizations are separate from each other or one another; *distinctive* organizations have qualities that set each apart from all others.

dive The past tense of the verb is either *dived* or *dove. Dived* is the more common in formal writing. The past participle is *dived.* Examples are: *They dived* (or *dove*) *into the water. After the contestants had dived from four platforms, their efforts were graded.*

done As an adjective meaning finished, this word is often found in speech or informal writing, though not confined to that level. In formal writing, *finished* or *completed* is usually preferable. Sometimes this meaning of *done* is not made clear in a given sentence; the word is capable of being construed as a form of *do,* expressing action, and confusion results: *The work will be done next year.* The intended sense (completed or finished) may not come through, and the reader may assume that the work will begin, as well as end, next year. *Finished* or *completed* is preferable in such examples.

don't   This contraction is not acceptable when used with a subject in the third-person singular. *Doesn't* is required: *It doesn't happen often. He* (or *she*) *doesn't really care. Smith doesn't know.*

doubt, doubtful   Clauses introduced by *that, whether,* and *if* often follow the verb and noun *doubt* and the adjective *doubtful: We doubt that the deadline will be met. It is doubtful whether the work will be completed on time.* In sentences having a negative sense or in the form of questions, what is expressed is not doubt but a denial of it; in such examples the clause almost invariably begins with *that: I have no doubt that he will succeed. Do you really doubt that he will succeed?* When the writer wants to express genuine doubt, *whether* and *if* are the better choices (and *whether* is usually considered better than *if* in formal writing): *It was considered doubtful whether the terms of the contract could be fulfilled.* In positive statements, such as the last example, use of *that* (for *whether* or *if*) conveys the sense of unbelief rather than genuine doubt. Reread the example, employing *that,* and note how the change of a single word seems to alter the sense—from uncertainty to unbelief. See also **but that, but what.**

doubtless, undoubtedly   *Doubtless* and *no doubt* are rather weak terms for expressing certainty or assurance, since they can also express presumption or probability. *Undoubtedly* and *without doubt* are much stronger; they convey only certainty and conviction. Contrast these examples: *He will doubtless leave. He will undoubtedly leave. No doubt she will be tired after the trip. Without doubt she will be tired.*

dove   See **dive.**

dozen   In modern usage, *dozen* is generally not followed by *of,* except when reference is made to a quantity that is part of a larger, specified quantity: *a dozen eggs; a dozen of those eggs; a dozen of her closest associates.* When the plural *dozens* is employed in the sense of an indefinitely large quantity of something specified, it is followed by *of: He showed his bravery on dozens of occasions.*

drag   The past tense and past participle is *dragged,* not *drug.*

drunk, drunken   As adjectives, these have separate

functions. *Drunk* is used predicatively after a form of the verb *be: She was always drunk.* In contrast, *drunken* is employed attributively (before a noun): *a drunken scoundrel; a drunken driver; drunken driving.* The combinations *drunk driver* and *drunk driving* have become stock expressions, especially in certain varieties of journalism, but they are not acceptable in serious writing on a formal level.

due to This phrase has two related meanings; in expressing them, it has different functions, one of which is always acceptable and the other of which is disputed. When *due to* means attributable to or caused by, *due* is a predicate adjective that follows a form of *be* or another linking verb: *His concern for her safety was largely due to his own lack of confidence.* Such examples are always acceptable. When *due to* means *because of,* the phrase functions adverbially to set forth a reason for, or cause of, some action expressed by a nonlinking verb: *The machine broke down due to faulty maintenance.* Constructions of the latter kind are very common (*game called due to rain*), but this adverbial usage is better avoided in formal writing. Alternative ways of expressing the same sense include the substitution of *because of, on account of, owing to,* or *through.* For example: *The machine broke down because of faulty maintenance.* Or such examples can be rephrased by employing the adjectival construction: *The breakdown was due to faulty mainte-nance.*

On any level of usage, when *due to* means because of, the unnecessarily wordy expression *due to the fact that* should be avoided; *the fact that* adds nothing.

dye   The present participle is *dyeing: He is still dye-ing his hair these days.*

each   When the pronoun is used as a subject, it takes a singular verb in formal usage: *Each is involved to some extent.* The verb is also singular when *each* is followed by *of* and a plural noun or pronoun: *Each of the men was implicated.* When related pronouns or pronominal adjectives occur in such sentences, they are likewise singular in form: *Each of the four is liable for his own part in the shady transaction.* (In-formally, especially in speech, such an example might be phrased *each . . . are liable for their own part.*)

When *each* occurs after a plural subject with which it is in apposition, the verb is generally plural: *They each need expert counsel. The company president and treasurer each have retained special legal staffs.* In examples having compound subjects, such as the sec-ond, a singular verb sometimes occurs: *each has re-tained a special legal staff.*

each and every   This is a wasteful expression, and it is preferable to use either *each* or *every* singly. When *each* *and every* is employed in that form, however, it takes a singular verb and related modifying words: *Each and every girl is expected to do her part.* See also **between each, between every.**

each other, one another   In practice, these expressions are used interchangeably in most examples, and acceptably so. Some grammarians and usage authorities make a distinction, however. They recommend *each other* when the reference is to only two persons or things, and *one another* when more than two are present: *The boxers pounded each other furiously for two rounds. Employees in such a large company regard one another impersonally.*

The possessive forms of the expressions are written as follows: *each other's* (not *others'*); *one another's*.

eager   See **anxious, eager.**

earthly, earthy   Both adjectives express relationship to the earth. *Earthly,* however, is most often a categorizing term used to distinguish something from what is heavenly or divine: *earthly considerations.* Or the term may mean conceivable or possible: *no earthly reason for such unreasonable delay* (that is, no reason on earth). *Earthy* distinguishes something from what is spiritual. It applies to what is down to earth in the more special sense of being concerned with the satisfaction of material wants and the more primitive human instincts: *earthy pleasures; earthy creature* (that is, uninhibited).

easily, easy *Easily* is only an adverb, whereas *easy* is principally an adjective. As an adverb, *easy* occurs for the most part in the expression *easy come, easy go,* and informally in *go easy on, take it easy,* and *easier said than done.* Otherwise *easy* and the comparative form *easier* are not acceptable in examples such as: *The lock works easily. The matter can be settled easily. Your problem is more easily resolved than mine.*

economic, economical In usage, *economical* is largely restricted to the sense of not wasteful; prudent in management: *an economical way to recycle tin. Economic* is applied more generally to matters of economics (the science), finance, and to the necessities of life: *economic goals; an economic formula.*

effect See **affect, effect.**

egoism, egotism The two nouns are closely related, and in some examples either is possible. In their primary senses, however, they are not identical. *Egoism* is the tendency to think or act with only oneself and one's personal interests in mind. *Egotism* is the tendency to speak or write of oneself excessively and boastfully. *Egoism* is related to self-interest, as is the corresponding noun *egoist. Egotism* is related to conceit, as are the corresponding *egotist, egotistic,* and *egotistical.*

either Particularly in formal writing, the pronoun *either,* used as a subject, takes a singular verb and related pronouns or pronominal adjectives: *Either is capable of reversing its course automatically.* The rule applies when *either* is followed by *of* and a plural noun or pronoun: *Either of the unmanned space vehicles is capable of reversing its course.* The singular verb prevails also when the sentence has a negative sense or is in the form of a question: *We doubt that either of them is really practicable. Is either of them practicable?* In informal speech, examples such as the last two often employ plural verbs.

As pronoun and adjective, *either* is preferably limited to constructions specifying two persons or things: *Take either* (one of two). *Either course* (of two) *presents difficulty.* Although *either* sometimes occurs in sentences involving more than two, *any* or *any one* (written as two words) is preferable to *either* in them. The conjunction *either,* used in combination with *or,* is likewise most appropriate to statements involving two alternative elements. The elements themselves may consist of more than one component, in which case the components, taken together, have the sense of one: *The consent of either the patient or a parent or guardian is required.*

either . . . or   When the alternative elements within an *either . . . or* construction are both singular, the verb governed by the elements is singular: *Either coffee or tea is served.* When the elements are both plural, the verb is plural: *Either apples or oranges are suitable.* When the elements differ in point of number, the verb agrees in number with the element to which it is nearer, or with the final component of the nearer element: *Either coffee or soft drinks are available. Either soft drinks or beer is provided. Either the patient or the patient's parents or legal guardian is required to sign a statement of consent.* When the nearer element is a personal pronoun, the verb agrees with it. *Either Harry or I have the necessary authority. Either he or I am authorized to grant permission.* Examples with personal pronouns, such as the last, often produce clumsy or unnatural-sounding phrasing, and a more desirable course is to rephrase by discarding the *either . . . or* formula: *He and I are both authorized to grant permission.*

When possessive pronouns or pronominal adjectives appear in *either . . . or* constructions, they agree in number with the verb: *I can provide the necessary money if either Frank or Jim has forgotten to bring his* (not *theirs*).

elder, eldest, older, oldest   As forms of adjectives, *elder* and *eldest* refer only to persons; *older* and *oldest* can refer to both persons and things. *Elder* and *eldest* are now used only attributively (before a noun or proper noun), unlike *older* and *oldest: He is older than I. She is the oldest member. Elder* and *eldest* are further limited in usage to references to members of a specific family or business establishment, as indications of age or seniority: *the elder Harris; my eldest brother; the elder partner. Elder* is always the form used in the term *elder statesman*.

elegy, eulogy   An *elegy* is a poem written to mourn one who is dead. A *eulogy* is a tribute to one recently deceased, and usually has the form of an oration.

elicit, illicit   These merely sound alike. *Elicit* (verb) means to bring out or draw forth: *questions designed to elicit straightforward responses. Illicit* (adjective) is applied to what is improper, in the sense of being not sanctioned by custom (*an illicit love affair*) or illegal (*illicit traffic in drugs*).

else   The possessive forms of combinations with *else* are usually written: *anyone* (or *anybody*) *else's; everyone* (or *everybody*) *else's; no one* (or *nobody*) *else's; someone* (or *somebody*) *else's*. Both *who else's* (followed by a noun) and *whose else* are in use, but not *whose else's: Who else's work might it be? Whose else could it be?*

elude   See **allude, elude.**

emend See **amend, emend.**

emigrate, immigrate, migrate Persons *emigrate from* a country or region when they leave it to settle in another. Persons *immigrate* to a country or region upon moving and settling there. Persons, and certain birds and animals, are said to *migrate from* one place, an old home, or to *migrate to* another, a new home. The corresponding nouns are *emigrant, immigrant,* and *migrant.*

eminent, imminent Someone or something *eminent* towers over others, either literally (*an eminent building*) or in the sense of achievement, rank, or talent (*an eminent physician; eminent discoveries*). Something that is *imminent* is about to occur: *the imminent arrival of fresh combat forces.*

enormity This noun denotes outrageousness or great wickedness, or an offense that reflects such qualities: *the enormity of an assassination plot.* Mere size or physical extent is not conveyed by *enormity* but by words such as *enormousness* or *hugeness.*

enquire, enquiry These are variant forms of *inquire* and *inquiry,* which are the more common spellings.

en route The term, meaning *on the route,* is written thus.

ensure See **assure, ensure, insure.**

enthuse This verb, a back-formation from *enthusiasm,* is for informal use only: *She enthused* (showed enthusiasm) *over the rise in membership. She was even more enthused* (made more enthusiastic) *by the caliber of the newcomers.* More acceptable wording is indicated within the parentheses.

envelop, envelope *Envelop* is the verb: *enemy forces enveloping the peninsula; mist that envelops the hilltops.* The noun is *envelope* with a plural form *envelopes.*

enviable, envious Someone or something *enviable* arouses envy through being highly desirable: *an enviable record.* Someone who is *envious* feels or shows envy: *envious friends plotting his downfall.*

envy, jealousy The nouns name qualities that are related but not identical. *Envy* is discontent and resentment arising over one's awareness of another's possessions, which one covets. *Jealousy,* which has wider range, may denote bitterness arising from rivalry, a fearful or suspicious attitude stemming from possible loss of position or affection, or close watchfulness that reflects overpossessive or oversolicitous tendencies.

epithet In its primary sense, the noun means a term used to characterize a person or thing. The term may not be derogatory. President Kennedy, for example, spoke of "that seemingly unending war to which we have given the curious epithet 'cold.' " Increasingly, however, *epithet* is used, without elaboration or description, to convey a much narrower meaning: an abusive or contemptuous word or phrase employed to describe a person. This usage is still in dispute, though it is now common, and a surer way to express the narrower meaning is to say *shouted abuse,* or *words of contempt,* instead of *shouted epithets.*

equable, equitable   *Equable* can describe something, such as a climate, that is steady and unvarying, or something, such as a person's nature, that is tranquil. *Equitable* is applied to something, such as a settlement or arrangement, that is impartial and just.

equal   By definition, the adjective *equal* seemingly defies comparison, in the sense of being preceded by the words *more* or *most.* To all appearances it is an absolute term. In usage, however, it is often qualified by *more* and *most,* and acceptably so: *a more equal distribution of the burden.* As used thus, *equal* is equated with *equitable* and *nearly equal.*

Omissions can also create problems when *equal* is used in comparisons. The words *to* and *of* in the following examples are essential to acceptable usage but are often omitted: *equal (to) or better than mine; the equal (of) or better than his.*

equitable   See **equable, equitable.**

errata   This plural noun, from Latin, is regularly employed in the collective sense of a list of errors. The word is nevertheless construed as plural in choice of a verb and when preceded by an adjective: *these errata are . . .*

escalate   For better or worse, the war in Vietnam established this verb, in both transitive and intransitive usages, in the sense related to increasing, enlarging, or intensifying: *Both sides in the conflict escalated the fighting. The war has escalated with each succeeding year.* The antonym (word having an opposite sense) is *de-escalate,* not *descalate.*

escape   When the verb means to break out of confinement, it is used with *from: He escaped from the prison* (not *escaped the prison*). In other senses, *escape* is used without *from: escaped harm; a clue that escaped him at the time; a sigh that escaped her lips.*

especial, especially, special, specially   *Special* and *specially* are the more general of these pairs and therefore have wider use. They are always the choice when the desired sense is merely the opposite of ordinary or routine, without particular emphasis: *dress appropriate to special occasions; personnel specially trained for such emergencies. Especial* and *especially* are often preferred to indicate pre-eminence or exceptional de-

gree: *an especial friend; especially bright children.*
Here *special friend* would be somewhat weaker; *specially,* used with reference to *bright children,* would not be in accord with established idiom. *Specially* is used most often to modify a verb form, such as *trained,* rather than a word, such as *bright,* that is only an adjective. *Especial* and *especially* are the choice to express individuality or a particular circumstance: *This is for her especial benefit. Smith especially is at fault. Prudence is the best policy, especially now.* In these last examples, *special* could replace *especial* in modifying *benefit,* though the substitution would make the desired sense less strong; but *specially* could not replace *especially* in the two sentences that follow, or in like examples.

et al. The abbreviation meaning *and others* is written thus, with a period after the second element only. The term is very useful in bibliographies, and also is employed in some special areas, including legal writing. Otherwise it has rather little use in more general formal writing, and as a rule should not be used as a substitute for the words *and others* (aside from listings such as bibliographies). Occasionally it is employed for humorous effect: *Mencken et al.* The abbreviation is applied only to persons, not to things.

etc. This abbreviation stands for *unspecified things of the same class.* It is not appropriate to formal writing in general but is found in technical reporting and business correspondence. When it is used anywhere, *etc.* should suggest a reasonably clear idea of what additional things the writer has in mind; it should never be a lazy way of finishing a thought whose meaning the reader can only guess. The abbreviation should be written once, not as *etc., etc.* or as *and etc.* (since *and* is inherent in the meaning).

ethical, moral   Both describe proper human behavior, but from somewhat different points of view. *Ethical* implies a philosophical standpoint and stresses more objectively defined, though essentially idealistic, standards such as those applied to the conduct of doctors, lawyers, and people in business. *Moral* is applied especially to sexual conduct and suggests a rather subjective code of right and wrong.

eulogy   See **elegy, eulogy.**

ever   The word is usually hyphenated in combinations used attributively (before nouns): *ever-rising waters; ever-growing problems.* But no hyphen is used when such combinations come after verbs: *waters were ever rising; problems that are ever growing in scope.* See also **rarely.**

ever so often, every so often   These expressions have different meanings and are therefore not interchangeable. *Ever so often* is the equivalent of frequently;

repeatedly. *Every so often* means occasionally; now and then.

everybody, everyone, every one When they are used as subjects, the pronouns *everybody* and *everyone* take singular verbs in formal writing, and accompanying personal pronouns and pronominal adjectives are correspondingly singular in form: *Everybody raised his* (or *her*) *hand in hearty approval. Everyone is entitled to sufficient time to make up his own* (or *her* or *his* or *her*) *mind.* Informally, especially in speech, *their hand* (or *hands*) and *their own mind* (or *minds*) appear in such examples, but formal writing requires a consistently singular construction. Objection is sometimes taken to the masculine *his* when it refers to a group including both sexes. *His* can be justified in examples such as these, both on the ground of long usage and on the ground that it is used indefinitely with reference to the indefinite pronouns *everybody* and *everyone*. Use of *his and her* is a possible solution to the problem of accounting for both sexes, though a rather cumbersome one. Where the writer has strong feeling against use of *his,* perhaps the best solution is to rephrase, abandoning *everybody, everyone,* and such other problem words as *anyone* and *someone: All hands were raised in hearty approval. One is entitled to sufficient time to make such a decision.*

Everyone and the two-word form *every one* are distinguished in usage. *Everyone* is the choice when *everybody* can be substituted for it—when the sense is that of every person considered indefinitely: *Everyone was aware of her presence. Every one* refers to each person or thing of a specific group; it is typically followed by *of,* or else *of* and an object are implied: *Every one of them is at fault* (or *Every one is to blame*). *There were four choices, every one of which presented serious problems.*

everyplace, every place   The adverb *everyplace,* written as a single word, is an informal term for *everywhere;* in formal usage, make it *everywhere. Every place,* written as two words, has a different meaning— that of every one of a group of places specified or understood: *Every place was taken. We shall try to visit every place that the book mentions.* The two-word form is acceptable on all levels of usage.

every way   Write it as shown, not as one word: *We found something difficult about every way she mentioned.*

everywhere   This is the only acceptable spelling— not *everywheres.*

except   When the word means with the exclusion of, other than, or but, it is construed as a preposition. A pronoun following *except,* used in that meaning, is therefore in the objective case: *No one except me was affected. Every member of the committee was implicated except him.*

As a conjunction, *except* can mean *if it were not for the fact that*. In that sense, especially in formal writing, *except* is followed by *that: She would have accepted the invitation, except that the trip was very expensive*. See also **accept, except.**

except, excepting   As prepositions, both words mean excluding. In theory, *excepting* can replace *except* in all examples expressing that meaning, including those in the preceding entry: *No one excepting me was affected. Every member was implicated excepting him.* In practice, in modern usage, *except* is almost always used in examples of that kind. But *excepting* is still employed in negative constructions to the exclusion of *except: All employees, not excepting part-time ones, must be familiar with the emergency procedures.*

exceptionable, exceptional   These are often confused, and unfortunately so, since they have quite different meanings. That which is *exceptionable* is open or liable to objection: *He insisted that there was nothing exceptionable about the requirement he set.* That which is *exceptional* is uncommon (out of the ordinary): *The job calls for exceptional skills, but there was nothing exceptional in her performance.*

exodus   In careful usage, the term applies only to a departure of a large number of people.

expect   As a synonym for the verbs presume or suppose, *expect* is used informally: *We will hear from* *them soon, I expect*. This usage is characteristic of speech. It is related to, but different from, *expect* used in *We expect to hear from them soon*. The latter example, appropriate to all levels, including formal, employs *expect* in the primary sense of looking forward to the probable occurrence of (something).

explicit, express These adjectives both apply to something clearly stated rather than implied. *Explicit* applies more particularly to that which is carefully spelled out: *explicit instructions*. *Express* applies particularly to a clear expression of intention: *an express promise*.

eye The present participle of the verb is either *eyeing* or *eying: He is said to be eyeing* (or *eying*) *an ambassadorship as a possible reward*.

farther, farthest, further, furthest In examples dealing with literal (actual) distance, *farther* and *farthest* are the better choices, though *further* and *furthest* are also possible: *The arrow traveled farther* (adverb) *than we expected. The ride is farther* (adjective) *than I thought. This is the farthest* (adjective) *point from the center of the city*. Where figurative extent is involved (opposed to measurable distance), *further* and *furthest* are preferable and more common, though *farther* and *farthest* cannot be ruled out: *further from the truth; the furthest flight of the imagination. Further* is more common than *farther* when they are used as adjectives meaning additional: *no further reason for* *delay. Further* and *furthest,* as adverbs, express the sense of *to a greater extent* or *more: went further in debt; carried the investigation furthest.* As adverbs, both *further* and *farther* may be employed with the meaning of in addition or furthermore, but *further* is much more common: *She disliked the idea in general and felt, further, that this example was especially ill-timed.* A major distinction between *farther* and *further* is that only *further* is a verb, meaning to help the progress of; to forward; advance: *discoveries that further the cause of preventive medicine.*

Note that the related word *furthermore,* meaning moreover or in addition, is always spelled thus, not *farthermore.*

fatal, fateful Although there is considerable overlapping of meaning between these adjectives, usage has given them rather well-differentiated roles. In the following examples, the word given is the more common one in that sense, though by definition the other could be substituted: *a fatal wound* (causing death; mortal); *something fatal to our hopes* (causing ruin; disastrous); *a fateful decision* (affecting one's destiny). *Fateful* is the choice when the sense is related clearly to the operation of fate: *no escaping a fateful conclusion* (seemingly controlled by fate; predetermined); *a fateful sign* (full of significance; in particular, foreboding or ominous).

fault Like *author,* this word is now widely employed

as a transitive verb after a lengthy period of disuse. As such, *fault* means to find a fault in (a person or something pertaining to the person); to criticize or blame. Like that of *author,* this usage is disliked by many writers and editors, though it has long had dictionary sanction.

feasible, possible *Possible* is the more general of these adjectives; it describes what is capable of happening or existing. *Feasible* is applied to that which is capable of being accomplished or brought about; in that sense the word implies practicability and applicability to need or purpose. *Feasible* also can describe what is capable of being utilized or dealt with successfully, in which case it implies suitability.

feel The verb is followed by an adjective when the sense relates to a person's perception of his or her condition of being: *I was ill last week but now I feel different; today I feel strong again.* The adjectives *different* and *strong* describe the subject; *feel* serves as a linking verb. When the sense relates to having strong emotional involvement through an opinion or conviction, an adverb often follows: *She has always felt strongly about women's rights. He once agreed with her position, but he feels differently now.* In these examples, *strongly* and *differently* qualify *feel* with respect to degree and condition. See also **bad, badly.**

feel like This phrase is for informal usage: *did not feel like going to work; felt like a round of golf in-*

stead. In formal writing, the corresponding meaning is expressed by one of these: want; be in the mood for; have a desire for.

fellow   Terms such as *fellow citizen, fellow student,* and *fellow worker* are written thus, as two words without hyphens. *Fellow* is an adjective in such expressions. The same rule applies to *fellow feeling, fellow servant,* and *fellow traveler. Fellow man* is written thus or as one word (no hyphen).

female, feminine   *Female,* like *male,* is largely limited to classifying by sex: *the female population; female* (biological) *characteristics; female birth,* or *death, rate; female diseases. Feminine* is less frequently used as such a categorizing word: *the feminine lead in a play or film.* It often precedes nouns naming things considered characteristic of women (and thus corresponds to *masculine*): *feminine charm; a feminine taste for finery.* In grammar, *feminine* is always the term that describes words or forms classified as *female: feminine nouns such as "confidante" and "protégée."*

fewer, less   Use *fewer* when referring to numbers or units considered individually and therefore capable of being counted or enumerated. Use *less* in references to collective quantity and to something abstract. For example, *fewer jobs, less opportunity; fewer teachers, less individual instruction. Fewer* is seldom misused but *less* often is, and tends to take over the functions of both words. In the following examples, *less* should not replace *fewer* (though it often does in the hands of unskilled writers): *fewer people in a period of declining birth rates; no fewer than ten applicants seeking information; fourteen fewer seats in Congress. Less* is generally the choice in sentences setting forth periods of time, sums of money, and measures of distance, weight, and the like; here the sense is collective, even though the nouns qualified by *less* name things that can be counted or enumerated: *less than two months; less than forty years of age; less than $1,000; weighing less than 100 pounds.*

figure As a verb bearing on mathematics, *figure* is used formally when it means to calculate or compute: *figure the distance between two planets.* In several related usages, the verb is for informal writing only. Among them are *figure out* for solve or decipher, and *figure on* for depend on or expect: *figure on her to be a big help; figure on having sufficient time to finish the job.* Also informal is *figure* for conclude, believe, or predict (*figure that they may leave*), and *figure* for interpret or see: *figured him for a coward.* Informal, at best, is the expression *it figures* as the equivalent of it is to be expected: *It figures that Congress won't pass such a tax bill in an election year.*

finalize The verb has widespread use, almost invariably in quite formal settings. It is so roundly disliked by many writers, editors, and students of language, however, that its users take what amounts to a calculated risk. The dislike stems from the word's association with coinages that suggest bureaucracy and self-importance. The meaning of *finalize,* moreover, is readily expressed by *complete, conclude, make final, put in final form,* or the like, most of which are no less economical.

fine   The adverb *fine* occurs principally in compounds such as *fine-wrought* and *fine-cut* to express the sense of discriminatingly or minutely. As the equivalent of *very well,* as in *doing fine,* the adverb is for informal use only.

first, last   In modern usage, the adjectives *first* and *last* almost invariably precede the numeral in collective expressions such as *the first three pages* and *the last two chapters.* There is an alternative way of expressing the same ideas: *the three first pages* and *the two last chapters.* The alternative way is the older one; it is still acceptable usage when only low numbers are employed. Especially in formal writing, however, this older form is now less desirable, for it occurs rather infrequently and tends to puzzle some readers, who are liable to confuse a reference such as *two last chapters* with the idea of two versions of the last chapter—that is, with alternative modes of presenting the same unit.

fit   The past tense and past participle of the verb is *fitted* or *fit. Fitted* is the more common form, but idiom is also a determining factor in making a choice to express different senses. The following examples illustrate the various meanings of the verb: *The suit fit (or fitted) him very well. The punishment fit (or fitted) the crime. The equipment was fitted to their needs. The training fitted her for the ordeal. They fitted him out for the journey. She fitted it into the last part of the program. He fitted the washer in the valve. The explanation fitted (or fit) in with the rest of the account.*

flagrant See **blatant, flagrant.**

flail, flay To *flail* is to thresh, beat, or wave (the arms, in particular). To *flay* is to strip off the skin of, plunder, or criticize savagely.

flair, flare *Flair* denotes natural talent or instinctive discernment. *Flare* is the term for a blaze of light and for a device that produces the light. Only *flare* is a verb: *The torches flared. The suggestion that she was malingering caused her to flare up.*

flammable, inflammable These are alike in meaning and interchangeable when they describe something actually capable of burning. But only *inflammable* can refer to a nature quickly or easily aroused to strong emotion. The popularity of *flammable* in literal usage is due to the feeling that the word expresses a warning more clearly than *inflammable,* which is sometimes mistaken for nonflammable or noncombustible. *Flam-*

mable is therefore especially appropriate in technical writing and where it serves as a warning (as a label).

flare See **flair, flare.**

flaunt, flout To *flaunt* something is to exhibit it ostentatiously: *flaunt power; flaunted her diamonds.* To *flout* is to show contempt for (something), to scorn or scoff at it. In examples dealing with showing disregard for laws, rules, and regulations, especially in a contemptuous way, *flaunt* is often misused for *flout: repeatedly flaunted the no-parking ordinance.* Only *flout* is acceptable in such examples.

flay See **flail, flay.**

flier, flyer The second is a variant spelling of *flier.* Both forms are in widespread use in most senses of the noun.

flounder, founder *Flounder* is the verb expressing clumsy movement. *Founder* refers to becoming disabled, collapsing or giving way, and sinking below the surface of a body of water.

flout See **flaunt, flout.**

flyer See **flier, flyer.**

folk, folks *Folk* is the singular and plural form when the noun denotes a people (ethnic group or race) and people of a specified group or kind: *city folk* (collective plural). The plural *folks* is informal and is applied to one's relatives and to people in general: *Folks are a pretty good lot, all told.*

(as) follows The established and unchanging form of the expression preceding a listing is *as follows,* not *as follow.* This is true regardless of the grammatical number of the noun that comes before: *The text is as follows. The components of the remedy are as follows.* In such examples the subject of *follows* (singular) is construed as *it* unexpressed: *as it follows.*

foot *foot* (singular) and its plural *feet,* as units of measure, are distinguished in usage according to the following typical examples: *a six-foot man; a man six feet tall* (or *six feet in height*); *a two-foot space; a gap two feet wide; a ledge six feet below; a crevice about a foot above him.*

forbear, forebear As nouns, both denote an ancestor. Only *forbear* is a verb meaning to refrain or desist from or to be tolerant: *Despite much provocation, the police forbore* (or *have forborne*) *retaliating* or *forbore from retaliation.*

forbid This verb is used with an infinitive or a gerund to express the same idea: *forbid her to leave; forbid her leaving.* The common misuse, with *from,* should be avoided: *forbid her from leaving.* The usual past tense is illustrated by *they forbade.* The usual past participle is *forbidden: they have* (or *had*) *forbidden.*

forceful, forcible *Forceful* describes what is characterized by or full of force and therefore effective: *a forceful argument. Forcible* is applied to what is accomplished by force: *forcible entry; forcible ejection.*

forebear See **forbear, forebear.**

forecast Constructions in past time are illustrated by *forecast,* or *forecasted, trouble; has forecast,* or *forecasted, trouble; trouble was forecast,* or *forecasted.*

forego, forgo *Forego,* spelled only as given, is the verb meaning to precede or go before in time or place. *Forgo,* less often spelled *forego,* is the verb meaning to relinquish or abstain from: *forgo* (or *forego*) *worldly pleasures.*

foregoing This is the adjective meaning just past; preceding; previously mentioned: *the foregoing statement.*

foregone conclusion The expression for an end or result regarded as inevitable is written thus.

foremost This can be applied to one person or thing to indicate undisputed leadership. Or the adjective can describe a small group regarded as representing the front rank, which permits expressions such as *the foremost writers* and *one of the foremost writers of the time.*

foresee The verb meaning to see or know beforehand is written thus. The corresponding noun is *foresight*.

foreswear See **forswear.**

foreword The noun meaning preface or introductory note is spelled thus.

forgo See **forego, forgo.**

former As a term corresponding to *latter,* use *former* only with reference to the first of two: *Paderewski and Hess were noted pianists, and the former* (Paderewski) *was also famous outside music.* When three or more occur in an enumeration, reference to the first should be by means of *the first* or *first-named.* Often it is more desirable to repeat the name of the indicated person or thing in such constructions, as an aid to the reader; especially if the second reference to the given person or thing is far from the first, such repetition will spare the reader the pause otherwise necessary to determine who or what is meant by *former* or *first-named.*

forswear This is the preferred spelling of the verb meaning to renounce, disavow, or swear falsely. The alternative form is *foreswear.*

fortuitous, fortunate *Fortuitous* is used only to describe something happening by accident or chance and thus unplanned. It does not mean fortunate or lucky.

A *fortuitous* thing is sometimes fortunate and sometimes not. To employ *fortuitous* in examples in which there is no clear indication of chance or accident is loose usage. *Fortunate* means occurring by good fortune or favorable chance, or having unexpected good fortune (and therefore lucky).

forward, forwards   The adjective is always written *forward,* in all senses: *a forward cabin; forward movement; a forward* (presumptuous; bold) *person; a forward* (progressive) *country. Forward* is the usual form of the adverb (when the word follows a verb that it qualifies). But either *forward* or *forwards* is possible when the meaning is toward the front, or frontward: *Drive forward* (or *forwards*) *a bit.* In other adverbial senses, the only form is *forward: look forward to seeing you* (that is, toward the future); *came forward from obscurity* (into view or prominence).

founder   See **flounder, founder.**

free   The word is both an adjective and an adverb. The comparative and superlative forms are *freer* and *freest;* the corresponding forms for the adverb *freely* are *more freely* and *most freely.* The expression *for free* is a slang, and wordy, variant of *free.*

froze, frozen   Froze is the past tense of *freeze,* and *frozen* the past participle: *The storm froze the citrus crops,* or *has frozen them. The crops were frozen.*

fulsome Especially in the expression *fulsome praise,* this adjective is often misused as a synonym of full and abundant. In modern usage *fulsome* combines the idea of fullness or abundance with that of excess or insincerity. *Fulsome praise* is therefore praise so lavish that it has a false ring. In a related sense *fulsome* means loathsome or disgusting.

fun A newer use of the word, as an adjective, is informal: *Mayor Lindsay called New York a fun city.*

further, furthest See **farther, farthest.**

gage See **gauge.**

gamut In its most familiar sense, the word means the complete range of anything. The expression *run the gamut* should not be confused with *run the gantlet* (or *gauntlet*).

gantlet, gauntlet These words are found most often in several stock expressions, of which *run the gantlet,* or *gauntlet,* is the most familar. In earlier times, as punishment a person was sometimes forced to run between two lines of men facing each other and armed with sticks or other weapons. The two lines made up the *gantlet* (*gauntlet*). Though people are seldom subjected to such beatings at present, the word's figurative sense of a severe trial or ordeal survives, and so does the expression: *run the gantlet* (*gauntlet*) *of criticism; legislative sponsors who ran the gantlet* (*gauntlet*) *of* *economy-minded legislators.* Both spellings of the noun are commonly used, and both are acceptable, though some usage authorities insist on or prefer *gantlet.* *Gauntlet* is the preferred spelling of the glove worn with medieval armor; that term survives in the expressions *fling* (or *throw*) *down the gauntlet* and *take up the gauntlet*—to issue a challenge and to accept such a challenge.

gauge   *Gauge* is the first spelling, and *gage* an acceptable alternative, of the noun meaning a standard of measurement, an instrument for measuring or testing, the position of a vessel, the distance between two rails or between two wheels, the diameter of a shotgun barrel, thickness (of metal or wire), and fineness of knitted cloth. The corresponding verb meaning to measure or evaluate is spelled only *gauge.*

get   The past tense is *got,* the past participle *got* or *gotten.* (In British English, *got* is virtually the sole form of the participle.) In usage, the constructions *has* (or *have*) *got* and *has* (or *have*) *gotten* are distinguished as follows: *got* indicates possession (*has got two cars*), without indication of time, and *gotten* usually implies, besides possession, the idea of recent acquisition (*has gotten two cars*). Especially in writing, the idea of mere possession is better expressed without *got*—by *has* or *have* alone: *has* (or *have*) *two cars.*

gibe, jibe As verbs and nouns, both words express the sense of taunting or scoffing. Only *jibe* is used for the verb expressing agreement and for the lesser-known nautical (sailing) term.

gift The word's use as a transitive verb—to present (a person) with a gift—is informal. In such constructions, the recipient is the direct object: *gifted his niece on her confirmation.*

glamour This is the preferred spelling; the alternate is *glamor.* But the usual forms of the adjective and verb are *glamorous* and *glamorize.*

glassful The plural is *glassfuls.*

good In formal usage, as a descriptive word *good* is only an adjective, not an adverb. As an adjective it can qualify a noun attributively by preceding the noun (*a good aircraft*), or it can follow a linking verb such as *be, feel, seem, smell, sound,* and *taste: The soup smells good. The news sounds good.* In such examples *good* once more describes a noun, the subject of the sentence, though its position in the sequence of the wording is different. Adverbs, rather than adjectives, qualify nonlinking verbs, but *good* may be used as an adverb only in dialogue or other deliberately informal usage, as in *She speaks good.* On a formal level, *well* replaces *good* in such examples: *speaks well; sings well; dances well; a machine that runs well,* or *works* *well.* The expression *good and,* preceding an adjective, is acceptable informally: *good and tired.*

got, gotten See **get.**

graceful, gracious *Graceful* is applied to persons, animals, or things that show beauty or charm of movement, form, or proportion. *Gracious* principally describes human demeanor that reflects a kind and compassionate nature or, less often, elegance of taste.

graduate The idea of successfully completing a course of study is expressed by either *graduated* or *was graduated: He graduated* (or *was graduated*) *from college.* Both constructions are acceptable on a formal level, and both require *from. He graduated college* is not acceptable on any level.

grisly, grizzly What is *grisly* is horrifying or gruesome. That which is *grizzly* is grayish or flecked with gray. *Grizzly* (noun) is also the term for the grayish form of the brown bear.

groom In all but the most formal contexts, this noun is an acceptable substitute for *bridegroom.*

ground, grounds An area of land set aside for a particular purpose is denoted by either the singular or plural form in many cases: *burial ground(s); fairground(s).* In some, however, only the plural appears: *baseball grounds. Grounds* is always used to designate land surrounding or forming part of a building: *the rectory grounds.* Either form may be employed to denote the foundation for an argument, belief, or action, in the sense of basis or premise: *little ground for dispute; the grounds cited by Charles Darwin in expounding his theory of evolution.* The plural form is generally employed in the case of an underlying condition that prompts an action: *grounds for divorce; grounds for impeachment.*

group Like most collective nouns, *group* can be construed as singular or plural in determining the grammatical number of the verb that *group* governs. A singular verb is used when the persons or things forming the group are considered as one or as acting as one, or when they are related by membership in a class or category. A plural verb occurs when reference is made to persons thought of as acting individually. The grammatical number of related pronouns or pronominal adjectives agrees with that of the verb: *The group* (of persons), *though varied in many respects, is bound together by an all-powerful common interest in maintaining its secular form of education. This group* (of animals) *manifests many of its characteristics most clearly in second-generation offspring. The group* (of persons) *were divided in their sympathies.*

hail, hale *Hail* (noun and verb) is the term for precipitation, literal and figurative (*a hail of abuse; hailed curses at the enemy*); it is also the verb meaning salute, designate, and signal (*hailed the new president;*

hailed her queen of the tribe; hailed a cab). Hail from, meaning come from, is written thus. *Hale* has the narrower application: as an adjective describing good health and as a verb meaning compel to go (*haled them into court*).

half In written usage, *a half glass of water* is preferable to *half a glass,* though the latter form is acceptable (but not *a half a glass*). The expression *in half* means into halves. It is good usage, therefore, to write *cut a cake in half.* The construction is not only acceptable but more natural to most persons than *cut a cake in halves.*

handful The plural is *handfuls.*

hanged, hung When the verb *hang* refers to execution (capital punishment), the past tense and past participle is *hanged,* not *hung: The outlaw was hanged. The dictator's forces hanged many political prisoners.* In all other senses of the verb, the corresponding past tense and past participle is *hung: hung the clothes, the drapes, a flag, a scythe* (to its handle); *hung her head in shame; after the wallpaper was hung; a jury that was hung* (deadlocked); *an argument that hung* (depended) *on slim evidence; a listener who hung on every word as the verdict hung in the balance.*

happen, occur, take place Each of these refers to the coming about of something. *Happen* and *occur* are used when the action is spontaneous, accidental, or unforeseen: *The accident happened an hour ago. It occurred a mile south of the bridge.* Action that is pre-arranged is preferably expressed by *take place: An inquiry into the cause of the accident will take place on Monday. Happen* and *occur* are often interchangeable, as in the preceding examples. But *happen* is especially applicable to what is accidental; *occur* also works in such examples and is the better choice when the action is traceable to a clear cause. In sentences in which *occur* could be misconstrued to mean come to mind, *happen* is mandatory: *Something like that might have happened to them.* When the desired sense is to be met with or appear, *happen* cannot express it; *occur* is the choice (and less often *take place,* in the case of prearrangement): *Violence frequently occurs* (or *takes place*) *in the later plays of Tennessee Williams. Widespread sickness of this kind seldom occurs* (not *takes place*) *now.*

hardly Since the word has a sense verging on the negative, it is not used with another negative in the same construction: *They could hardly hear* (not *couldn't hardly*). *She accepted the verdict with hardly a sign of emotion* (not *without hardly*). *Hardly* is followed by clauses introduced by *when* or, less often, *before,* but not by *than* or *until: They had hardly arrived when* (or *before*) *the call came.*

harebrained The adjective meaning giddy or flighty is spelled thus, not *hairbrained.*

have In phrases such as *could have seen* or *might have gone,* have rather than *of* is correct.

head When the verb is used transitively, meaning to be in charge of (something), *head* is preferable to *head up,* especially in formal writing: *head a committee; head an investigation.*

headquarter, headquarters The noun *headquarters,* plural in form, is more often used with a plural verb (*headquarters are located*), though a singular one is also possible. As a verb, *headquarter* is informal in both intransitive and transitive senses: *The company will headquarter in Providence. It has headquartered the sales department in an outlying district.*

healthful, healthy *Healthful* is applied to what promotes or encourages good health: *a healthful climate; healthful working conditions. Healthy* expresses the same meaning, and could be substituted in the preceding examples, but primarily it describes someone or something that possesses good health.

hectic By extension of its medical meanings, this adjective has come to describe that which is characterized by feverish activity, confusion, or haste: *a hectic day.* The word is well established in that sense, on all levels of usage.

height The word is spelled as given. *Heighth,* an earlier spelling, is now a misspelling.

help The expression *cannot help but,* especially common in speech, is found in examples such as *We cannot help but regret it*. In formal writing, preferable ways of expressing the same idea are *cannot help regretting it* and *can* (or *cannot*) *but regret it*.

here The adverb meaning in this place follows the noun (never precedes it) in constructions introduced by the demonstrative *this: this house here* (not *this here house*). Constructions introduced by *here is* and *here are* are similar to those beginning *there is* and *there are* with respect to determination of the grammatical number of the verb. For an explanation of the procedure, see **there.**

hero The plural is *heroes*.

hers The possessive pronoun is written thus, without an apostrophe: *The money is hers.*

herself, himself Like other *-self* pronouns, these have a variety of functions that are never disputed. As reflexives they form the direct or indirect object of a verb or the object of a preposition: *She cut herself. He wants it for himself.* They are used for emphasis: *She did it herself. He himself did the work.* They are also employed as an indication of real, normal, or healthy condition or identity: *He's more like himself again.* In written usage they are less appropriate than *her* or *him* as elements of compound objects: *Mary expressed the hope that they would give Frank and* *her* (preferable to *herself*) *enough time.* The *-self* words are even less acceptable as parts of compound subjects: *If the tests prove negative, Mrs. Ford and he* (not *himself*) *will leave the hospital tomorrow.*

historic, historical   Use *historic* when the thing it describes is important in or contributes to history: *the historic* (history-making) *moon landing in 1969. Historical* refers more broadly to what is concerned with history: *historical novel.*

homogeneous, homogenous   The general senses related to likeness in nature or kind and to uniformity in structure or composition can be expressed by either word. *Homogenous* is the term used in biology to indicate homogeny (correspondence between organs and parts).

hopefully   When the adverb means with hope or in a hopeful manner (*looked forward to the meeting hopefully*), it is always used acceptably. A much newer usage employs the word as the equivalent of it is to be hoped, or let us hope: *Hopefully we are on the right track.* The newer sense is now very common but is still not accepted by many usage authorities.

host   Employed as a transitive verb meaning to serve as host for (a party, convention, or television program, for example), *host* is informal. In formal writing, *serve as host for* or *be host to* are preferable.

however   Avoid using *but* just before *however* when the conjunction means nevertheless: *The votes are in; however* (not *but however*) *they have not yet been counted.*

human   The noun is acceptably employed, on a formal level, in the sense of human being.

human, humane, humanitarian   As descriptive words, *human* is essentially a classifying term relating to individuals or people collectively (*human achievement; human events*); *humane* implies having the qualities of kindness and compassion (*humane treatment*); and *humanitarian* applies to what actively promotes the needs and welfare of people (*humanitarian concerns*).

hung   See **hanged, hung.**

I   See **between you and me; me.**

idle   As a verb in the sense of to make inactive or unemployed, *idle* is acceptable on all levels of spoken or written English.

if   Both *if* and *whether* are used to introduce noun clauses, though *whether* is preferred by many writers and editors in formal writing: *By Friday he will learn whether* (or *if*) *he has succeeded.* When such a clause comes at the start of a sentence, *whether* is always the choice: *Whether he has succeeded is not certain.* Use of *if* in such an example very likely would confuse a reader and make a rereading of the sentence necessary.

illicit See **elicit, illicit.**

illusion See **allusion, delusion, illusion.**

imaginary, imaginative Something *imaginary* has existence only in the imagination and is therefore unreal. *Imaginative* primarily describes persons having creative imagination or ingenuity, or things reflecting such qualities.

immigrate See **emigrate, immigrate, migrate.**

imminent See **eminent, imminent.**

impassable, impassive Something *impassable* cannot be traveled across or through. Someone *impassive* experiences no emotion or shows none and is characteristically expressionless.

imply, infer In modern usage these are carefully distinguished. To *imply* something is to state it indirectly, to hint or suggest it. *Implication* is the corresponding noun: the act of implying or that which is implied (an indirect indication or hint). *Imply,* in another sense, means to involve by logical necessity or to entail: *Continued success generally implies something more than luck.* To *infer* is to conclude (something) from evidence, or to deduce: *inferred from her actions that she didn't believe my story. Infer* is often misused for *imply,* in the sense of stating indirectly, just as *inference* is misused for *implication.* An *inference* is a deduction or conclusion, something that is inferred.

important, importantly *Important,* not *importantly,* is the choice in examples such as the following: *The move will hinder this project and, more important, will ruin the morale of the entire staff. More important* is a shortened form of *what is more important;* thus an adjective, *important,* following *is*—not the adverb *importantly.*

impracticable, impractical *Impracticable* describes what cannot be done or carried out. *Impractical* can be used in the same sense, but more often is applied to what would be unwise to carry out or maintain in practice. The distinction is that between what is impossible and what is not desirable or worthwhile.

in, into, in to As a preposition, *in* primarily indicates position, location, or condition: *He was in the library. She was in a bad mood.* Used correspondingly, *into* indicates direction or movement to an interior location or, figuratively, change of condition: *She went into the lobby. He flew into a rage. In* is also possible in such examples, but conveys the desired sense less clearly and less forcefully. The two-word form *in to* is used in examples, such as the following, in which *in* is an adverb: *We went in to supper. You may go in to see them now.*

in addition to See **along with.**

include Unlike *comprise,* this verb does not imply that all components are enumerated; generally it implies an incomplete listing: *New York comprises the boroughs of Manhattan, the Bronx, Queens, Brooklyn, and Richmond. The cake's ingredients include butter and egg yolks.* When a complete listing is made, *comprise* is a better choice than *include*.

incredible, incredulous   What is *incredible* is unbelievable. *Incredulous,* often misused in that sense, properly describes a person or something about a person that shows skepticism or disbelief.

indefinitely   Although the word describes a condition or action that lacks precise limits, in many contexts it makes the implication of lengthy duration: *She expects to be stationed in Puerto Rico indefinitely.* In such examples, *indefinitely* suggests continued residence (or other action) in the foreseeable future and is acceptably so used except when lack of clarity might result.

individual   As a noun, *individual* means person but should not be used as an all-purpose substitute for *person. Individual* is most appropriate in examples in which a single human being is distinguished from a group or mass, by contrast or stress on individuality: *the individual's right to a nonconformist view; an individual to the core* (an independent, strong-willed person). When those conditions do not exist in the example at hand, *person* is the better choice.

indoor, indoors *Indoor* is an adjective only, and *indoors* an adverb: *indoor sports; an indoor football field; went indoors; a field built indoors.*

infer See **imply, infer.**

inferior Persons and things are said to be *inferior to* others—not *inferior than.*

inflammable, inflammatory In their most common application, *inflammable* applies to what ignites readily and burns rapidly, and *inflammatory* to what stirs strong emotion—a speech, for example. See also **flammable, inflammable.**

ingenious, ingenuous Both are said of persons and the attributes and creations of persons. *Ingenious* indicates inventive skill or imagination; *ingenuous,* the absence of worldliness or sophistication, or a tendency to be open and honest in dealing.

inhuman, inhumane, nonhuman The first two adjectives are close synonyms and refer to persons or things that are cruel and lacking in compassion. *Nonhuman* is basically a categorizing term applicable to things not human, but lacks a suggestion of their nature in other respects.

inside As a preposition, *inside* is capable of functioning without a following *of: remained inside the house.* In written usage such a construction is preferable to the variant *inside of the house*. With reference to time and distance, *inside of* is perhaps the more common construction, but *inside* is likewise able to express the desired sense: *inside* (within) *a mile; inside an hour*.

insignia   Though plural in form, this noun is acceptably used with a singular verb: *This insignia is attractive*. The plural form, meaning more than one such badge or distinguishing sign, is either *insignia* or *insignias*. The English singular *insigne,* from Latin, is extremely rare in current usage.

insure   See **assure, ensure, insure.**

intend   This verb is often followed by an infinitive (*intend to go*) or by a clause introduced by *that* and with a subjunctive form of verb: *intended that he call her* (but not *intended for him to call her*).

intense, intensive   *Intense* most often describes what is extreme in degree (*intense pain; intense emotion*), usually in the sense of being deeply felt; it can also indicate intensity, as in *intense effort* and *a very intense person*. In a corresponding sense, *intensive* is synonymous with concentrated and exhaustive: *intensive care; intensive study*.

interment, internment   *Interment* refers to burial, *internment* to detaining or confining, especially in wartime, or to training or serving as an intern (in medicine).

internecine The word describes something mutually destructive, ruinous or fatal to both sides; or it can refer to internal struggle, within a nation or an organization, that is not necessarily fatal or mutually destructive, though intense.

interpretative, interpretive These are alike in meaning, and both are acceptable on a formal level.

into See **in, into, in to.**

intrigue As a transitive verb meaning to arouse interest or curiosity (*a tale that intrigued us*), the word occurs on all levels. It is still resisted by some usage authorities, however, on the ground that it displaces words that would express the desired sense more precisely: *excite, interest, puzzle, fascinate,* and *titillate,* for example.

invent See **discover, invent.**

inward, inwards Only *inward* is the adjective: *an inward force.* The corresponding adverb is *inward* or *inwards: turned inward,* or *inwards.*

irregardless This double negative is not acceptable. Use *regardless.*

irrespective The phrase *irrespective of* (regardless of) is always written thus, not *irrespectively of.*

Israel, Israeli *Israel* is the name of the modern republic, and is sometimes used as an adjective relating to that nation. *Israeli* is more widely employed as an adjective in that sense; it (not *Israelite*) is the term for a native or inhabitant of modern Israel, with alternative plurals: *Israeli, Israelis*.

its, it's *Its* is the possessive form of the pronoun *it*: *a city and its people*. *It's* is the contraction of *it is* and *it has*: *It's not new; it's been done before*.

jealousy See **envy, jealousy**.

jibe See **gibe, jibe**.

judicial, judicious *Judicial* refers broadly to courts of law and the administration of justice: *judicial branch of government; the judicial process*. *Judicious* describes persons or things that show sound judgment: *judicious measures*.

jurist The term is more inclusive than *judge*. It denotes any person skilled in the law: an eminent judge, lawyer, or legal scholar, for example.

kind In formal written usage, *kind* is preferably employed in a consistently singular construction in examples such as *This kind of pen is quite useful*. (The demonstrative adjective *this* is singular, as are the following noun and verb, *pen* and *is*.) The alternative constructions, *these kind of pens are* and *this kind of* *pens are,* are more typical of spoken language, though they also have a long history of written usage. A preferable rendering of the example employing plural elements is *Pens of this kind are quite useful.* A more acceptable use of *kind,* with an accompanying plural noun and verb, occurs in interrogative constructions introduced by *what* or *which: What kind of pens are these?* Writers sometimes use *kinds* in sentences of this variety in an effort to justify accompanying plural elements—but *kinds* is possible only when the desired sense involves more than one class or variety. *Kinds* and plural verbs are required when *all* precedes *kinds: All kinds of aircraft are on display.*

(a) kind of, kind of *A kind of* indicates a rough approximation of the category stated: *a kind of early printing press.* Such examples are acceptable on all levels of writing. An informal use of *kind of* expresses the sense of somewhat (*kind of tired*) or after a fashion; to a degree: *kind of nodded.*

knot In nautical measure, *knot* is a unit of speed, with a built-in sense of "per hour." A ship is said to travel at ten knots (not knots per hour) and to cover ten nautical miles in an hour.

kudos The term means acclaim or prestige resulting from achievement or position. It is construed as singular in choice of a verb: *Kudos was not his lot.* There is no singular term *kudo* in standard usage.

lack See "Picking a Preposition."

last, latest Both can describe what is final: *the last* (or *latest*) *train to Chicago. Last* makes the clearer implication that nothing else follows; *latest train* might also be one in a continuing series. Both also mean most recent: *the last* (or *latest*) *word from Saigon. Latest* expresses that sense more clearly, for it stresses the expectation of further news. *Last word* implies that no other word may be forthcoming. See also **first, last.**

latter As a term corresponding to *former,* this word is applied only to the second of two. In referring to the last element in an example containing three or more, use *last-named,* not *latter.* In general, use all these terms only when the desired reference is clear without a rereading of what has gone before. Otherwise, a better course is to repeat the name of the person or thing to which a term like *latter* refers.

lay, lie The following examples illustrate these verbs in constructions in which errors commonly occur. *Lay* (to put, place, or prepare) always takes a direct object in the meanings indicated; *lie* (to recline or be situated) never does. Confusion occurs in part because the meanings are complementary, in part because of the overlapping of principal parts. The past tense and past participle of *lay* is *laid.* The past tense of *lie* is *lay,* the past participle is *lain.*

In the following, only *lay* and *laid* are possible, as indicated: *laid the letter on the desk; decided to lay the cards on the table; laid some cables and then the flooring; laid a burden on us; has laid the blame on her; laid plans and then a trap; laid much stress on several points; laid our case before the people; laid a bet; laid bare the scandal; laid claim to the property; had laid himself open to criticism; the hen that laid the eggs; a tale laid in Greece; a table laid for two; a ceiling laid with precious stones.*

In the next group, only *lie, lay, lain,* and *lying* are possible, as indicated: *decided to lie down for an hour; undressed and then lay on the couch; had lain there a few minutes when the bell rang; was lying half asleep; a dispute that lies unresolved; a site that lies between two small towns; property that lay between the frontier and an ancient fortress; accused of lying down on the job; lay in wait for them all night; advised us to lie low; a choice that lay with them alone.*

learn, teach In modern usage these are carefully distinguished. *Learn* is confined to the act of gaining knowledge. It is not acceptably used to express the act of instructing or imparting knowledge, a sense expressed only by *teach.*

leave, let The verbs are interchangeable only when followed by a noun or pronoun and *alone: Leave* (or *let*) *them alone.* The meaning thus expressed is to refrain from disturbing or interfering with. Both *leave* *alone* and *let alone* convey it acceptably. For reasons concerned in part with style and in part with clarity, some writers prefer *let alone* in such examples and confine *leave alone* to those in which the meaning is to depart and leave (one) in solitude (a sense *let alone* cannot convey). *Leave* is never interchangeable with *let* when the desired meaning is to allow or permit. Only *let* is acceptable in the following: *Let her go. Let me be. Let go of the rail. Let us not argue. Let it lie.* Note that *let* is followed by objective pronouns in the preceding examples and in *Let George and me* (not *I*) *help.*

lend.   See **loan, lend.**

less   See **fewer, less.**

let   See **leave, let.**

level, levy   These are confused in one sense of *level:* to direct emphatically or forcefully toward someone. One *levels* criticism, charges, accusations, and the like at another person. One does not *levy* such things; but taxes and war are *levied.*

liable   See **apt, liable, likely.**

libel, slander   *Libel* refers to injury through written, printed, or pictorial statements, and *slander* to similar injury through utterance of defamatory statements.

lie   See **lay, lie.**

like The verb *like* often occurs in constructions in which it is followed by an infinitive preceded by a noun or pronoun: *They would like us to report early* (but not *like for us to report early*). In conditional sentences, *would have liked* and *should have liked* are followed by a present infinitive: *She would have liked to remain* (not *to have remained*). But the perfect infinitive is possible when *like* is in the present tense: *She would like to have remained.* An unacceptable usage is that of *like* as a verbal auxiliary with a perfect infinitive: *I like to have died last night.* Make it *almost,* or *nearly, died.*

like, as As prepositions, *like* and *as* express different senses. *Like* most often indicates resemblance to the object mentioned: *run like a greyhound; a boy like him; not at all like her to give up.* (Note that the pronouns are in the objective case.) *As* indicates a role, capacity, or function: *serve as chairman.* In these usages, the words are not interchangeable. The distinction is illustrated by *act like a leader* and *serve as leader.* The object of *like* can be either a single word or a phrase: *felt like running away; looks like a good spring for gardening.*

A much less desirable use of *like* occurs when the word serves as a conjunction (to introduce a clause). In formal writing, the conjunctive *like* is usually acceptable only when it introduces an elliptical clause in which a verb is not expressed. The last example of the preceding paragraph is such a usage, as are: *The car looked like new. He took to politics like a fish to water.* If these examples were more fully expressed in the following ways, they would not be acceptable on a formal level: *looks like it will be a good spring; looked like it was new; like a fish takes to water.* To make them appropriate to formal writing, *like* must be replaced by *as, as if,* or *as though: as if it will be a good spring; as though it were new; as a fish takes to water.* Other typical examples: *Tell it as* (not *like*) *it is. The oatmeal tastes good, as* (not *like*) *cereal should. He had no authority but acted as if* (not *like*) *he did.*

Note that the last sentence could be recast: *but acted like one who did.* Here *like* is a preposition, and the usage is fully acceptable. Fear of misusing *like* should not tempt writers to employ *as* when *like* (preposition) is called for: *She acted like* (not *as*) *an idiot. They treated him like* (not *as*) *a child.* See also **along with; as if, as though.**

likely   When *likely* is employed as an adverb (meaning probably) in formal writing, idiom calls for it to be preceded by a qualifying word such as *quite, very,* or *most: He will very likely refuse to testify. Most likely it will rain tomorrow.* No such qualifying word is needed when *probably* replaces *likely* in such examples, nor is one called for when *likely* functions as an adjective following a linking verb such as *be, ap-*

pear, or *seem: It is likely to rain tomorrow. His refusal to testify now appears likely.* See also **apt, liable, likely.**

likewise The word is an adverb only, not a conjunction. Consequently it cannot take the place of connectives such as *and, as well as,* and *together with* in examples such as: *Her attractiveness and her good manners disarmed most of the questioners* (not . . . *attractiveness, likewise her good manners disarmed . . .*).

linage, lineage The noun meaning number of lines of printed or written material is usually spelled *linage,* though *lineage* is an acceptable variant. The noun pertaining to descent or derivation is spelled only *lineage.*

literally The following example illustrates a common misuse of *literally* (meaning actually): *Enraged, he literally spit fire.* The opposite of *literally*—that is, *figuratively*—is what is meant by writers of such sentences. But since *figuratively* would not be a comfortable choice idiomatically, a different course is desirable. One is to delete *literally;* another is to use as a substitute for it a less extreme phrase such as *seemed to* or *all but,* one of which is usually appropriate.

loan, lend As a verb, *loan* is acceptable, but *lend* is preferable, according to many writers and editors, especially when a given example does not deal with a transaction of money: *lent her some patterns.*

loath, loathe, loth *Loath,* or *loth,* is an adjective meaning unwilling, reluctant, or disinclined. *Loathe* is a verb meaning to detest or abhor.

lot The noun, meaning a considerably large number of persons or things, is found on all levels of usage: *A lot of modern music seems lacking in warmth.* In formal writing, *much* and *a great deal* are more frequent. The variant noun construction, *lots of,* occurs most often in informal writing, as does the adverbial usage: *lots of modern music; a lot better; lots better.*

loud, loudly *Loud* is both adjective and adverb. As an adverb it is often interchangeable with *loudly* after common verbs such as *laugh, play, roar, say, scream, shout, sing,* and *talk. Loudly* is the established form after *boast, brag, insist, proclaim,* and *exclaim,* among other verbs. In general, *loudly* is found more often than *loud* in formal usage, especially in writing.

luxuriant, luxurious *Luxuriant* is the choice when the sense is that of abundant growth (*luxuriant beard*), ornateness (*a luxuriant literary style*), or highly productive (*a luxuriant talent*). A *luxurious* taste reflects love of luxury; *luxurious* surroundings are marked by luxury.

majority The expression *great majority,* meaning most of, is always written thus, not *greater majority.* The expression *greater majority* is used only with reference to a comparison of two specific numbers. *Majority* is used with a singular verb when the reference is to a specific numerical figure: *Their majority is four votes.* When the meaning is the larger of two groups, the verb may be either singular (if unity or oneness is meant) or plural (if the members are considered as individuals): *The majority is determined to force a vote. The majority are of different minds on the issue.* When the term denotes most of a given group, it takes a plural verb: *The majority of the workers are without representation.*

male, masculine As an adjective, *male* (like *female*) is largely confined to classifying by sex: *male population figures; male ward of a hospital.* *Masculine* is applied to characteristics generally associated with men: *masculine force; masculine vigor; a typical masculine sense of self-importance.*

man The use of *man* to mean a human being regardless of sex has a long history, but many feel that the sense of male is predominant over that of person. Where it is necessary to avoid possible confusion, terms such as *men and women, human beings,* or *humans* can be used instead of *man.* Many occupational titles in which *man* occurs as an element are being replaced, sometimes officially, by terms that are neutral: *firefighter* (instead of *fireman*), *Member of Congress* (instead of *Congressman*).

mania, phobia Though often confused, the words are almost opposites. A *mania* is a desire or enthusiasm amounting to a craze. A *phobia* is a strong fear or aversion, often abnormal or illogical.

mantel, mantle *Mantel* is confined to fireplace terminology (facing and shelf). *Mantle* conveys all the many noun senses of these terms, including those of *mantel,* and it alone is the verb. Pertaining to fireplaces, *mantel* and *mantelpiece* are the more common spellings.

masculine See **male, masculine.**

masterful, masterly *Masterful* primarily describes what is forceful, vigorous, or domineering but can also mean skillful or expert, a sense that is expressed more precisely by *masterly.*

materialize In figurative usage this verb is sometimes employed to express the act of giving, or assuming, material or effective form. Plans and dreams can be said to *materialize* when they result in something real. But the verb is imprecise and pretentious as a mere substitute for *happen* or *occur,* which do not connote transformation into something actual.

may, might *Might* is the past tense of *may.* In modern usage, however, both verb forms are treated as subjunctives capable of expressing present and future time. When they are employed in the senses of possibility and permission, they are basically alike in meaning, and differ in intensity rather than in time. In both senses, *may* is stronger than *might: He may go. He might go.* The example with *may* suggests greater likelihood. The distinction holds with respect to permission: *May he go? Might he go?* The *may* example is the more forceful and direct. See also **can, may.**

maybe, may be   *Maybe* is the adverb meaning perhaps or possibly: *Maybe she will return. May be,* written as two words, is a verb form having a corresponding meaning: *It may be that she will return.*

me   This is the objective case of the pronoun *I.* Its principal uses are illustrated by the following: *injured me seriously* (direct object of a verb); *did me many favors* (indirect object of a verb); *gave the package to me* (object of a preposition). *I,* not *me,* is required after the verb *be,* in formal writing: *It was I who called you.* Informally, and in speech on all levels, *me* is used acceptably after a form of *be,* as a concession to speech patterns that seem more natural to most users of language: *It's me. The caller was me.* Rules of grammar, which govern formal writing, specify *I* in both examples. See also **between you and me; myself.**

mean   In expressing intention, *mean* is used with a clause introduced by *that: We did not mean that they should leave.* In written usage, particularly, the following variant of that sentence should not be used: *did not mean for them to leave.*

means   When *means* is used in the sense of resources such as money and property, it takes a plural verb: *His means are small.* When *means* has the sense of a way to an end, it may be used in either singular or plural constructions. The determination of grammatical number is influenced by the modifying words preceding *means. The means* may be followed by either a singular or a plural verb. *A means, any means, each means, every means,* and *one means* are followed by singular verbs. *All means, several means,* and *such means* (not *such a means*) are followed by plural verbs.

meantime, meanwhile   Each of these is a noun and an adverb, but in usage *meantime* is more often a noun: *In the meantime he waited. Meanwhile* is the more common as an adverb: *She went inside; meanwhile he waited.*

media   This plural form of the noun *medium* is applied in a collective sense to means of mass communication. Each means, considered individually, is a *medium: Television is a highly influential medium* (singular). *Together, television and radio, newspapers, and periodicals make up what we call the media* (plural). When it is used as a subject, *media* (plural) always takes a plural verb: *The media are often the target of public criticism.* As a collective plural, *media* expresses the sense of a group of things. Because some writers do not realize this, they sometimes seek to express the group sense by using *medias* —but *medias,* a superfluous term, is not accepted in standard usage.

might See **may, might.**

mighty As an adverb meaning very or extremely, *mighty* is informal: *a mighty fine day.* In formal writing, make it *very fine.*

migrate See **emigrate, immigrate, migrate.**

militate, mitigate *Mitigate* (to moderate or alleviate) is the one of this pair of verbs that is often misused, as in *prejudice that mitigated against his advancement. Militate against* (to have an adverse effect) is the proper choice in such examples. *Mitigate* is correctly used in *a surprise that mitigated his deep disappointment.*

million The plural is either *million* or *millions.* The first is almost invariably found when a specific number precedes: *fifty million Frenchmen. Millions* is used (with *of*) in the sense of an indefinitely large number: *millions of wasted opportunities.*

mishmash This is the only acceptable spelling.

mitigate See **militate, mitigate.**

mobile, movable *Movable* is applicable to what is capable of being moved, but does not imply great facility for movement. In contrast, *mobile* stresses such facility. For example, *mobile* equipment is that which is designed and built so as to be capable of being moved readily.

money *Moneys,* not *monies,* is the preferred plural. It is used in referring to the mediums of exchange of two or more countries or, within one country, in designating particular forms of money or specific sums.

moral See **ethical, moral.**

more, most In comparisons of two persons or things, one is said to be *more* talented, *more* efficient, or the like (or *the more* talented, *the more* efficient). *Most* is the corresponding term in such examples when more than two are present.

more than one Contrary to what logic would dictate, this expression is followed by a singular verb: *More than one man has tried and failed.*

Moslem, Muslim *Moslem* is found largely in journalism and popular usage in general. *Muslim* is preferred by scholars and English-speaking adherents of Islam. *Muslim* is the only form used by the organization of American blacks, Nation of Islam.

most As an adverb meaning almost, *most* is confined to informal usage: *Most everyone was present.* It is spelled thus—not *'most.* Of the two adverbial usages established on a formal level, one indicates a comparison: *the most skillful of all.* The other does not;

most functions as a mere intensive meaning *very: a most unfortunate occurrence.* Overuse of this last-named sense is often condemned as a stylistic weakness—as an affectation. See also **more, most.**

mostly This adverb conveys only one sense: for the most part, or almost entirely: *She wrote some fiction, but her work was mostly in biography.* It cannot replace the adverb *most* in examples in which the sense is to the greatest degree, very, or extremely: *She was most* (not *mostly*) *famous as a biographer.*

motif, motive *Motif* is the special word of this pair, applicable to a recurrent thematic element in the development of a work in architecture and the fine arts, music, or literature. That meaning can also be expressed by *motive,* though *motive* is used most often to denote something that serves to move a person to action.

movable See **mobile, movable.**

Ms. As a title of respect for a woman without regard to her marital status, *Ms.* is the equivalent of *Mr.,* the courtesy title for a man: *Ms. Smith; Ms. Judith Smith. Ms.* should not be used when a woman is addressed by her husband's given name and surname: *Ms. Green,* but not *Ms. Paul Green.*

Muslim See **Moslem, Muslim.**

mutual, reciprocal *Mutual* primarily refers to a relationship of two. Most often it describes intangibles of a personal nature, such as fear, respect, and obligation, and consequently expresses what two persons do, feel, or represent to each other. John Donne wrote: *The best league between princes is a mutual fear of each other.* In a few cases the word indicates a relationship between more than two. Examples are *mutual friend,* generally preferred to *common friend* in denoting a third party, and *mutual aid,* which often is not limited to two. *Reciprocal* most often is applied to two parties. But it usually describes terms with impersonal, tangible senses, notably *reciprocal trade* and *reciprocal tariff,* and strongly implies a balanced relationship in which one action is taken in return for another. It differs also in being applicable to a single action of one party, whereas *mutual* always implies a continuing interaction.

myself This pronoun sometimes replaces *me* and *I* in compound objects and compound subjects, but not acceptably so in formal writing: *They invited Mary and me* (not *myself*). *The mayor and I* (not *myself*) *are equally responsible.*

mysterious, mystic, mystical *Mysterious* has the widest application to anything that arouses wonder by being full of mystery and therefore difficult to understand or solve. *Mystic* and *mystical* are generally interchangeable as adjectives and are applied principally to highly unusual spiritual disciplines and religious practices, or to rites associated with the supernatural.

Native American *Native American* is the term many now prefer to designate the original inhabitants of the Western Hemisphere. Usage, however, varies according to tribe and region, and in Canada and Alaska in particular *American Indian* is still preferred as the term for all indigenous inhabitants other than the Eskimos.

nauseated, nauseous A person who is *nauseated* experiences nausea. Something or someone that is *nauseous* causes nausea and is therefore sickening in a physical sense or repulsive in an intellectual one. The second word is often misused for the first.

near See **close, near.**

nearest, next *Nearest* is the more general term; it indicates proximity in space, time, or kinship, but does not necessarily imply a sequence. *Next* always indicates direct succession in a series.

née This term is used when identifying a married woman by her maiden name. It literally means born; consequently it is followed only by a family name, the sole name a person has at birth: *Mrs. Helen Sloan, née Carver* (not *née Helen Carver*).

need *Need* is often employed as an auxiliary verb meaning be obliged or have to. As such it has several peculiarities. It is regularly followed by an infinitive (*need to sleep*), but in varying ways. When the example is a negative statement or a question, the infinitive that follows is sometimes expressed with *to,* and sometimes not: *You need not leave. Need we leave?* But: *You do not need to leave. Do we need to leave?* In all examples, *to* is always expressed when the infinitive follows the inflected forms *needs* and *needed: She needs to rest. They needed to stop.* In negative statements and questions, *need* as an auxiliary is not inflected in the third person singular, present tense, as it is in positive statements: *He need not try. He needs to try. Need it have occurred?*

neither As adjective and pronoun, *neither* is applied to one of two persons or things: *Neither shoe fits properly. Neither feels comfortable.* When more than two are present, use *none: Tax revision, welfare reform, and energy proposals all have high priorities, but none is likely to get definitive action in this session of Congress.* In formal usage the adjective or pronoun *neither* takes a singular verb: *Neither house was open; neither is available for inspection.* This is true even when a plural noun follows the subject *neither: Neither of the buildings is close to completion.* When accompanying possessive pronouns or pronominal adjectives appear in such sentences, they agree in number with the singular verb: *Neither of the women has her identification papers in proper order.*

The adverbial use of *neither,* for *either,* is not acceptable on any level, when it forms a double negative: *I could not go, and he didn't neither.*

neither . . . nor   In this construction, *neither* is a conjunction, and *nor* is always the second word of the pair to signify continuing negation: *Neither men nor machinery could remove the chief obstacle.* The construction is almost invariably used with two elements (*men* and *machinery* in the preceding example). But either of the elements may be compound; that is, either may consist of two or more components that, taken together, make up a single element. Two or more such closely related components may be joined by *or* within this *neither . . . nor* formula: *Neither United Nations sanctions nor unofficial threats or promises are likely to change such a dictator's course.*

The procedure for determining the number of a verb in such constructions is the same as that used in the case of *either . . . or.* For a discussion of this problem, and that of the agreement of accompanying personal pronouns and pronominal adjectives, see **either . . . or.**

never   Applied to action in the past, this adverb means not ever or on no occasion: *During his stay in*

Washington he never visited any of the governmental buildings. It implies action (or lack thereof) over a period of time and is not properly used to give a negative sense to a single action: *He was invited to yesterday's reception but never attended.* Make it *did not attend. Nor* is never paired with *ever* to emphasize the sense at no time whatsoever: *She promised never ever to do it again* (delete *ever*).

next See **nearest, next.**

nite, nitely These are not acceptable forms of *night* and *nightly.*

nobody See **no one.**

noisome, noisy These have no relationship in meaning. *Noisome* refers to what is extremely offensive or harmful: *a noisome odor. Noisy* refers only to noise. When *noisy* implies clamor or contention, in particular, *noisome* is often misused for it: *a noisy* (not *noisome*) *debate.*

nominal When applied to amounts, as in *nominal charge* or *nominal sum,* the term means not merely low, but so low in relation to value that the amount in question is merely a token.

none As a pronoun and subject, *none* is used with both singular and plural verbs, according to the meaning conveyed by *none.* When *none* stands for *no one* or *not one,* it is construed as singular and followed by a singular verb: *None is without some blemish. None of us is perfect.* A singular verb also occurs when *none* precedes a singular noun: *None of the laundry is really clean.* A plural verb is used when *none* has the sense of not any of a specified group of persons or things: *None were more deserving of pity than the survivors who returned hopelessly injured.* In many examples, a case can be made for either a singular or plural verb: *None of these proposals is* (or *are*) *a real solution.* Especially in earlier usage, a singular choice was invariably urged by conservative grammarians, but that position is much less widespread now. Whatever the choice, the singular or plural nature of the construction should be consistent throughout: *None has his work completed* (or *none have their*).

nonhuman   See **inhuman, inhumane, nonhuman.**

no one   When used as subjects, *no one* and *nobody* take singular verbs, and accompanying modifiers are also singular: *No one* (or *nobody*) *has complete control of his* (or *her,* or *his or her*) *future.*

nor   This conjunction is used primarily to express the sense of continuing negation. In varying examples it stands for *and not, or not, likewise not,* or *not either.* It is often paired with *neither,* and *nor,* not *or,* invariably follows *neither: She insisted that she was* *neither for it nor opposed. Nor,* not *or,* is always the choice to signify continuing negation in sentences having successive independent clauses: *She said she was neither for the proposal nor was she opposed. He had no experience in cost accounting, nor did the subject interest him.* Often such examples are expressed within a single independent clause, however; then *or,* rather than *nor,* is used following the opening negative statement, when it is clear that the negative sense carries over to the element introduced by *or: She was not strongly for or against the proposal. He had no experience or interest in cost accounting. He would not accept the explanation or even consider it.* See also **either . . . or; neither . . . nor; nor.**

normalcy There is no disputing the wide use of this word on a formal level or the fact that the usage has dictionary sanction. Among many writers, however, there is still considerable resistance to the noun. In part the adverse feeling traces to the belief that *normalcy* is a needless alternative to *normality* and *normal,* coined outside the usual pattern of the language. In part it also stems from the word's association with Warren Harding, who used it in a famous campaign speech preceding his ill-fated Presidency: *America's present need is not heroics but healing; not nostrums but normalcy.* He was not the coiner of the word, however; it was in standard usage before the address in Boston and so it remains, despite the controversy.

nothing When *nothing* is used as a subject, it takes a singular verb, even when it is separated from the verb by a qualifying passage introduced by *but, except,* or a like term that contains a plural noun or pronoun: *Nothing but bales of cotton was visible on the waterfront. Nothing except a few of their primitive tools survives today.*

nowhere This is the only acceptable form of the word. *Nowheres* and *noplace* are not in standard usage.

number Referring to quantity, *number* is used with a singular verb when preceded by *the.* In the expression *a number of,* meaning a large, indefinite quantity, a plural verb follows: *The number of applicants was smaller this year. A number of applicants were disqualified by the new rule.*

numerous This is an adjective only: *added numerous examples.* It is not acceptably used as a plural collective pronoun, as in *numerous of the pictures.*

O, oh *O* is the more special of these, except on those rare occasions when it is used as a variant of *oh.* In general the two have separate functions and are not interchangeable. The present-day writer has use for *O* principally in the exclamations *O dear!* and *O my!* (in which *oh* is also possible). In literature and in religious contexts, *O* is employed in direct address to express earnestness or solemnity: *O mighty ocean! O God on high!* In such usage *O* is always dependent on the words that follow it; unlike *oh,* it does not stand alone. *O* is always capitalized (usually as the first word of a sentence) and never followed directly by punctuation. The interjection *oh* has both wider use and greater range. Usually it expresses strong emotion but can also indicate merely a reflective pause. Most often it is part of a sentence, but it can stand alone as a one-word (elliptical) sentence. *Oh* is capitalized only when it begins a sentence; it is followed directly by a comma or, when the emphasis is strong, by an exclamation point: *Oh, I see. Oh! What a relief.*

obligate, oblige The two verbs are frequently used in passive constructions, and they are generally interchangeable when the prevailing sense is that of actual constraint. In other words, a person is *obligated,* or *obliged,* when under direct compulsion to follow a given course. A person is *obliged* (not *obligated*) upon feeling a debt of gratitude and nothing more: *We were obligated* (or *obliged*) *to follow all the terms of the contract. We were much obliged to them for their kindness.*

oblivious As an adjective corresponding to the noun *oblivion,* this word basically means forgetful of something that one has known in the past: *stayed at home, oblivious of the fact that he had tickets for a play that night.* But *oblivious* is also acceptably used in a broader sense equivalent to not conscious or aware of: *pursued her work oblivious of* (or *to*) *the distractions around her*.

observance, observation *Observance* refers to the keeping or celebrating of holidays, anniversaries, and customs, and to abiding by laws and regulations. *Observation* refers to close watch or study (of a person's actions, for example, or of current affairs or a branch of learning).

obsolescent, obsolete Something *obsolete* is no longer in use or in fashion, or no longer useful owing to outmoded design or construction or because of hard wear. Something *obsolescent* is in the process of passing out of use or usefulness, and is thus becoming obsolete.

occur See **happen, occur, take place.**

oculist, ophthalmologist, optician, optometrist *Oculist* and *ophthalmologist* are names for a physician who specializes in diseases of the eye. *Optometrist* names one skilled in testing the eyes and prescribing corrective lenses. *Optician* is the name for one who makes or sells optical goods.

odd Among the word's uses is that of indicating an indefinite amount in excess of a specified round number. The number and *odd* are usually joined by a hyphen, and invariably so when otherwise the meaning of *odd* might be misconstrued: *100-odd teachers*.

of   When it indicates possession or association, *of* is followed by either an uninflected noun (*friend of my brother; parts of a machine*) or by a noun or pronoun in the possessive case (*friend of my brother's; son of hers*).

off   When it is used as a preposition, *off* expresses its various meanings without being joined with *of*. In the following typical examples, use *off,* not *off of: stayed off the grass; lived off roots and herbs* or *off her pension; anchored a mile off shore. Off from* is as unnecessary as *off of* in examples such as *stepped off the curb. From,* not *off,* is the only acceptable preposition in expressions indicating a source: *got a loan from him.*

official, officious   *Official* is the general term used to indicate a position of authority or proper authorization: *official responsibilities; an official representative; official permission. Officious* describes a person who is excessively forward in offering services or advice to others, especially where they are unneeded or unwanted, and implies a tendency to be meddlesome.

oh   See **O, oh.**

O.K. or OK   This most popular of American coinages is used and understood throughout the world, but is best kept for informal writing and business correspondence. In general, the most acceptable usages are the noun, meaning approval, agreement, or consent (*got her O.K.*) and the verb: *O.K. this arrange-*

ment. The adjective has a more informal sound: *a partner who was O.K.* (preferable to *an O.K. partner*). The adverbial use is least desirable: *The engine is running O.K.* A variant form of the expression is written *okay* (lower-case *o*); another variant, *okeh*, is now seldom found. The plural noun forms are *O.K.'s, OK's* and *okays*. The inflected verb forms are *O.K.'d, OK'd, okayed; O.K.'ing, OK'ing, okaying; O.K.'s, OK's, okays*.

older, oldest See **elder, eldest.**

on, onto, on to Both *on* and *onto* indicate motion to a position, and in many examples they are interchangeable. But *onto* more clearly expresses movement toward the object specified: *leaped onto the platform; leaped on the platform*. *Leaped on* can also mean action in a given place. In constructions in which *on* is an adverb and *to* a preposition, they are not joined as one word: *move on to* (not *onto*) *other problems; hold on to* (not *onto*) *what we have*. In such usage, *on* may be considered part of a verb.

on, upon, up on Both *on* and *upon* can indicate a position of rest or movement in a given position or toward a specified object. *On* primarily implies rest: *The pillow lies on* (or *upon*) *the bed*. *Upon* is stronger in indicating movement toward: *He jumped upon the platform*. *Jumped on the platform* is less clear in that sense. *Jumped on* and *jumped upon* both convey the idea of movement in a single position. When *up func-*

tions adverbially and *on* as a preposition, the words are not joined: *climbed up on the roof.* Here *up* is, in effect, part of the verb, stressing elevation whereas *upon* would indicate only contact.

one another   See **each other, one another.**

one in every   A singular verb is employed in this phrase: *One in every four of these switches is defective.* The singular verb is in agreement with the subject *one.*

one of these (those)   The following examples illustrate a common construction that often gives difficulty: *It was one of these medicine bottles that have special caps to protect children. She is one of those women who like to walk their dogs in the park.* The form usually recommended is as given: the relative pronouns *that* and *who* are construed as plural (with reference to *bottles* and *women*), and the verb forms, *have* and *like,* are correspondingly plural. Sometimes the examples are written thus: *one of these bottles that has a special cap; one of those women who likes to walk her dog* (or *dogs,* if she has more than one). The alternative constructions are open to question grammatically, since *bottles* and *women* are the true antecedents, not *one,* in the view of most. But writers occasionally choose the singular form to emphasize the sense of *one.* Whatever the choice, the elements should be consistently plural or singular throughout.

oneself   This is the usual form of the pronoun, which may also be written *one's self*.

only   Often more than style is at stake in the proper placement of the adverb *only;* clarity is also an important consideration. Quite different senses are conveyed by these sentences: *Only I work here. I only work here.* Proper placement of *only,* adjoining the word it actually limits, is illustrated by the two examples (*I* in the first, *work* in the second). Other examples of recommended placement are: *She had only a few minutes. They arrived only an hour ago. A cure is possible only if you cooperate.*

Though *only* has a long history of use as a conjunction, meaning but or except that, the use does not occur often in good writing, but rather in everyday speech: *They would have gone, only his wife became ill.* In formal writing, *only* would be replaced by *but* or *except that,* or the second clause would be reworded: *had not his wife become ill.*

onto   See **on, onto, on to.**

onward, onwards   The adjective is only *onward: an onward movement.* The adverb is either *onward* or *onwards: moving steadily onward* or *onwards.*

ophthalmologist, optician, optometrist   See **oculist.**

or   When all elements of a sentence connected by *or* are singular, the verb they govern is singular: *This* *version or the other has to be correct. A tax increase or a subsidy or a reduction in services is indicated by today's testimony.* When the elements are all plural, the verb is correspondingly plural. When the elements do not agree in grammatical number, or when one or more is a personal pronoun, the verb agrees in number with the element to which it is nearer or nearest: *Cold symptoms or headache is the usual first sign. Nausea or fainting spells are often early indications. Baseball or football or similar games have little place in their program. He or I am most likely to be chosen.* In examples in which a pronoun causes awkwardness, it is better to rephrase even a sentence that abides by the rules as outlined above. This is a case in which being correct and being desirable are not necessarily compatible. See also **either . . . or; neither . . . nor; nor.**

oral, verbal *Oral* is the more precise term for specifying that something (an agreement or contract, for example) is by word of mouth. *Oral* refers only to what is spoken, whereas *verbal* can also apply to what is written. Nevertheless, the phrases *verbal agreement* and *verbal contract* generally signify something unwritten and are understood accordingly.

other than, otherwise The phrase *other than* is used both adjectively and adverbially to express difference or opposition: *firearms other than pistols; acted other* (or *otherwise*) *than perfectly.* It should not be used as the equivalent of *apart from* or *aside from* in examples such as: *He said nothing more, apart* (or *aside*) *from noting a minor change* (not *other than to note*). *She has a bad headache, but apart from that* (or *otherwise*) *her condition is favorable* (not *other than that*). See also **each other, one another.**

ought *Ought* is employed as an auxiliary verb and is not inflected. It is used with an infinitive, the choice of which is important in indicating time. Present time is expressed by a present infinitive: *They ought to comply.* Past time is conveyed by a perfect infinitive: *They ought to have complied.* A negative sense is indicated by using *not* immediately following *ought: ought not to have complied.* Other auxiliary verb forms, such as *did, could, had,* and *should,* are never used with *ought: She ought to go* (not *had ought*). *They ought not to complain* (not *hadn't ought* or *shouldn't ought*). Sometimes the infinitive (verb) following *ought* is omitted and only *to* is expressed, if the sense is clear from the context: *Shall we try again? We ought to.* Sometimes the reverse procedure holds true; the infinitive without *to* is used in negative sentences: *ought not complain; ought not have complied.* But the writer must not omit *to* in combinations such as the following: *She ought and can call. She ought and could have called.* The word *to* is necessary in these positive sentences, and structural revision is also in order. Make them read: *She can and ought to call. She could and ought to have called.* As corrected, the last example permits *could* and *ought* in a single sentence; as we have noted, however, *could* and *ought* are never joined as *couldn't ought*.

ourself, ourselves   *Ourself* is a singular form approximately equivalent in meaning to *myself*. It is used only when *we* is employed in the sense of *I*—when a monarch employs *we* or an editor uses the same term in speaking for a publication. Thus an editor might write: *We ourself favor the incumbent mayor for reelection, but we shall also present other opinions.* Though the average writer has little use for *ourself,* it is important to understand that the word cannot be substituted for *ourselves.* The latter term is the usual form of the first person plural pronoun, used in sentences such as the following: *We should not permit ourselves such liberties. We ourselves are not directly involved. We have not been ourselves since the accident.* (In none of the examples can *ourself* replace *ourselves.*) *Ourselves* should not replace *us* and *we* in compound objects and subjects, as in the following: *They have invited the Smiths and us* (not *ourselves*). *We* (not *ourselves*) *and the Smiths are invited.*

outdoor, outdoors   *Outdoor* is an adjective: *outdoor lighting. Outdoors* is an adverb (*went outdoors*) and a noun: *enjoying the great outdoors. Outdoors* is sometimes written *out-of-doors;* much less often, *outdoor* is written *out-of-door.*

outside   In formal writing, *outside* (preposition) is preferable to *outside of* in indicating physical limits, scope, or an exception: *stayed outside the house; a matter outside our jurisdiction; received no word outside what you already know.*

over As a preposition meaning more than (a specified amount), *over* is well established on all levels of usage: *cost over three dollars; over age sixty-five.* It is clearly out of place in an example having a sense of decrease: *attendance figures down five per cent over last year's* (properly *down . . . from*).

overlay, overlie Though both verbs are transitive, and are related in meaning, they are carefully distinguished in usage. *Overlay* expresses the sense of superimposing; a carpenter *overlays* plywood with veneer, and a writer might *overlay* a narrative with much symbolism. *Overlie* refers to lying over or resting upon (something), as one layer of rock *overlies* another. The past tense and past participle of *overlay* is *overlaid*. The past tense of *overlie* is *overlay,* the past participle is *overlain,* and the present participle *overlying.* Both verbs are often used in the passive voice: *wood that was overlaid with silver; bedrock overlain with sand.*

overly This adverb, meaning to an excessive degree, is established on all levels of usage though it is disliked by many writers on the stylistic ground that it is a superfluous word. Many adjectives and adverbs formed with *over-* express the same sense more concisely: *overcautious* (for *overly cautious*) and *over-fast* (for *overly fast*).

pair　In formal usage, the plural is *pairs: three pairs of shoes.* Informally, the same sense is conveyed by *three pair.* When *pair* is used as a subject it always takes a singular verb when the meaning stresses one-ness or unity of components: *This pair* (of socks) *is not mine.* A plural construction occurs when the members are considered individually: *The pair were seldom in agreement on anything.*

palate, palette　*Palate* denotes the roof of the mouth. *Palette* is a board for mixing colors.

partially, partly　Often these adverbs are interchangeable; in many cases a choice is determined by prevailing idiom. In general *partially* is found most often before a word describing the condition of a person: *partially blind; partially dependent. Partly,* which has much wider application, could replace the other term in the second example. Other examples: *a house partly* (or *partially*) *completed; mail sorted partly* (or *partially*) *by hand; partly to blame; partly at fault.* Only *partially* has the sense of showing favorable prejudice or bias, but that meaning is now expressed more often by the noun *partiality.*

party　In formal usage, the word as the equivalent of person is confined to legal material. Informally *party* is applied to a particular person, often in a jocular sense: *a strange old party.*

pass, past   The past tense and past participle of the verb *pass* is *passed: They passed* (or *have passed*) *our home. Time had passed slowly. Past* is the corresponding adjective (*in centuries past*), adverb (*drove past*), and preposition (*past midnight; past the crisis*).

pedal, peddle   As a noun, *pedal* most often denotes a lever operated by the foot; as an adjective, it refers to a foot, as in *pedal extremities;* as a verb it applies to riding a bicycle and to operating levers in other machines and in musical instruments. *Peddle* is a verb only (to sell wares). The corresponding noun is *peddler* (or *pedlar* or *pedler*).

people   The plural of this noun is usually also *people.* When the noun refers to a nationality, however, or to a body having a common religion, culture, language, or inherited condition of life, the plural is *peoples: Germanic peoples; nomadic peoples.* The possessive form in such cases is *peoples': the Semitic peoples' goals.* When *people* is the plural form, the possessive is written *people's: the people's best interests.*

people, persons, public   *People* (not *persons*) is the choice in referring to a large body collectively and indefinitely—people in general: *People do strange things. Persons* is applicable to a specific, relatively small number: *Ten persons are affected by the change.*

Persons is considered by some usage authorities the better word in such an example, but *people* is also acceptable. *The people* and *the public* are often interchangeable, but only *the people* has the political sense of an electorate.

per cent, percentage Both terms express quantity with relation to a whole. *Per cent* (which may also be written *percent*) is specific and used with a number or numeral. *Percentage* is nonspecific; it is never preceded by such a figure, but should be qualified by an adjective such as *small* or *large,* since *percentage* does not necessarily connote smallness. The grammatical number of the noun that follows these terms, or is understood to follow them, determines the number of the verb: *Twenty per cent of the estate has been distributed. The first five per cent of the profits* (a sum, singular) *is tax-exempt. Fifty per cent of these claims are fraudulent. A small percentage of the mail orders were unfulfilled.*

perfect In a few of its meanings bearing on scientific and technical subjects, this adjective is construed rigidly: *a perfect specimen* (lacking nothing essential); *a perfect gem* (without a defect). In those senses it would be illogical to call one animal, plant, or stone *more perfect* than another since *perfect* (like the adverb *perfectly*) is an absolute term. In most usage, however, *perfect* and *perfectly* are not used in absolute senses but in those that only approach the absolute. When *perfect* is the equivalent of *altogether excellent,* it is acceptably used with *more* and *most: no more perfect day; the most perfect tribute imaginaable.*

persecute, prosecute To *persecute* is to ill-treat someone, or to annoy persistently. In a corresponding sense, to *prosecute* is to bring legal action against a person.

person In formal usage, a consistently singular construction is required in examples such as: *A person should be permitted to make up his* (or *her* or *his or her,* but not *their*) *own mind.* See also **people, persons, public.**

personage, personality In the senses in which the words correspond, *personage* refers to a person of distinction, and *personality* to one of prominence or notoriety. *Personage* is quite formal; *personality* is largely informal.

personnel Like most collective nouns, *personnel* may be construed as singular (and take a singular verb) when unity of the group is stressed, and as plural when the component members are considered individually. The term is never used with a specific number as in *six personnel of the police department.* Make it *members, employees,* or *representatives.*

persuade See **convince, persuade.**

phobia See **mania, phobia.**

piteous, pitiable, pitiful All three describe something that arouses pity. *Pitiable* and *pitiful* also apply to what arouses or deserves disdain or contempt.

place, put The verb *place* usually implies care and precision in bringing something to a desired position. *Put* makes no such suggestion of exactness.

plan This verb plus an infinitive is the usual construction in expressing intention: *plan to leave*. An alternative, *plan on leaving,* is not recommended for formal writing.

plead In legal usage, a person *pleads guilty* or *pleads not guilty;* the expression *plead innocent* is not used, though it often appears in general usage.

plenty The word *plenty* is always used as a predicate (following a verb): *This is plenty*. It is not employed before a noun, as in *have plenty money*. Make it *have plenty of money*. Sometimes the noun *plenty* appears acceptably in the expression *in plenty: goods in plenty*. An informal adverbial use occurs in expressions such as *plenty tired* and *plenty hot,* in which *plenty* means very or sufficiently.

plus When it expresses the sense of *added to, plus* is a preposition, not a conjunction. Consequently a verb that follows *plus* is not invariably plural. The grammatical number of the verb is determined by that of the subject: *Two* (the numeral, construed as singular) *plus two equals four. His skill* (singular) *plus their* *material resources makes them a formidable foe. Their possessions* (plural) *plus his ingenuity constitute a considerable advantage.* The element introduced by *plus* does not affect the verb. A recent use of *plus* as a conjunction is not acceptable in formal writing: *She has a great deal of talent, plus she is willing to work hard.* Instead of *plus,* use *and, in addition, besides,* or *moreover.*

P.M. See **A.M., P.M.**

politics Though plural in form, this noun is usually used with a singular verb in present-day writing. A singular verb occurs especially when *politics* is used in the sense of a science or profession and when it is followed by a singular predicate noun: *Politics is a strange business.* A plural construction is used when *politics* means opinions or principles: *His politics are his own business.*

poor, poorly *Poor* is an adjective only, not an adverb. It cannot qualify a verb, as in *did poor* and *never played poorer. Poorly* and *more poorly* are required in such examples.

pore, pour *Pore* means to read or study carefully. *Pour* applies to the flowing of liquid and to sending or going forth: *poured the milk; rain that poured down; troops who poured into the capital's streets.*

possible See **feasible, possible.**

practicable, practical *Practicable* means capable of being done. *Practical* carries the idea beyond possibility or capability by connoting that what is done is worthwhile in the given circumstances or that it has value in proportion to required means and is economical or efficient in execution.

practically, virtually Both can express the sense of in every important respect, to all intents, or in effect. Because *virtually* means that and nothing more, it is preferred by many writers and editors: *virtually* (or *practically*) *completed*. In that example and many others, *practically* could be misconstrued as completed in a practical way—since that is a primary and often used sense of *practically*.

precede, proceed *Precede* means to come before in time, order or rank, or physical position, or to preface or introduce. *Proceed* means to go forward or onward or to undertake an action.

precipitant, precipitate, precipitous *Precipitant* and *precipitate* are both applied, as adjectives, to rash, overhasty human actions and to the related sense of headlong movement. *Precipitous* can be used in those senses also, but primarily it describes things whose steepness suggests a precipice: *a precipitous descent*. These distinctions apply also to the corresponding adverbs ending in *-ly*.

predominant, predominate The adjective that describes something that has greatest importance, influence, or force, or that is most common or conspicuous, is *predominant*. The corresponding noun is *predominance*. The verb meaning to be most important or outstanding, or to have authority or controlling influence, is *predominate*. In most examples the adverbs formed from these words are interchangeable: a *predominantly* (or *predominately*) *male occupation; predominantly* (or *predominately*) *blue in color and small in size.*

prefer This verb is often followed by an infinitive: *prefer to leave early.* When the object is not an infinitive, the object is usually followed by *to,* never by *than: prefer tennis to golf; prefer leaving early to getting in a traffic jam.* When an infinitive is the object, the usual construction for an elaborate sentence is *rather than* (not merely *than*) plus a second infinitive, sometimes without *to: prefer to leave early rather than get in a traffic jam.*

premiere The verb usage (to present or have the first performance) is not established in formal writing.

preparatory to The phrase means *in preparing for,* and in careful usage is restricted to what calls for actual preparation. It does not mean merely *before* or *prior to.*

prescribe, proscribe Prescribe expresses the act of establishing rules or directions, or of recommending remedies. *Proscribe* means to denounce or prohibit. The nouns *prescription* and *proscription* have corresponding senses.

presently The safest course is to use this adverb only in the sense of *in a short time, soon,* or *directly.* It is also widely employed in the sense of *currently* or *now,* but that usage is not approved by many writers.

presume See **assume, presume.**

prevent This verb is most often followed by *from: prevents us from seeing properly.* When, instead, a gerund (the *-ing* form of a verb) follows, the noun or pronoun preceding the gerund is in the possessive case: *prevents our seeing properly; prevented the emissary's going; prevented Smith's leaving.*

preventative, preventive Both forms of the adjective are acceptable. *Preventive* is the more common.

principal, principle *Principal* is both an adjective meaning leading or chief and a noun, most often denoting a leader or person in charge; or, in finance, the capital or main body of an estate, and a sum owed as a debt. *Principle* is only a noun applicable to basic truths, rules of human conduct, and fundamental laws governing the operation of a thing.

prioritize Although many consider *prioritize* to be jargon and so avoid its use, in recent times it has become firmly established in the language.

proceed See **precede, proceed.**

prophecy, prophesy The *-cy* form is a noun meaning prediction. The *-sy* form is the corresponding verb meaning to predict or foreshow.

proportion The noun *proportion* deals principally with relationship—of a part to the whole, between things or their parts, and between quantities in the sense of a ratio. It can also mean harmonious relation, or balance. The plural *proportions* is also acceptably used in the less specialized sense of dimensions or size: *a job of such proportions.*

proscribe See **prescribe, proscribe.**

prosecute See **persecute, prosecute.**

protagonist Applied to a drama or other literary form, this noun denotes the leading character. It is improper to use the plural form *protagonists* with respect to a single such work. The noun in an extended sense can refer to any leading figure (in a cause or movement, for example) but does not necessarily mean that the person is the opposite of the noun *antagonist* (adversary). In this sense *protagonist* is not always the equivalent of the words *advocate, champion,* or *partisan.*

proved, proven Both are past participles of the verb *prove,* but *proved* is the preferred one in actual verb usage: *She had proved her point. Their worth was proved on many occasions. Proven* is the more common when used as an attributive adjective before a noun: *a proven record; a proven remedy.* It is also the form used in the phrase *not proven.*

provided, providing As conjunctions these mean on the condition: *There will be no trouble provided the contract is fulfilled. Provided* is preferable to *providing* in this sense, especially in formal writing. Both are often used with *that: provided that the contract is fulfilled.*

public See **people, persons, public.**

put See **place, put.**

quarter With reference to the time of day, *a* in the following phrase is optional: *(a) quarter of* (or *to* or *before*) *ten; (a) quarter past* (or *after*) *five.*

quick, quickly Though both are adverbs in good standing, *quickly* is found more often in formal writing and *quick* in speech and dialogue.

quite In its primary senses the adverb means to the greatest extent or entirely (*quite alone*) and actually or truly (*quite happy*). But it is also used acceptably in the less rigid sense of somewhat or rather: *quite cool for August.* The expressions *quite a* and *quite an,* indicating indefinite quantity (*quite a few*), are also acceptable on all levels, but only informal when they indicate extraordinary quality: *quite an actor.*

quote The noun *quote,* for *quotation,* is for informal writing. See also **cite, quote.**

rack, wrack As noun and verb, *rack* is the more common, associated with the senses of framework, torture machine, mental torture, and straining with great effort. Thus, *nerve-racking, on the rack, rack one's brain,* and *rack up* (in sports). *Wrack* (verb) is the form for causing ruin, but the corresponding noun for destruction is either *wrack* or *rack. Wrack and ruin* has the variant form *rack and ruin.*

raise, rear Both verbs are acceptable in formal writing in expressing the sense of bringing up (children).

raise, rise In the sense of moving upward or to a higher position, *raise* is transitive and *rise* intransitive: *Raise the window. The window rises easily.* As nouns, both words mean an increase in salary; *raise* is the more common in American English and *rise* in British.

rare, scarce *Rare* implies special quality and value enhanced by permanent shortness of supply. *Scarce* describes things not plentiful at the moment, though they may have no great and lasting value in themselves.

rarely In the expressions *rarely ever* and *seldom ever, ever* is redundant and should not be used, especially in writing: *They rarely* (or *seldom*) *go.* But the following combinations are possible: *rarely* (or *seldom*) *if ever; rarely* (or *seldom*) *or never;* but not *rarely* (or *seldom*) *or ever.*

rather In modern usage, *rather* is usually preceded by *would* or *should* in expressing preference: *would rather stay home.* The construction *had rather* is an acceptable alternative in such examples.

ravage, ravish *Ravage* has the wider application; it means to destroy or devastate. *Ravish,* sometimes misused in that general sense, properly refers to the act of violating by rape or to enrapturing.

re This preposition and the variant form *in re* mean in reference to. They have little place outside business correspondence and legal writing.

rear See **raise, rear.**

reason Since *because* and *why* are inherent in the noun *reason,* the expressions *the reason is because* and *the reason why* are better avoided in formal writing: *The reason for her hesitating was that she was unable to see* (preferable to *The reason why she hesitated was because she was unable to see*).

reciprocal See **mutual, reciprocal.**

reclaim, re-claim The verb meaning to reform (a person), make (land) suitable for cultivation, and procure (usable things) from refuse or waste products is *reclaim*. To *re-claim* is to claim again or back.

recount, re-count *Recount* means to narrate the facts of. *Re-count* means to count again.

recourse, resource The act of turning to a person or thing for aid and the person or thing turned to are inherent in *recourse: He had recourse* (not *resource*) *to the courts. The law was his only recourse* (not *resource*). *His knowledge of the law was among his resources.*

recover, re-cover To *recover* is to regain; to *re-cover* is to cover anew: *re-covered the sofa.*

recreate, re-create To *recreate* is to refresh or take recreation; to *re-create* is to create anew.

reform, re-form *Reform* applies to improvement by eliminating defects, and *re-form* to the act of forming again or becoming formed again.

regard, respect The expression *in* (or *with*) *regard to* is written thus (singular *regard*). But the corresponding expression is *as regards*. *Respect,* not *regard,* is the better choice in examples in which the noun means a particular feature: *They differ in some respects.* The verb *regard* (meaning to consider in a particular way) is used with *as: regarded her as a friend* (not *regarded her a friend* or *regarded her to be a friend*).

regretful, regrettable   A *regretful* person feels regret or sorrow. Something *regrettable* calls forth regret. The distinctions also apply to the adverbs *regretfully* and *regrettably: a regrettably long wait.*

relay, re-lay   *Relay* means to send along: *relayed the message. Re-lay* means to lay again: *re-laid the tiles.*

reluctant, reticent   A *reluctant* person shows unwillingness in a given respect. A *reticent* one shows uncommunicativeness by being silent or restrained or reserved. *Reluctant* is the desired adjective in expressions such as *reluctant to discuss the matter.*

repel, repulse   Both verbs mean to drive back or off, as in *repel* (or *repulse*) *a commando raid. Repulse* also applies to rebuffing or rejecting by discourtesy; *repel* alone means to cause distaste or aversion: *repulsed this newcomer whose forwardness repelled them all.*

replete   This adjective means abundantly supplied with—not merely complete with or equipped with.

replica   Strictly, this refers to a copy of a work of art by the original artist. But it is also acceptably applied to any close reproduction, including one in miniature, such as a model.

repulse See **repel, repulse**.

resign, re-sign To *resign* is to quit or to force (one-self) to acquiesce. *Re-sign* means to sign anew.

resource See **recourse, resource**.

respect See **regard, respect**.

respectfully, respectively *Respectfully* means with respect or esteem: *treated the hostages respectfully; respectfully yours. Respectively* means singly in the order designated: *willed cash and securities to Joan and Ellen, respectively*.

restive, restless Both adjectives are applicable to uneasiness. *Restive,* however, especially suggests impatience under restriction or pressure and resistance to control, in which sense the word is more nearly interchangeable with *unruly* or *balky*.

reticent See **reluctant, reticent**.

revenge See **avenge, revenge**.

right, rightly Both are adverbs, but *right* has the wider application. They are often interchangeable when correctly is the sense: *answered her right* (or *rightly*). *Rightly* is used most often when the desired sense is either properly or uprightly: *quite rightly refused the request; can rightly claim title to the land*. In the last example, *rightfully* could also be used; *right* would be impossible in either one.

ring   When the verb pertains to sound, the past tense is *rang,* not *rung,* particularly in written usage: *when the telephone rang.* The past participle is *rung: when it had rung several times.*

rise   See **raise, rise.**

rob, steal   Errors occur most often in passive usage. Persons and establishments are *robbed;* property, including money and goods, is *stolen,* not *robbed.*

round   The adverb and preposition are spelled thus, not *'round: as they gathered round; make the turn round the bend; worked round the clock.*

rung   See **ring.**

said, same   In the following, *said* (adjective) and *same* (pronoun) refer to someone or something mentioned earlier: *The said tenant is given two keys and is expected to return same.* The example, from a lease, illustrates two usages that should be confined to legal and commercial writing. *Said* is almost never needed; if clarity demands it, *said* can be replaced by *aforementioned* or *specified.* For *same,* use *them* (or another pronoun in a different example) or repeat the noun (here, *keys*).

sanatorium, sanitarium   Though these may be used interchangeably, there is some distinction in their primary meanings. A *sanatorium* (also spelled *sanatarium*) is devoted to treatment of chronic diseases and to medically supervised recuperation. A *sanitarium* is a health resort.

sank See **sink.**

savings The plural noun *savings* should not be preceded by the article *a: a savings of three dollars.* Make it *a saving* or delete *a.*

scan This verb can be used acceptably in senses that are poles apart: to examine (something) closely and to look over or leaf through hastily. Examples are *scan a road map* (closely); *scan a newspaper or the headlines* (hastily). Care must be taken to see that the intended sense is clear.

scarce See **rare, scarce.**

scarcely Since this adverb has a sense verging on the negative, it is not used with another negative in a single statement: *could scarcely make it out* (not *couldn't scarcely*); *listened with scarcely a change of expression* (not *without scarcely*). In examples such as the following, *scarcely* is followed by *when* or, less often, *before* but not by *than: They had scarcely departed when the storm broke.*

Scot *Scot* and *Scotsman* (the preferred terms), together with *Scotchman,* all denote a native or inhabitant of Scotland. The corresponding plural terms are *Scots* and (*the*) *Scotch.* The adjectives preferred in Scotland are *Scottish* and *Scots; Scotch* is also in com-

mon usage (but not *Scot,* which is not an adjective).
Certain combinations have been established by idiom.
We speak of Scotch broth, Scotch whisky, Scottish rite,
and Scots Guards.

seasonable, seasonal   Use *seasonable* when the thing
it describes is appropriate to a season (*light frost,
seasonable in the North in early fall*) or timely (*seasonable rains welcomed by farmers*). Use *seasonal* to
describe what depends on and is controlled by seasons
or a given season: *seasonal employment; seasonal
variations in precipitation.*

seeing as how   See **being as.**

seldom   See **rarely.**

sensual, sensuous   Both adjectives apply to gratifica-
tion of the senses but differ in the level of the senses
affected. *Sensual* has strong reference to physical (especially sexual) appetite; *sensuous,* though neutral by
definition, is more often associated with aesthetic pur-
suits.

series   Depending on how it is construed, *series* can
take either a singular or a plural verb. When it has the
singular sense of one set, it is followed by a singular
verb, even though it is also followed more immediately
by *of* and a plural noun: *The series of plays is open
to the public.*

serve, service *Service* is the more specialized of these verbs, used especially in the sense of making (something) fit for use, as by repairing or maintaining: *serviced the household appliances.* But most services —of broadcasters, newspapers, the medical profession, and utility companies, for example—are expressed by *serve: served the city.*

set, sit The verb *set* is most often transitive (it takes a direct object), whereas *sit* is largely intransitive. The most common errors involving the pair are uses of *set* for *sit.* In the following, forms of *sit* are correct and *set* would be incorrect: *Sit with us. The bird sat on a low branch. The town sits in a valley. Her duties and a hostile environment sat heavily on her. Neither the dinner nor the speeches that followed sat well with me.* Either verb is possible in these examples: *The hen sets (or sits) on eggs. The coat sets (or sits) well.*

sew, sow One *sews* an article of clothing and *sews up* a business deal or the rights to something. One *sows* seed or the like.

sewage, sewerage The waste material carried off in sewers is usually called *sewage,* though *sewerage* is also possible in that sense. *Sewerage* more often denotes a system of sewers and the process by which the system removes waste.

shall, will In formal writing these verbs are employed as auxiliaries according to a formula that distinguishes mere future time from the expression of a variety of conditions. In the first person, singular and plural, *shall* indicates simple futurity (unstressed intention or normal expectation): *I shall leave tomorrow*. In the second and third persons, the same sense of futurity is expressed by *will: He will come this afternoon*. Use of the auxiliaries is reversed when the writer wants to indicate any of the following conditions: determination, promise, obligation, command, compulsion, permission, or inevitability; *will* is employed in the first person, and *shall* in the second and third. Thus, *I will leave tomorrow* (meaning: am determined to leave, or obligated, compelled, or fated). *He shall come this afternoon* likewise can express any of the conditions enumerated, such as promise, permission, command, or compulsion.

In actual practice, the restrictions on the use of *shall* and *will,* in indicating mere futurity, are observed by most careful writers and should be the rule in all writing on a formal level. But the roles of the auxiliaries in the expression of the various conditions is not widely understood by the average reader. Consequently a more realistic (and recommendable) course is to use other constructions. For example, to indicate determination, compulsion, or obligation, use *must* or *have to;* or use an intensifying word, such as *certainly* or *surely,* with *shall* or *will* to express one of the other conditions. In informal usage, *will* is generally employed in all three grammatical persons to express futurity and any of the conditions listed. On a variety of usage levels, *shall* is sometimes employed, regardless of grammatical person, to emphasize resolve, as in *We shall overcome* and Churchill's memorable speech after Dunkirk: *"We shall fight on the beaches, we shall fight on the landing grounds . . . ; we shall never surrender."*

shambles   The word can denote a slaughterhouse or a place or scene of bloodshed. It is even more widely, and acceptably, used in the extended sense of a scene or condition of complete disorder or ruin.

shine   The past tense and past participle are *shined* or *shone: The sun* (or *moon* or *a diamond* or *a light*) *shone brightly. The truth shone through. He shined a light in the closet. They shined their boots. She had shined as both scholar and athlete.*

short   See **brief, short.**

should, would   Of these auxiliary verbs, only *should* is employed to express obligation or necessity. Both are used in sentences expressing simple conditions (contingency of one clause or phrase on another), but *would* is much more common in American usage: *If she had objected, we would* (or *should*) *have made other plans. I would* (or *should*) *not have proceeded without her consent.* To indicate condition (but not obligation), *would* is used in such examples in all three grammatical persons, whereas *should* is limited to the first person. In the same way, either *would* or *should* is used in the first person as an auxiliary with *like, be inclined, be glad, prefer,* and related verbs: *I would* (or *should*) *like to change my vote.* Again *would* is more common in American usage. In such examples, the present and perfect infinitives are frequently found: *I would* (or *should*) *have preferred to stay. I would* (or *should*) *like to have stayed.* But not *I would* (or *should*) *have liked to have stayed.*

sick   The idea of experiencing nausea is expressed acceptably by *sick at* (or *to*) *one's stomach.*

Sierra   The preferred form for reference to a mountain range such as the Sierra Nevada is the full name or *the Sierras* (not *Sierra mountains*).

similar   This is an adjective only. It can follow a linking verb and thus modify the subject to which it is linked: *The mechanism seems similar to ours.* But it cannot acceptably modify a nonlinking verb, a job for an adverb: *The mechanism works similarly to that in our refrigerator.*

simultaneous   This adjective, like *similar,* is often misused in examples that require the adverb *simultaneously.* Only the adverb is acceptable in *physical examinations conducted simultaneously with student registration.*

since   Though clauses introduced by *since* (referring

to time) are in the past tense, the corresponding verb in the clause joined by *since* must be in a perfect tense: *It has been* (not *was*) *two years since I last visited my home. It had been two years since she departed.* See also **ago.**

sink   In formal writing, the preferred past tense is *sank: as the ship sank from view. Sunk* is the preferred past participle: *after it had sunk from view.* The alternative past participle, *sunken,* is more often used as an adjective: *sunken cheeks; sunken treasure.*

sit   See **set, sit.**

slander   See **libel, slander.**

slow, slowly   Both are adverbs. Where they are interchangeable, *slowly* is generally preferred in formal writing; *slow* occurs more often in speech, in commands and exhortations (*drive slow*), and when emphasis is desired. Established idiom is important in determining a choice. In the following senses, only *slow* conveys the meaning, and it should be used on all levels: *My watch runs slow* (loses time). *The trains are running slow* (behind schedule). *Go slow* or *Take it slow* (referring to a course of action, not to speed of a vehicle).

smell   When the verb means to have or emit an odor, it is a linking verb followed by an adjective: *The milk smells good,* or *fresh,* or *sour.* An adverb may occur

in constructions such as *smells strongly of vinegar.*
When *smell* means to have or emit an unpleasant odor
(to stink), it may be modified by an adverb: *The fish
smells disgustingly.* Here the adverb indicates a degree
of foul smell; in contrast, *smells disgusting* merely
specifies an odor, as in the first example.

sneak The only acceptable past tense is *sneaked: as
he sneaked* (not *snuck*) *behind the screen.*

so When the conjunction *so* introduces a clause that
gives the purpose of, or reason for, an action stated
earlier, it is usually followed by *that,* in formal writing: *He worked late so that he could complete the
shipment.* Informally, the same thought is often expressed by *so* used without *that. So* is used alone when
the clause that it introduces states a result or consequence of something preceding: *He had to complete
the shipment, so he worked late.* See also **as . . . as,
so . . . as.**

so-called This hyphenated adjective precedes a noun
that is not enclosed in quotation marks, even when
sarcasm is intended: *this so-called leader.* Alternative
ways of expressing the same thought are *this "leader"*
and *this leader, so called.*

some As an adverbial substitute for *somewhat,* this
word is used informally: *feeling some better.* In formal writing, make it *somewhat better.* In those ex-

amples in which *somewhat* cannot replace *some,* the desired meaning (of indefinite degree or extent) must be expressed by other wording in formal usage: *plays golf sometimes* (for *plays golf some*).

somebody, someone, some one   In formal usage, *somebody* and *someone* take singular verbs, and accompanying pronouns and pronominal adjectives are also singular: *Someone has lost his way.* (*Her* or *his or her* can replace *his,* but *their* cannot.) *Somebody* and *someone* refer indefinitely to some person unspecified or unknown. The reference is general, whereas *some one* (two words) refers specifically to a person or thing singled out of a group: *Some one of them will be called on to explain.* In such an example, *someone* cannot be used.

someday, sometime   These adverbs express future time indefinitely, not specifically: *They hope to return home someday* (or *sometime*). The two-word forms *some day* and *some time* are for reference to a specific day or time: *We should choose some day* (or *some time*) *when reduced fares are in effect.* In such examples *someday* and *sometime* cannot be used. See also **sometime.**

some place, someplace   In formal writing, *somewhere* is the proper choice rather than one of these in making an indefinite reference. But when reference is made to a specific place, rather than to one not specified or definitely known, the two-word form *some place* is acceptable on all levels: *seeking some place* (not *someplace*) *better served by public transportation.*

sometime   When this word serves as an adjective, it means former: *a sometime public official.* It should not be used as a synonym of *occasional,* as in *an economist and sometime writer on public finance.* See also **someday, sometime.**

some way, someways, someway   The adverbs *someway* and *someways* are for informal usage. In formal writing, the desired sense is expressed by *somehow: must raise the money somehow.* The two-word form *some way,* indicating a more specific course, is acceptable on all levels, as in *some way that is less difficult. Someway* cannot be used in such an example.

somewhere   The adverb is written thus, not *somewheres.* See also **some place, someplace.**

sooner   In sentences such as the following, *no sooner* is followed by *than,* not by *when: She had no sooner departed than her true identity became known.*

sort   When the noun *sort* means a group or collection, it is a synonym of *kind.* The information provided in the entry for *kind* also applies to *sort.* See also **kind; type.**

sow See **sew, sow.**

special, specially See **especial, especially.**

spoonful The plural is *spoonfuls.*

stamp See **stomp.**

stanch, staunch *Staunch* is the usual spelling of the adjective, though *stanch* is possible: *staunch friends. Stanch* (less often *staunch*) is the verb meaning to stop a flow.

stationary, stationery *Stationery,* denoting writing materials, is a noun only. *Stationary* is usually an adjective referring to fixed position or condition.

steal See **rob, steal.**

stomp The verbs *stomp* and *stamp* are interchangeable in the sense of trampling or violent treading: *stomped to death; stomping horses.* Either is acceptable in such examples. In formal usage, however, only *stamp* is acceptable in the sense of striking the ground with the human foot, as in anger.

strait In modern usage *strait* is never interchangeable with *straight.* It is a noun denoting either a passage of water or a position of difficulty or need: *in dire straits.*

strata This is the plural of *stratum.* We speak of a *stratum* (layer) of rock and of a *stratum* (category) of society, literature, or the like. *Strata* is properly preceded by *all, the,* or another modifier appropriate to a plural form, but never by *a.* To denote more than one *stratum,* only *strata* is acceptable; *stratas* is not a standard form.

sunk, sunken See **sink.**

superior A person or thing is said to be *superior to* (not *superior than*) another.

swim In modern usage the past tense is *swam,* the past participle *swum: swam a mile before breakfast; had never swum that early before.*

tablespoonful The plural is *tablespoonfuls.*

take See **bring, take.**

take place See **happen.**

tasteful, tasty In usage, *tasteful* is applied to that which shows a sense of what is proper or seemly, and *tasty* to what has a pleasing flavor.

teach See **learn, teach.**

tear The past participle of the verb is *torn: He has torn the page. The page is torn. Tore* is the past tense: *He tore the page.*

teaspoonful The plural is *teaspoonfuls.*

tend to When this phrase expresses the sense of

applying attention (*tended to his chores*), it is informal. *Attend to* is the formal equivalent.

than In formal writing, *than* is generally construed as a conjunction rather than as a preposition in constructions that make comparisons. Accordingly, the inflected word following *than* is not necessarily in the objective case; case is determined by the word's grammatical function: *She dances better than I do.* The same rule applies to elliptical clauses introduced by *than,* in which unexpressed words are plainly indicated: *She dances better than I* (subject of unexpressed *do*). *She is a better dancer than I* (subject of unexpressed *am*). *The children liked no one more than her* (that is, *than they liked her*). In informal usage, the word following *than* is more often in the objective case. In some examples, an argument can be made for either the nominative or the objective case; both *They had no more devoted follower than she* and *They had no more devoted follower than her* are acceptable. The objective case always occurs in the expression *than whom: Lee, than whom no more admired general ever lived.*

that, which, who (whom) All these are relative pronouns, whose function is to introduce subordinate clauses. Rules of usage guide the writer in choosing the right relative pronoun for a given example.

That has for its antecedent persons, animals, and

things; *which* now refers only to animals and things; and *who* and *whom* refer to persons (and occasionally to animals).

The choice in formal writing is determined by the nature of the clauses introduced by the pronouns. *That* is used almost exclusively to introduce restrictive clauses, that is, clauses that define and limit the antecedent by providing information necessary for a real understanding of the sentence: *The book that you ordered has just arrived.* Such clauses are never set off by commas; a good test of a restrictive clause is that the relative pronoun can be unexpressed. *Who* and *whom* also may be used in restrictive clauses: *I met the girl (whom) you spoke of. Who, whom,* and especially *which* are employed to introduce nonrestrictive (nondefining) clauses, or those that provide incidental or nonessential information: *The book, which received excellent reviews, is much in demand. Later I spoke to my teacher, who has a German accent.* Such nonrestrictive clauses are set off by commas; in theory they are capable of being enclosed within parentheses. *Which* is always used for clauses of both types when the relative pronoun is preceded by *that* used as a demonstrative pronoun: *We often long for that which is impossible.*

Sometimes it is hard to decide whether a clause is restrictive or nonrestrictive, and use of either *which* or *that* can be justified. But *that* should be employed when a clause is clearly restrictive; those who invariably choose *which* in all examples because they think it alone is appropriate in formal writing are misguided. Sometimes careful discrimination between *which* and *that* is essential to clarity: *The typewriter, which needs cleaning, is on the front table. The typewriter that needs cleaning is on the front table.* Unlike the first example, the second strongly implies the presence of more than one typewriter. See also **this.**

this Both *this* and *that,* as demonstrative pronouns, represent, in single summarizing words, thoughts expressed earlier: *She had good intentions, but that* (or *this*) *cannot excuse the wrong she did.* Either *that* or *this* is acceptable in most such examples. In formal writing, however, many authorities consider *that* the better choice in referring to what has gone before (a prior action or its basis, as in the example); *this* is preferably employed in referring to what is about to be stated: *That is what she intended, but this is what she did. This* tends to be much overworked in such sentences without regard to consideration of time. Neither *that* nor *this* should be used when the one chosen is so far removed from the thought it represents that the reference is unclear; in such cases, restate what is meant. The use of *this* should also be avoided to refer to a person: *This is a public official of real integrity* (preferably *he* or *she is,* or *here is*).

though When *though* is an adverb meaning however

or nevertheless, it usually occurs at the end of a sentence or clause: *Its owners said the great liner could never sink; it did, though.* Such usage is more typical of speech and informal writing than of formal writing, in which *however* or *nevertheless* would be more likely to occur. A more clearly informal usage is the spelling *tho* for *though* in all the word's various senses. See also **although, though.**

thrash, thresh *Thrash* is applied principally to the acts of beating, defeating, and lashing out with the arms or legs, and *thresh* to beating grain. To discuss or go over (something) is to *thresh over* it. The act of resolving by intensive discussion is expressed by either *thresh out* or *thrash out.*

through As an adjective meaning finished, *through* has a less formal sound than its synonym *finished* but may be used on all levels: *Call when you are through.* The word is largely confined to informal usage in the senses of having no further relationship and having no further effectiveness: *He and I are through. As a serious contender he's through.* The spelling *thru* is also informal.

thus, thusly *Thus* is always the choice. *Thusly* is not only a needless variant of *thus* (itself an adverb) but also a nonstandard one.

tie The past tense and past participle of the verb is

tied, the present participle *tying: tied the parcels; tying the score in the baseball game.*

till, until These are usually interchangeable, and each is found in formal writing. The shortened form *'til* is a third possibility but hardly a necessary one. *'Till* is nonstandard and should be avoided.

together with See **along with.**

tonite This variant spelling of *tonight* is not acceptable in formal usage.

too The use of *too* preceded by *not* or another negative is an acceptable means of conveying humor or sarcasm through understatement: *He was not too bright. They were not too pleased by the slight.* But *not too,* used indiscriminately to mean *not very,* is not appropriate in formal usage: *His health isn't too good* (preferably *very good* or *is none too good*). *Not too,* in such casual usage, can create ambiguity; the intended sense is generally *not very,* but the construction can be construed as meaning *not excessively: We cannot say too much for her effort.*

tore See **tear.**

tortuous, torturous Keep these straight by remembering that *torturous* is associated with the pain and anguish of torture. *Tortuous* means winding, highly involved or complex, or not straightforward (and thus deceitful or devious).

toward, towards Either form is acceptable, though *toward* is more common in American formal writing.

transient, transitory *Transient* usually describes persons who remain in a given place only a short time: *a transient guest in a hotel; transient labor. Transient* can also mean short-lived or impermanent, inherently or otherwise, but that sense is generally expressed by *transitory: transitory exercise of power*.

transpire Apart from scientific usage, this verb should be employed in the sense of becoming known or coming to light. It is more widely employed to mean happen or occur, but that usage is considered improper by many authorities.

troop, troupe As noun and verb, *troupe* is applied only to stage performers. *Troop* has wider application, to persons, animals, or things, especially when they are on the move. It has particular reference to soldiers and Boy Scouts and Girl Scouts.

try In formal usage, *try* is followed by *to,* not by *and,* in expressing an attempt to accomplish something: *Try to finish on time*.

turbid, turgid *Turbid* means muddy, cloudy, dense, or muddled. *Turgid* describes what is swollen, bloated, or excessively ornate in language or style.

type As a noun denoting a group, *type* is used most precisely when it refers to a specific, clearly definable category; resemblance between members is marked, and so is difference from other groups. In contrast, *kind* and *sort* refer to less sharply definable categories. In expressions such as the following, *type* is always followed by *of* in formal usage: *this type of flower.*

unaware, unawares *Unaware* is the adjective, followed by *of* (expressed or implied): *She seemed unaware of the danger. Unaware, she hastened ahead.* The adverb *unawares* qualifies a verb: *The storm caught them unawares. They made the discovery unawares.*

underestimate Like *minimize,* this verb is often misused and conveys a meaning exactly opposite to that intended: *His worth cannot be underestimated.* To express the sense of great worth, make it *cannot be overestimated.*

underwater The word is both an adjective (*underwater exploration*) and an adverb (*exploration performed underwater*). The adjective usually occurs before the noun it modifies. In examples such as the following, the two-word form is used: *Much of the town was under water after torrential rains.* The adverbial example could also be written *performed under water.*

under way The phrase is written thus (two words).

undoubtedly See **doubtless, undoubtedly.**

unexceptionable, unexceptional These are not inter-changeable. *Unexceptionable* means not open to objection or above reproach. *Unexceptional* means either not exceptional (and therefore usual or ordinary) or not permitting exceptions to a rule.

uninterested See **disinterested, uninterested.**

unique Something *unique* is in a class by itself, being the only one of its kind or without an equal. In careful usage, the adjective is construed as absolute; the quality it expresses cannot be said to vary in degree or intensity, and is consequently incapable of comparison. Therefore expressions such as *more unique* and *most unique,* indicating comparison, should be avoided, as should *rather* (or *somewhat*) *unique* and *very unique.* Each of these modifiers may be used with adjectives such as *unusual, remarkable, rare,* or *exceptional,* which are not absolute. *Unique* may be modified by terms that do not imply degree in the sense noted; each of these is acceptable: *really* (or *quite,* meaning truly) *unique; almost* (or *nearly*) *unique; more* (or *most*) *nearly unique.*

until See **till, until.**

up, upon See **on, upon, up on.**

upcoming In formal writing, *forthcoming, coming,*

approaching, and *anticipated* are preferable to *up-coming.*

upward (or **upwards**) **of** This expression means more than or in excess of. It should never be used to convey the sense of somewhat less than, about, or almost.

us See **we.**

usage, use *Usage,* a specialized term, has particular reference to what is customary practice or procedure and to the employment of language. When the desired meaning is related to employment or usefulness in a much more general way, *use* is the proper choice: *gave her car hard use; a new use for nylon.*

use(d) to To express the meaning of regular practice or custom in past time, the verb *use* occurs in the inflected form *used,* or as *use* when coupled with *did.* For example: *He used to walk to work. He used not to ride* (or *did not use to ride*). *Did* (or *didn't*) *he use to ride?*

various This is an adjective only: *wrote to various officials; her reasons were various.* It is not acceptably used as a plural collective pronoun, as in *wrote to various of the officials.*

verbal See **oral, verbal.**

virtually See **practically, virtually.**

wake, waken See **awake, awaken.**

want The phrase *want for* is standard usage in expressing need: *She did not want for funds.* The same phrase is unacceptable in the sense of wish or desire: *She wants him to leave* (not *wants for him to leave* or *wants he should leave*).

way Referring to distance in general, the singular noun *way* is the only acceptable form in an example such as *a good way* (not *ways*) *to go.*

we The choice between the nominative pronoun *we* and the objective *us* is governed by the grammatical function of the pronoun in a given example. The same method of determination applies when *we* and *us* are followed by nouns, as in: *We officers were not consulted* (subject of verb). *They gave us officers no hearing* (indirect object).

well, well- The adverb *well* appears in many modifiers that are hyphenated when they stand before nouns: *the well-known actress.* A hyphen is not used when the modifier follows a verb: *The actress is well known for Shakespearean roles.*

were As the past subjunctive of the verb *be,* *were* appears in statements expressing conditions that are clearly hypothetical or contrary to fact: *if I were you.* Such statements frequently express a wish: *I wish that the operation were over.* Often they are introduced by *if* and *as if* (or *as though*): *If the economy were more healthy, we would proceed. She acted as though everything were settled.* In formal writing, *were* is required in such examples; in speech and informal writing, the indicative form *was* is often found. But more errors probably occur through misguided use of *were.* Such misuse is especially common in mere conditional statements (not contrary to fact) and in indirect questions. In each of the following, *was,* not *were,* is proper: *They said that if the report was true, changes would be necessary. I tried to determine whether the emergency was over. They asked if he was agreeable.*

what The relative pronoun *what,* as the subject of a sentence or clause, can be either singular or plural in construction, according to the sense involved. It is construed as singular when *what* is the equivalent of *that which* or *a* (or *the*) *thing that;* it is plural when *what* stands for *things that* or *those which.* How *what* is construed governs the grammatical number of the verb or verbs that follow. For example: *He is involved in what seems to be an outright fraud. They are making what appear to be signs of welcome. What impresses me most is his honesty. What were intended as gestures of friendship appear to have aroused suspicion.* Note that in the last two examples, the verbs preceding and following *what* agree in number. In some examples, either a singular or a plural construction of *what* is possible, especially when the elements

318

following the second verb can be construed collectively or abstractly and *what* has the meaning *that which:* *Sometimes what really commands respect is power and the willingness to use it effectively.* Or two plural verbs could be used.

when   This word and *where* should not be used to define other words, as in *a rupture is when* (or *where*) *there is a tear in bodily tissue.* A noun is defined in terms of another noun: *A rupture is a tear.*

whence   Since *whence* has a built-in sense of *from,* it is not preceded by *from* except redundantly: *the land whence* (not *from whence*) *he came.*

where   Use *where* with *from* to indicate motion from a place: *Where did she come from?* Use *where* alone in a corresponding sentence to indicate direction or motion to a place: *Where did she go* (not *go to*)? Use *where* alone to indicate location or position of rest: *Where is she now* (not *where is she at now*)? *Where* is improperly used as a conjunction, in place of *that,* in sentences such as *I see where* (properly *that*) *he has resigned.* See also **when.**

which   In sentences such as the following, *which* means a thing or circumstance that: *He seemed unhappy, which was understandable. Which* refers to an entire preceding clause instead of to a single word. This usage is acceptable when the reference is clear, as in the preceding example. It should be avoided when the reference is unclear. Ambiguity occurs most often when *which* follows a noun that could be construed as the antecedent: *She refused our offer, which caused much surprise.* If the surprise stemmed from the refusal rather than from the nature of the offer, rephrasing is desirable: *She refused our offer, and that caused much surprise.* See also **that, which, who (whom).**

while   As a conjunction, *while* is used most often, and most safely, to indicate a period of time: *He slept while I worked.* It is also acceptably used to mean although: *While we dislike her, we did respect her talent.* It is acceptable too in the sense of whereas, to imply opposition or difference: *The main figure is red, while the background is blue.* In such examples, when something other than time is intended but a reference to time can easily be read into them, *while* should be replaced by a more specific conjunction: *While he had rifles of his own, he believed strongly in control of firearms* (preferably *Although he had*). *He spent his youth in Ohio, while his father grew up in England* (preferably *whereas his father grew up*). *While* should never be used as a mere substitute for *and,* as in *They took steak, my brother had veal, while I ordered fish.* See also **awhile, a while.**

whiskey, whisky   *Whiskey* is the more common spelling in American usage, particularly for American and Irish liquor. *Scotch whisky* and *Canadian whisky* are spelled thus.

who, whom   In written usage, especially on a formal level, the grammatical distinctions between these pronouns are closely observed. *Who* (and *whoever*) are nominative forms employed to represent a subject or a predicate after a form of the verb *be*. *Whom* (and *whomever*) are corresponding objective pronouns, used principally to represent an object of a verb or of a preposition. In speech and informal writing, *who* often replaces *whom* in questions (*Who did they choose?*) and in sentences in which the object of a preposition precedes the preposition: *He wanted to know who he should speak to.* In both examples, on a formal level, *whom* is required. Misuse of *whom,* when *who* is indicated, is a more glaring error; it occurs most often when the pronoun is misconstrued as the object of a verb when in fact it is the subject of a clause: *I talked to a man who I think is much interested in the job.* The choice between *who* and *whom* depends always on the pronoun's function in its clause, even though the entire clause may be the object of a verb or of a preposition: *Who shall we say is calling? They will accept whoever is chosen. They will accept whomever the delegates name. We should give our support to whoever is selected. We should give our support to whomever the delegates express a preference for.* See also **than; that, which, who (whom).**

whose   *Whose* functions as the possessive form of both *who* and *which*. As such it can refer to things as well as to persons: *It is the only work whose author-*

ship is in doubt. The alternative possessive form *of which* is also possible in referring to things: *the only work the authorship of which is in doubt.* In that example, as in most others, the alternative is too cumbersome to be desirable.

why   See **reason.**

wide   See **broad, wide.**

will   See **shall, will.**

-wise   In certain combinations, such as *taxwise* and *timewise, -wise* means with reference to. The usage is informal outside business writing, where its conciseness is considered an asset. On other levels, such combinations are objectionable particularly if they are formed indiscriminately and overused, thus giving the effect of commercial jargon.

with   See **along with.**

would   *Would have* is frequently misused for *had* in conditional clauses introduced by *if.* The following illustrate correct forms: *They could have come if they had wanted to* (not *if they would have wanted to*). *If they had come, this would not have occurred* (not *if they would have come*). *Had* is also the proper auxiliary in clauses following *wish: I wish that she had called* (not *that she would have called*). See also **should, would.**

wrack   See **rack, wrack.**

wrong, wrongly In the meaning erroneously, *wrong* is the more common adverb, but *wrongly* is used before a verb or participle that it modifies: *advised us wrong; spelled it wrong; a wrongly conceived arrangement.*

Xmas Although the word is by no means the creation of modern advertising, it is now largely confined to that medium and to commercial writing. It is not appropriate to formal usage.

yet As an adverb meaning up to the present, thus far, or in the phrase *as yet,* this word is used with a perfect tense rather than with the simple past tense: *She has not called yet. Have you made plans yet?*

yourself, yourselves In formal usage, these are not interchangeable with *you* in sentences such as *They are expecting the Smiths and yourself. Yourselves and our neighbors come from the same town.* Make it *you* in both examples.

Picking a Preposition

The following list contains forms of verbs, adjectives, and nouns that regularly appear in combination with certain prepositions. Following each entry word are the prepositions which are idiomatically linked with that word.

Picking the right preposition is often a matter of idiom. Related verbs such as *acquiesce, agree,* and *concur* might be thought to agree in every detail in the choice of prepositions, but they do not. So consulting a list of idiomatic expressions is the only sure method of avoiding error. Even people who work with the language every day—such as professional writers and speakers—often consult such a list. The list is not intended to imply that the entry word must be followed or preceded by a preposition, but rather that in certain contexts it is often used with that preposition. Only usages that commonly give difficulty are treated.

The prepositions listed are the ones most often used with the words in question; where the choice is determined by a particular sense of the entry word, the sense is indicated and illustrated when an example of the particular combination is not likely to come to the reader's mind readily. No adverbial usage is included, nor are the countless combinations of entry words followed by infinitives. Phrasal verbs, such as *bottom out* and *carry forward,* are also omitted.

abashed at
abhorrence of
abhorrent to
ability at or *with*
  (*at mechanics; with tools*)
abound in or *with*
absolve of or *from*
accede to
access to
accessible to
accession of or *to*
  (*of property; to the throne*)
acclimate or *acclimatize to*
accommodate to or *with*
  (*to changing circumstances;
  with everything she requested*)
accompanied by or *with*
  (*by her husband; with every
  difficulty imaginable*)
accord (n.) *between, of,* or *with;*
  (v.) *to* or *with* (*accord every
  consideration to her; a statement that accords with the law*)
account (v.) *for* or *to*
  (*for things; to persons*)
accrue to
acquiesce in
acquit of
adapt for, from, or *to*
addicted to (plus noun, but not
  plus infinitive): *addicted to
  heroin; to taking heroin; not to
  take heroin*
adept at or *in*
adequate for or *to* (*for a goal* or
  purpose; to a need)
adjacent to
admit to, into, or *of* (*admit one
  to* or *into a club; a passage
  admitting to the lobby; a matter
  that admits of several views*)
adverse to

advocate (n.) *of;* (v.) *for*
affiliate (v.) *with* or *to*
affinity of, between, or *with*
akin to
alien (adj.) *to* or *from*
ally (v.) *to* or *with*
aloof from
amenable to
amused by or *at*
analogous in, to, or *with* (*in
  qualities; to* or *with each other*)
analogy of, between, to, or *with*
angry at, with, or *about*
antidote to, for, or *against*
antipathy to, toward, or *against*
anxious for or *about*
apprehensive of or *for*
  (*of danger; for one's welfare*)
apprise of
apropos of
arrogate to or *for*
aspiration toward or *after*
aspire to, toward, or *after*
assent to
attempt (n.) *at* or *on* (*at realizing
  an achievement; on a person's
  life*)
attended by or *with* (*by persons;
  by* or *with conditions* or
  circumstances)
attest to
attune to
augment by or *with*
averse to
aversion for, to, or *toward*
basis for, in, or *of* (*for a rumor;
  in fact* or *in law; of a medicinal
  compound; of* or *for an official's
  authority*)
bid (v.) *for* or *on*
  (*for nomination; on property*)
blame (v.) *for* or *on* (*blame her*

for the delay; blame the delay on him)

blink (v.) *at* (sense of *connive*; without preposition, sense of *ignore* or *overlook*)

boast (n., v.) *of* or *about*

boggle at

capacity of or *for* (*of four quarts for growth*)

capitalize at or *on* (*at $4 million; on an opponent's mistakes*)

careless about, in, or *of* (*about her attendance; in her speech; of* or *about the children's welfare*)

caution (v.) *about* or *against*

center (v.) *on, upon, in,* or *at* (but not *around*)

charge (v.) *for* or *with* (*for services; with manslaughter; with a duty; with strong emotion*)

clear (adj.) *of;* (v.) *of* or *from*

climb up (though usually redundant), *down*

coincide with

common (adj.) *to*

comparable to or *with*

compare with or *to* (like things that are strictly comparable, *with* each other; unlike things *to* each other in sense of *liken;* things *with* each other in sense of *be worthy of comparison*)

compatible with

complementary to

compliment (n., v.) *on*

concern (n., v.) *about, in,* or *with*

concur in or *with* (*in a plan or policy; with a person or view*)

conducive to

confide in or *to*

conform or *conformity to* or *with*

connive at or *with* (*at a fraud; with an accomplice*)

consequent (adj.) or *consequential to, on,* or *upon*

consist of or *in* (*an alloy consisting chiefly of nickel; treason, which consists in aiding the enemies of one's country*)

consistent with

contemporaneous with

contemporary with

contemptuous of

contend with, against, about, or *over* (*with* or *against rivals, enemies,* or *unfavorable circumstances; about* or *over disputed matters*)

contiguous to

contingent on or *upon*

contrast (n.) *between, to,* or *with* (*between things; in contrast to* or *with*); (v.) *with*

conversant with

convict (v.) *of*

correspond to or *with* (*a statement not corresponding to* or *with his earlier account; a part that corresponds to the bore of a musket; when I corresponded with her*)

culminate in

cure (v.) *of*

decide on, upon, for, or *against* (*on* or *upon a matter or issue; for* or *against a principal in a legal action*)

deficient in

deprive of

derive from

desire (n.) *for*

desirous of

desist from

despair (v.) *of*

destined for (for an end, use, or
  purpose; for a locality)
destitute of
destructive to or *of*
deviate (v.) *from*
devoid of
devolve from, on, to or *upon*
differ from, on, over, or *with*
  (from another person in out-
  look; on or over issues; with a
  second party to an argument)
different from or *than* (a job
  different from his; an outcome
  different from what we expected;
  how different things seem now
  than yesterday). *Different
  from* is the preferred form
  when it works readily—when
  from is followed by a single
  word or short clause. *Different
  than* is most acceptable when
  it aids conciseness—when *from*
  could not be used except
  ponderously and when *than* is
  followed by a condensed clause.
differentiate between, among, or
  from
diminution of
disappointed by, in, or *with*
  (by or in a person; in or with
  a thing)
discourage from
disdain (n.) *for*
disengage from
disgusted with, at, or *by* (with a
  person or an action; at an action
  or behavior; by a personal
  quality, action,* or *behavior)
dislike of
dispossess of or *from*
disqualify for or *from*
dissent (n., v.) *from*
dissimilar to

dissociate from
dissuade from
distaste for
distinguish from, between, or
  among (distinguish one species
  from another; distinguish
  between or among shades of
  meaning)
distrustful of
divest of
dote on
emanate from
embellish with
emigrate from
empty (adj.) *of*
enamored of or *with*
encroach on or *upon*
end (v.) *with* or *in* (with a light
  dessert or with a benediction;
  in divorce)
endow with
entrust to or *with* (entrust
  a mission to a confidant; entrust
  a friend with a mission)
envelop in
envious of
essential (adj.) *to* or *for;* (n.) *of*
estrange from
exclusive of
excuse (v.) *for* or *from* (for a
  fault; from an obligation or duty)
exonerate of or *from*
expect from or *of* (expect an
  apology from a mistaken person;
  expect integrity of a partner)
experience (n.) *in* or *of*
expert (adj., n.) *in, at,* or *with*
  (in or at weaving; with a loom)
expressive of
exude from
favorable to, toward, or *for*
fear (n.) *of* or *for* (of death; for
  my safety)

fond of
fondness for
foreign to
free (adj., v.) of or from
freedom of or from
friend of or to
frightened at or by
fugitive (n., adj.) from
grateful to or for (to a person; for a benefit)
grieve for, after, or at
habitual with
hanker after
heal by or of
hinder from
hindrance to
hint (v.) at
honor (v.) by, for, or with (by or with a citation for bravery; for his bravery; with one's presence)
hope (n.) for or of; (v.) for
identical with or to
identify (oneself) with (with the hero of a play)
immigrate to
impatient at or with (at a condition of affairs; with a person)
impervious to
implicit in
impressed by or with
improve on or upon
inaccessible to
incentive (n.) to or for
incidental to
incongruous to
inconsistent with
incorporate in, into, or with
independent (adj.) of
infer from
inferior to
infested with
influence (n.) on, upon, over, or of

infuse with
inimical to or toward
initiate into
innocent of
inquire about, after, or into
inroad into
insight into
inspire by or with
instruct in
intention of
intercede with, for, or (on behalf of)
intrude on, upon, into
inundated with
invest in or with (in bonds; with the rank and duties of an office)
involve in
isolate from
jealous of or for (of his power; for her rights and welfare)
justified in
lack (v.) in (lacking in support); or transitive usage (lack support),
laden with
lament (n., v.) for or over
laugh (n.) at or over; (v.) at
level (v.) at or with (level a gun or a charge at a person; level wood with a plane; with a person—that is, be honest in dealing)
liable for or to (for an act; for or to a duty or service; to a superior)
liken to
martyr (n.) to; (v.) for
mastery of or over (of a subject; of or over an adversary or obstacle)
means of, for, or to
meddle in or with
mediate between or among

meditate on or *upon*

militate against or (rarely) *for*

mindful of

mistrustful of

mock at

monopoly of

muse on, upon, or *over*

necessary (adj., n.) *for* or *to*

necessity for, to, or *of*

need (n.) *for* or *of*

neglectful of

negligent in or *of*

oblivious of or *to*

observant of

obtrude on or *upon*

occasion for or *of* (*for rejoicing; of my visit*)

occupied by or *with*

offend against

opportunity of or *for*

opposite (adj.) *to* or *from*; (n.) *of*

opt for or *against*

original (adj.) *with*

originate in or *with*

overwhelm by or *with*

parallel (adj.) *to*; (n.) *between* or *with*

partake in or *of*

patient (adj.) *with* or *of*

peculiar to

permeate into or *through*

permeated by

permit (v.) *of* (*a rule that permits of two interpretations*)

persevere in or *against*

persist in

persuaded by, of, or *into*

pertinent to

pervert (v.) *from*

possessed of, by, or *with* (*of great wealth; of a keen wit; by or with an urge to kill*)

possibility of or *for*

precedence of or *over*

precedent (adj. *to*; (n.) *for* or *of* (*for a ruling; of seating members according to rank*)

preclude from

prefer to (*prefer concerts to opera*)

pregnant by or *with* (*by a person; with significance*)

prejudicial to

preoccupied by or *with*

preparatory to

prerequisite (adj.) *to*; (n.) *of*

preside at or *over*

presume on or *upon*

prevail over, against, on, upon, or *with* (*over* or *against an adversary; on, upon,* or *with a person to provide a service*)

prodigal (adj.) *of*

productive of

proficient in or *at*

profit (v.) *by* or *from*

prohibit from

prone to

provide for, against, or *with* (*for* or *against an emergency; for a dependent child; for annual elections, by law; with food and medicine*)

pursuant to

qualify for or *as*

receptive to

reconcile to or *with* (*to hard times; one's belief with another's*)

redolent of

regard (n.) *for* or *to* (*for a person; in* or *with regard to a matter*)

repent of

replete with

329

respect (n.) *for*, *to*, or *of* (*for a person*; *with* or *in respect to*; *in respect of*)

responsibility *for*

restrain *from*

revel *in*

rich *in*

rob *of*

satiate *with*

saturate *with*

scared *at* or *by*

secure (adj.) *in*

similar *to*

slave (n.) *to* or *of*

solicitous *of*, *about*, or *for*

subject (adj.) *to*

suffer *from*

suitable *for*; *to*

superior (adj.) *to*

sympathetic *to* or *toward*

sympathy *for*, *toward*, or *with* (*for* or *toward a person* or *cause*; *in sympathy with a cause*)

tendency *to* or *toward*

thrill (v.) *to*, *at*, or *with* (*to* or *at a source of delight*; *with delight*)

tolerance *for*, *toward*, or *of* (*for*, *toward*, *of persons* or *causes*; *of pain*; *of a scientific instrument*)

treat (v.) *as*, *to*, *of*, or *with* (*as a friend*; *to a meal*; *of a subject* or *topic*; *with another person in negotiations*)

vary *from*

vest (v.) *in* or *with* (*authority vested in an official*; *an official vested with authority*)

vie *with*

void (adj.) *of*

vulnerable *to*

wait (v.) *for* or *on* (*for one who was delayed*; *on a customer* or *patient*)

want (n.) *of*; (v.) *for* (*did not want for money*)

wanting (adj.) *in*

wary *of*

yearn *for*, *after*, or *over*

zeal *for* or *in*

Prefixes and Suffixes

In today's world of mass communications, big business, and high technology, new words are constantly being formed. Many of these words are old terms to which a prefix or a suffix has been added. A knowledge, therefore, of the meanings of common prefixes and suffixes is an invaluable aid to anyone dealing with words. The following lists are designed to serve as a convenient reference.

Prefixes

a-[1], an-	Without; not: *amoral.*
a-[2]	1. On; in: *abed.*
	2. In the direction of: *astern.*
ab-[1]	Away from: *aboral.*
ab-[2]	Used to indicate a centimeter-gram-second system electromagnetic unit: *abcoulomb.*
ac-, ad-	Toward; to: *admit.*
acro-	1. Height: *acrophobia.*
	2. Tip; beginning: *acronym.*
aero-	1. Air; atmosphere: *aeroballistics.*
	2. Aviation: *aeronautics.*
agro-	Field; soil: *agrology.*
all(o)-	1. Other; different: *allopatric.*
	2. Isomeric: *allocholesterol.*
ambi-	Both: *ambidexterity.*
amphi-	1. Both: *amphibiotic.*
	2. Around: amphitheater.
ana-	1. Again; anew: *anamnesis.*
	2. Backward; back: *anaplasia.*

ante-	1. Earlier; prior to: *antebellum.*
	2. Before; in front of: *anteroom.*
anti-	1. Opposite; against: *antibody.*
	2. Reciprocal: *antilogarithm.*
apo-	Away from: *apogee.*
archaeo-, archeo-	Ancient; primitive: *archaeology.*
archi-, arch-	Chief; highest: *archduke.*
astro-	Star; outer space: *astrodome.*
audio-	1. Hearing: *audition.*
	2. Sound: *audiophile.*
auto-	1. Self; same: *autobiography.*
	2. Automatic: *autopilot.*
bacterio-	Bacteria: *bacteriogenic.*
baro-	Weight; pressure: *barometer.*
bathy-, batho-	Deep; deep-sea: *bathysphere.*
bi-, bin-	Two: *biannual.*
biblio-	Book: *bibliophile.*
bio-	Life; living organisms: *biomass.*
calci-	Calcium; calcium salt: *calcification.*
carbo-	Carbon: *carbohydrate.*
cardio-	Heart: *cardiovascular.*
cata-	1. Down: *catapult.*
	2. Reverse; degenerative: *cataplasia.*
centi-	1. One hundredth: *centimeter.*
	2. One hundred: *centipede.*
centro-	Center: *centrosphere.*
cephalo-	Head: *cephalopod.*
cerebro-	Brain; cerebrum: *cerebrovascular.*
chemo-	Chemicals; chemical: *chemotherapy.*
chromato-	Color: *chromatophore.*
chromo-	Color: *chromogen.*
chrono-	Time: *chronometer.*
circum-	Around; about: *circumscribe.*
cis-	On this side: *cisatlantic.*
co-, com-, col-, con-	Together; with: *coeducation.*

contra-	Against; opposite: *contraposition*.
cosmo-	Universe; world: *cosmochemistry*.
counter-	Contrary; opposite; opposing: *counteract*.
cranio-	Skull: *craniotomy*.
cryo-	Cold; freezing: *cryogenics*.
crypto-	Hidden; secret: *cryptogram*.
cyclo-	Circle; cycle: *cyclometer*.
cyto-	Cell: *cytoplasm*.
de-	1. Reverse: *decriminalize*.
	2. Remove; remove from: *delouse*.
	3. Reduce; degrade: *declass*.
deca-, deka-	Ten: *decade*.
deci-	One tenth: *deciliter*.
demi-	Half; partly: *demigod*.
dendro-	Tree; treelike: *dendrochronology*.
denti-	Tooth; dental: *dentifrice*.
dextro-	On or to the right: *dextrorotatory*.
di-	Two; twice: *diacid*.
dia-, di-	Through; across: *diagonal*.
dis-	1. Not: *dissimilar*.
	2. Undo: *disarrange*.
	3. Used as an intensive: *disannul*.
dys-	Bad; impaired; abnormal: *dysfunction*.
ecto-	Outer; external: *ectoparasite*.
electro-	Electric: *electromagnet*.
en-[1], em-	1. To put or go into or on: *entrain*.
	2. To cause to be: *endear*.
	3. Thoroughly: *entangle*.
en-[2], em-	In; into; within: *enzootic*.
endo-	Inside; within: *endogenous*.
entero-	Intestine: *enteropathy*.
epi-	On: *epidermis*.
equi-	Equal; equally: *equidistant*.
ethno-	Race; people: *ethnology*.
eu-	Good: *eugenics*.

ex-, e-	Out of; away from: *exceed.*
extra-, extro-	Outside; beyond: *extraordinary.*
ferro-	Iron: *ferromagnetic.*
fibro-	Fiber; fibrous tissue: *fibroid.*
fore-	1. Before; earlier: *foredoom.*
	2. Front; in front of: *foredeck.*
geo-	Earth; geography: *geochronology.*
gyro-	Spinning; circle: *gyroscope.*
hecto-	One hundred: *hectogram.*
helio-	Sun: *heliograph.*
hemo-, hema-, hem-	Blood: *hemocyte.*
hepta-	Seven: *heptagon.*
hetero-	Other; different: *heterogynous.*
hexa-	Six: *hexagon.*
holo-	Whole; entire: *holography.*
homo-	Same; like: *homophone.*
hydro-	1. Water; liquid: *hydrodynamics.*
	2. Hydrogen: *hydrocarbon.*
hyper-	Over; beyond; excessive: *hypercritical.*
hypno-	1. Sleep: *hypnophobia.*
	2. Hypnosis: *hypnoanalysis.*
hypo-	Below; under: *hypodermic.*
ideo-	Idea: *ideomotor.*
in-[1], il-, im-, ir-	Not: *inarticulate.*
in-[2], il-, im-, ir-	In; into; within: *inbreed.*
infra-	Below; beneath: *infrasonic.*
inter-	Between; among: *international.*
intra-	Within: *intracellular.*
intro-	In; inward: *introjection.*
iso-	Equal; uniform: *isobar.*
kilo-	One thousand: *kilowatt.*
lacto-	Milk: *lactoprotein.*
leuko-, leuco-	White; colorless: *leukocyte.*
levo-	On or to the left: *levorotatory.*
litho-	Stone: *lithosphere.*

macro-	Large; long; inclusive: *macronucleus*.
magneto-	Magnetism; magnetic: *magnetoelectric*.
mal-	Bad; abnormal: *maladminister*.
mega-	1. Large: *megaphone*.
	2. One million: *megahertz*.
meta-	1. Change: *metachromatism*.
	2. Beyond: *metalinguistics*.
micro-	1. Small: *microbiology*.
	2. One-millionth: *microcalorie*.
milli-	1. One-thousandth: *millisecond*.
	2. One thousand: *millipede*.
mis-	1. Bad; wrong; failure: *misconduct*.
	2. Used as an intensive: *misdoubt*.
mono-	One; single; alone: *monocline*.
multi-	Many; much; multiple: *multicolored*.
nano-	1. One-billionth: *nanosecond*.
	2. Extremely small: *nanoplankton*.
neo-	New; recent: *Neolithic*.
neuro-	Nerve; neural: *neurocyte*.
nitro-	Nitrogen: *nitrobacterium*.
non-	Not: *noncombatant*.
ob-	Inverse; inversely: *obcordate*.
octo-, octa-, oct-	Eight: *octane*.
oligo-	Few: *oligopoly*.
omni-	All: *omnidirectional*.
oo-	Egg; ovum: *oology*.
ortho-	Straight; correct: *orthodontia*.
paleo-	Ancient; early: *paleobotany*.
pan-	All; whole: *panorama*.
para-, par-	1. Beside; near: *parathyroid*.
	2. Beyond: *paranormal*.
	3. Resembling: *paratyphoid*.
	4. Subsidiary; assistant: *paraprofessional*.
pedo-	Child: *pedodontia*.
penta-	Five: *pentagon*.

per-	Thoroughly; completely; intensely: *perfervid*.
peri-	Around: *periscope*.
philo-	Loving: *philosophy*.
phono-	Sound; speech: *phonology*.
photo-	Light; radiant energy: *photosynthesis*.
physio-	Natural; physical: *physiography*.
phyto-	Plant: *phytogenesis*.
pico-	1. One-trillionth: *picosecond*.
	2. Very small: *picornavirus*.
poly-	Many; more than usual: *polychromatic*.
post-	After; behind: *postdoctoral*.
pre-	Earlier; before; in front of: *prehistoric*.
pro-¹	Forward: *proceed*.
pro-²	Supporting: *prorevolutionary*.
pseudo-	False; deceptive: *pseudoscience*.
psycho-	Mind; mental; psychology: *psychogenic*.
pyro-	Fire; heat: *pyrotechnics*.
quadri-, quadr-	Four: *quadrilateral*.
quasi-	In some manner: *quasi-scientific*.
re-	1. Again: *rebuild*.
	2. Back: *react*.
	3. Used as an intensive: *refine*.
retro-	Back: *retrograde*.
schizo-	Split: *schizophrenic*.
semi-	1. Half: *semicircle*.
	2. Partially: *semiconscious*.
	3. Resembling: *semiofficial*.
somn-	Sleep: *somnolence*.
spectro-	Spectrum: *spectrogram*.
spermato-	Sperm: *spermatocyte*.
spor-	Spore: *sporocyte*.
steno-	Narrow; small: *stenographer*.
stereo-	1. Solid: *stereotropism*.
	2. Three-dimensional: *stereoscopic*.
sub-	1. Below: *subsoil*.

	2. Secondary: *subplot.*
	3. Not completely: *subhuman.*
super-	1. Over: *superimpose.*
	2. Exceedingly: *superfine.*
supra-	1. Above; over: *suprarenal.*
	2. Greater than: *supramolecular.*
	3. Earlier than: *supralapsarian.*
sur-	1. Above: *surpass.*
	2. In addition: *surtax.*
syn-, sym-, syl-	Together: *synchronize.*
tele-	Distance: *television.*
tetra-	Four: *tetrahedron.*
theo-	God: *theology.*
thermo-	Heat: *thermodynamics.*
topo-	Place: *topography.*
tox-	Poison: *toxemia.*
trans-	1. Across; beyond: *transatlantic.*
	2. Change: *translate.*
tri-	Three: *triad.*
tricho-	Hair: *trichosis.*
ultra-	1. Beyond: *ultraviolet.*
	2. Excessively: *ultraconservative.*
un-[1]	1. Not: *unhappy.*
	2. The opposite of: *unrest.*
un-[2]	1. To reverse: *unbind.*
	2. Used as an intensive: *unloose.*
uni-	Single; one: *unicycle.*
vaso-	Blood vessel: *vasodilator.*
veno-	Vein: *venous.*
xeno-	Stranger; foreigner: *xenophobic.*
xero-	Dry: *xeroderma.*
xylo-	Wood: *xylophone.*
zoo-	Animal: *zoology.*
zygo-	Paired: *zygomorphic.*

Suffixes

-able, -ible	Capable of: *debatable*.
-age	1. Collection; mass: *sewerage*.
	2. Relationship; connection: *parentage*.
	3. Condition; state: *vagabondage*.
	4. Result of an action: *breakage*.
	5. Residence or place of: *vicarage*.
	6. Charge or fee: *cartage*.
-al	Of or relating to: *parental*.
-algia	Pain: *neuralgia*.
-an	Of or relating to: *librarian*.
-ance	State or action: *continuance*.
-ant	Causing or being: *deodorant*.
-ar	Of or relating to: *polar*.
-ate	Of or relating to: *collegiate*.
-chrome	Color: *monochrome*.
-cide	1. Killer: *insecticide*.
	2. Act of killing: *matricide*.
-cracy	Government: *democracy*.
-cy	1. State of being: *bankruptcy*.
	2. Rank: *baronetcy*.
-dom	1. Condition: *stardom*.
	2. Domain; rank: *dukedom*.
-ectomy	Surgical removal: *appendectomy*.
-ed	Having: *blackhearted*.
-eer	One concerned with: *profiteer*.
-en[1]	1. To cause to be: *cheapen*.
	2. To cause to have: *lengthen*.
-en[2]	Made of: *earthen*.
-ence	State or condition: *dependence*.
-ent	Causing or being: *absorbent*.
-er, -or	1. One that performs an action: *swimmer*.
	2. Native or resident of: *New Yorker*.

-ese	From or relating to: *Vietnamese.*
-ess	Female: *lioness.*
-est	Most: *nearest.*
-ferous	Bearing: *carboniferous.*
-ful	Full of: *playful.*
-fy	To cause to be: *electrify.*
-gamous	Marrying: *monogamous.*
-gamy	Marriage: *bigamy.*
-gram	Something written: *telegram.*
-graph	1. An instrument that writes: *seismograph.*
	2. Something written: *monograph.*
-hood	Condition or state: *manhood.*
-ia	Disease: *anorexia.*
-ian	Of or resembling: *Bostonian.*
-iatric	Relating to medical treatment: *geriatric.*
-iatry	Medical treatment: *psychiatry.*
-ic	Of or relating to: *Icelandic.*
-ine	Of or resembling: *canine.*
-ing	Used to form the present participle: *singing.*
-ion	Act or process: *admission.*
-ish	1. Of or like: *childish.*
	2. Tending toward: *greenish.*
-ism	1. Action or process: *terrorism.*
	2. Characteristic behavior: *heroism.*
	3. Doctrine; theory: *pacifism.*
-ist	1. One that produces: *novelist.*
	2. A specialist: *biologist.*
	3. An adherent of a doctrine: *anarchist.*
-ite	1. A native of: *New Jerseyite.*
	2. One associated with: *socialite.*
-itis	Inflammation or disease: *laryngitis.*
-ive	Of or tending toward: *demonstrative.*
-ize, ise	1. To cause to be: *dramatize.*
	2. To become: *materialize.*
	3. To treat with: *anesthetize.*

-lepsy	Seizure: *epilepsy.*
-less	Without: *blameless.*
-let	Small: *booklet.*
-lith	Stone: *monolith.*
-logy	1. Science: *biology.*
	2. Discourse: *phraseology.*
-ly	Like: *friendly.*
-mania	Exaggerated enthusiasm: *pyromania.*
-ment	1. Action or process: *appeasement.*
	2. Result of an action or process: *advancement.*
-meter	A measuring device: *pedometer.*
-metry	Science of measuring: *geometry.*
-most	Most: *innermost.*
-ness	State; quality: *brightness.*
-nomy	A body of knowledge: *astronomy.*
-oid	Resembling: *spheroid.*
-opsy	Examination: *biopsy.*
-osis	Abnormal condition: *neurosis.*
-ous	Characterized by: *joyous.*
-proof	Impervious to: *bulletproof.*
-sect	To cut: *bisect.*
-ship	1. State or condition: *scholarship.*
	2. Rank or office: *professorship.*
-some	Characterized by: *bothersome.*
-stat	A stabilizing instrument: *thermostat.*
-tion	Act or process: *absorption.*
-tomy	Act of cutting: *lobotomy.*
-tude	Condition or state: *exactitude.*
-ule	Small: *globule.*
-ure	Act or process: *failure.*
-ward	In a direction: *downward.*
-wide	Throughout a specified area: *citywide.*
-wise	1. In a manner or direction: *clockwise.*
	2. In regard to: *dollarwise.*

Foreign Words and Phrases

The English language has grown by incorporating words from many different languages. However, many such words and phrases retain a distinctly foreign flavor. The following list contains foreign words and phrases commonly used in English. Key to terms: French (F), Greek (G), Italian (I), Latin (L).

à bon marché (F)	At a bargain price
ad astra per aspera (L)	To the stars through difficulties
ad nauseum (L)	To a ridiculous extreme
annus mirabilis (L)	A year of wonders or disasters
après moi le déluge (F)	After me the deluge
à propos de rien (F)	Apropos of nothing
au contraire (F)	On the contrary
au courant (F)	Up to date
au fait (F)	Skilled or knowledgeable
aurea mediocritas (L)	The golden mean
au revoir (F)	Good-by
aussitôt dit, aussitôt fait (F)	No sooner said than done
autre temps, autres moeurs (F)	Other times, other customs
ave atque vale (L)	Hail and farewell
avec plaisir (F)	With pleasure
beau geste (F)	A noble but empty gesture
bête noire (F)	Something or someone that one particularly dislikes
bon mot (F)	A clever saying
carpe diem (L)	Enjoy the present

casus belli (L)	An event justifying a declaration of war
causa sine qua non (L)	An indispensable condition
caveat emptor (L)	Let the buyer beware
cave canem (L)	Beware of the dog
c'est-à-dire (F)	That is to say
c'est la vie (F)	Such is life
chacun à son goût (F)	Everyone to his own taste
chef de cuisine (F)	Head cook
cherchez la femme (F)	Look for the woman
cogito ergo sum (L)	I think, therefore I am
compte rendu (F)	Report, account
coup de grâce (F)	A death blow
coûte que coûte (F)	Cost what it may
de facto (L)	In reality or fact
de gustibus non est disputandum (L)	There is no arguing about tastes
Dei gratia (L)	By the grace of God
Deo gratias (L)	Thanks be to God
Deo volente (L)	God willing
de trop (F)	Too much or too many; superfluous
Deus vobiscum (L)	God be with you
Dieu avec nous (F)	God with us
Dieu defend le droit (F)	God defends the right
Dieu et mon droit (F)	God and my right
Dominus vobiscum (L)	The Lord be with you
dulce et decorum est pro patria mori (L)	It is sweet and fitting to die for one's country
ecce homo (L)	Behold the man
en famille (F)	In one's family; informally
en plein jour (F)	In full daylight, openly
en rapport (F)	In sympathy or accord
e pluribus unum (L)	One out of many
ex cathedra (L)	With the authority derived from one's office
ex more (L)	According to custom
fait accompli (F)	An accomplished fact or deed

faux pas (F)	A social blunder
femme de chambre (F)	A chambermaid
festina lente (L)	Make haste slowly
fin de siècle (F)	End of century
gaudeamus igitur (L)	Let us then be joyful
genius loci (L)	Guardian deity; the distinctive character of a place
hic jacet (L)	Here lies
hic sepultus (L)	Here lies buried
hinc illae lacrimae (L)	Hence those tears
hoc anno (L)	In this year
hoi polloi (G)	The common people
honi soit qui mal y pense (F)	Shame to him who thinks evil of it
humanum est errare (L)	To err is human
in extremis (L)	At the point of death
in loco parentis (L)	In the place of a parent
in medias res (L)	In or into the middle of a sequence of events
in omnia paratus (L)	Prepared for all things
in perpetuum (L)	Forever
in propria persona (L)	In one's own person
in rerum natura (L)	In the nature of things
in situ (L)	In its place
in statu quo (L)	In the state in which it was before
integer vitae scelerisque purus (L)	Upright in life and free from wickedness
in toto (L)	Altogether; entirely
in vino veritas (L)	There is truth in wine
ipso jure (L)	By the law itself
jure divino (L)	By divine law
jus canonicum (L)	Canon law
justitia omnibus (L)	Justice for all
j'y suis, j'y reste (F)	Here I am, here I stay
labor omnia vincit (L)	Work conquers all things

la dolce vita (I)	The sweet life
laus Deo (L)	Praise be to God
le roi est mort, vive le roi (F)	The king is dead! Long live the king!
le style, c'est l'homme (F)	The style is the man
le tout ensemble (F)	The whole (taken) together
locus in quo (L)	The place in which
loquitur (L)	He or she speaks
ma foi (F)	Really!
mal de mer (F)	Seasickness
mal du pays (F)	Homesickness
mens sana in corpore sano (L)	A sound mind in a healthy body
miles gloriosus (L)	A bragging soldier
mirabile dictu (L)	Wonderful to say
mirabilia (L)	Miracles
mise en scène (F)	A stage setting; environment
modus operandi (L)	Method of operating
mon ami (F)	My friend
morituri te salutamus (L)	We who are about to die salute you
mutatis mutandis (L)	The necessary changes having been made
nemine contradicente (L)	No one contradicting
nemine dissentiente (L)	No one dissenting
n'est-ce pas? (F)	Isn't that so?
nolens volens (L)	Whether willing or not
nom de guerre (F)	A pseudonym
non possumus (L)	We are not able
non sequitur (L)	Conclusion that does not follow
obiit (L)	He or she died
objet d'art (F)	A work of art
omnia vincit amor (L)	Love conquers all
opere citato (L)	In the work cited
O tempora! O mores! (L)	O times! O customs!

pari passu (L)	With equal pace
pax vobiscum (L)	Peace be with you
persona grata (L)	Fully acceptable
pièce de résistance (F)	An outstanding accomplishment
pied-à-terre (F)	A secondary or temporary lodging
pis aller (F)	The last resort
pleno jure (L)	With full authority
plus ça change, plus c'est la même chose (F)	The more it changes, the more it's the same thing
primus inter pares (L)	First among equals
pro bono publico (L)	For the public good
pro forma (L)	Done in a perfunctory way
pro tempore (L)	For the time being; temporarily
quid pro quo (L)	An equal exchange
qui s'excuse, s'accuse (F)	He who excuses himself accuses himself
quod vide (L)	Which see
quo jure? (L)	By what right?
raison d'état (F)	For the good of the country
raison d'être (F)	Reason for existing
requiescat in pace (L)	May he or she rest in peace
sans doute (F)	Without doubt
sans gene (F)	Without embarrassment
sans pareil (F)	Without equal
sans peine (F)	Without difficulty
sans peur et sans reproche (F)	Without fear and without reproach
sans souci (F)	Carefree
savoir-faire (F)	To know what to do
scripsit (L)	He or she wrote (it)
sculpsit (L)	He or she sculptured (it)
secundum (L)	According to
semper idem (L)	Always the same

semper paratus (L)	Always ready
sic passim (L)	Thus throughout
sic semper tyrannis (L)	Thus always to tyrants
sic transit gloria mundi (L)	Thus passes away the glory of the world
sine die (L)	Without a day specified for a future meeting
sine qua non (L)	Something essential
splendide mendax (L)	Nobly untruthful
sub verbo (L)	Under the word
summum bonum (L)	The greatest good
suo jure (L)	In one's own right
suo loco (L)	In one's rightful place
suum cuique (L)	To each his own
tabula rasa (L)	A clean slate
tant mieux (F)	So much the better
tant pis (F)	So much the worse
tempora mutantur, nos et mutamur in illis (L)	Times change, and we change with them
tempus fugit (L)	Time flies
timeo Danaos et dona ferentes (L)	I fear the Greeks even when they bear gifts
tout le monde (F)	Everyone
trompe l'oeil (F)	Illusionary; deceive the eye
ut infra (L)	As below
ut supra (L)	As above
vade mecum (L)	Go with me; guidebook
vae victis (L)	Woe to the conquered
vale (L)	Farewell
verbatim et literatim (L)	Word for word and letter for letter
vive la différence (F)	Three cheers for the difference
vive le roi (F)	Long live the king
voilà (F)	Look! See!

How it is
Written

Forms of Address

Forms of address do not always follow set guidelines; the type of salutation is often determined by the relationship between correspondents or by the purpose and content of the letter. However, the following general styles apply to most occasions. For informal salutations, use "Mr." for a man; use "Ms." or "Mrs." or "Miss" for a woman, according to her stated preference. For formal salutations, avoid gender-specific forms in favor of simpler forms that can be used to address either a man or a woman.

	Form of Address	Salutation
Academics		
assistant professor, college or university	Dr. (*or* Mr., Ms.) Joseph (Jane) Stone Assistant Professor Department of _____	Dear Professor Stone:
associate professor, college or university	Dr. (*or* Mr., Ms.) Joseph (Jane) Stone Associate Professor Department of _____	Dear Professor Stone:
chancellor, university	Chancellor Joseph (Jane) Stone	Dear Chancellor Stone:

dean, college or university	Dean Joseph (Jane) Stone *or* Dr. (*or* Mr., Ms.) Joseph (Jane) Stone Dean, School of ———	Dear Dean Stone: Dear Dr. (*or* Mr., Ms.) Stone:
president, college or university	President Joseph (Jane) Stone *or* Dr. (*or* Mr., Ms.) Joseph (Jane) Stone President, ———	Dear President Stone: Dear Dr. (*or* Mr., Ms.) Stone:
professor, college or university	Professor Joseph (Jane) Stone *or* Dr. (*or* Mr., Ms.) Joseph (Jane) Stone Department of ———	Dear Professor Stone: Dear Dr. (*or* Mr., Ms.) Stone:

Clerical and Religious Orders

abbot, Roman Catholic	The Right Reverend Joseph Stone, O.S.B. Abbot of ———	Right Reverend Abbot:
archbishop, Armenian Church	His Eminence the Archbishop of ———	Your Eminence: *or* Your Excellency:
archbishop, Greek Orthodox	His Eminence Archbishop Joseph Stone	Your Eminence:
archbishop, Roman Catholic	The Most Reverend Joseph Stone Archbishop of ———	Your Excellency:

349

	Form of Address	Salutation
archbishop, Russian Orthodox	His Eminence the Archbishop of ____ *or* The Most Reverend Archbishop of ____	Your Grace: Right Reverend Joseph:
archdeacon, Episcopal	The Venerable Joseph (Jane) Stone, Archdeacon of ____	Dear Archdeacon Stone:
archimandrite, Russian Orthodox	Very Reverend Father Joseph Stone	Very Reverend Father: Very Reverend Father Stone:
archpriest, Russian Orthodox	Very Reverend Father Joseph Stone	Very Reverend Father: Very Reverend Father Stone:
bishop, Episcopal	The Right Reverend Joseph (Jane) Stone Bishop of ____	Dear Bishop Stone:
bishop, Greek Orthodox	The Right Reverend Joseph Stone	Your Grace:
bishop, Methodist	Bishop Joseph Stone	Dear Bishop Stone:
bishop, Roman Catholic	The Most Reverend Joseph Stone Bishop of ____	Your Excellency: Dear Bishop Stone:
brother, Roman Catholic	Brother Joseph Stone, C.F.C.	Dear Brother: Dear Brother Joseph:
canon, Episcopal	The Reverend Canon Joseph (Jane) Stone	Dear Canon Stone:
cantor	Cantor Joseph (Jane) Stone	Dear Cantor Stone:

cardinal	His Eminence Joseph Cardinal Stone	Your Eminence: Dear Cardinal Stone:
clergyman, Protestant	The Reverend Joseph (Jane) Stone *or* The Reverend Joseph (Jane) Stone, D.D.	Dear Dr. (*or* Mr., Ms.) Stone:
elder, Presbyterian	Elder Joseph (Jane) Stone	Dear Elder Stone:
dean of a cathedral, Episcopal	The Very Reverend Joseph (Jane) Stone Dean of ――	Dear Dean Stone:
metropolitan, Russian Orthodox	His Eminence the Metropolitan of ―― *or* The Most Reverend Metropolitan of ――	Your Grace: Right Reverend Joseph:
monsignor, Roman Catholic	The Right Reverend Monsignor Joseph Stone	Right Reverend Monsignor: Dear Monsignor: Dear Monsignor Stone:
patriarch, Armenian Church	His Beatitude the Patriarch of ――	Your Beatitude:
patriarch, Greek Orthodox	His All Holiness Patriarch Demetrios	Your All Holiness:
patriarch, Russian Orthodox	His Beatitude the Patriarch of ――	Your Beatitude:
pope	His Holiness Pope John Paul II *or* His Holiness the Pope	Your Holiness: Most Holy Father:

351

Form of Address — Salutation

	Form of Address	Salutation
president, Mormon Church	President Joseph Stone Church of Jesus Christ of Latter-day Saints	Dear President Stone:
priest, Greek Orthodox	Reverend Father Joseph Stone	Dear Reverend Stone: Dear Reverend Father:
priest, Roman Catholic	The Reverend Joseph Stone	Dear Reverend Father: Dear Father: Dear Father Stone:
priest, Russian Orthodox	The Reverend Joseph Stone	Reverend Father: Reverend Father Stone:
protopresbyter, Russian Orthodox	Very Reverend Father Joseph Stone	Very Reverend Father: Very Reverend Father Stone:
rabbi	Rabbi Joseph (Jane) Stone *or* Joseph (Jane) Stone, D.D.	Dear Rabbi (*or* Dr.) Stone:
sister, Roman Catholic	Sister Mary Stone, C.S.J.	Dear Sister: Dear Sister Mary:
supreme patriarch, Armenian Church	His Holiness the Supreme Patriarch and Catholicos of all Armenians	Your Holiness:

Diplomats

ambassador, U.S.	The Honorable Joseph (Jane) Stone Ambassador of the United States	Dear Ambassador Stone:
ambassador to the U.S.	His (Her) Excellency Joseph (Jane) Stone The Ambassador of _____	Excellency: Dear Ambassador Stone:
chargé d'affaires, U.S.	Joseph (Jane) Stone, Esq. American Chargé d'Affaires	Dear Mr. (Ms.) Stone:
chargé d'affaires, to the U.S.	Joseph (Jane) Stone, Esq. Chargé d'Affaires of _____	Dear Mr. (Ms.) Stone:
consul, U.S.	Mr. Joseph (Jane) Stone American Consul	Dear Mr. (Ms.) Stone:
minister, U.S.	The Honorable Joseph (Jane) Stone The Minister of the United States	Dear Mr. (Ms.) Stone:
minister to the U.S.	The Honorable Joseph (Jane) Stone The Minister of _____	Dear Mr. (Ms.) Stone:
secretary-general, United Nations	His (Her) Excellency Joseph (Jane) Stone Secretary-General of the United Nations	Excellency: Dear Secretary-General Stone:
U.S. representative to the United Nations	The Honorable Joseph (Jane) Stone United States Representative to the United Nations	Dear Mr. (Ms.) Stone: Dear Ambassador Stone:

Federal, state, and local officials (government)

	Form of Address	Salutation
alderman	The Honorable Joseph (Jane) Stone	Dear Mr. (Ms.) Stone:
assistant to the President	The Honorable Joseph (Jane) Stone Assistant to the President The White House	Dear Mr. (Ms.) Stone:
Attorney General, U.S.	The Honorable Joseph (Jane) Stone Attorney General of the United States	Dear Attorney General Stone:
attorney general, state	The Honorable Joseph (Jane) Stone Attorney General State of _____	Dear Attorney General Stone:
assemblyman, state	The Honorable Joseph (Jane) Stone _____ Assembly State Capitol	Dear Mr. (Ms.) Stone:
cabinet member	The Honorable Joseph (Jane) Stone Secretary of _____	Dear Secretary Stone:
assistant secretary of a department	The Honorable Joseph (Jane) Stone Assistant Secretary of _____	Dear Mr. (Ms.) Stone:
undersecretary of a department	The Honorable Joseph (Jane) Stone Undersecretary of _____	Dear Mr. (Ms.) Stone:
deputy secretary of a department	The Honorable Joseph (Jane) Stone Deputy Secretary of _____	Dear Mr. (Ms.) Stone:

chairman, House Committee	The Honorable Joseph (Jane) Stone Chairman, (Chairwoman), Committee on _____ United States House of Representatives	Dear Mr. Chairman: *or* Dear Madam Chairwoman:
chairman, Senate Committee	The Honorable Joseph (Jane) Stone Chairman, (Chairwoman) Committee on _____ United States Senate	Dear Mr. Chairman: *or* Dear Madam Chairwoman:
chief justice, U.S. Supreme Court	The Chief Justice of the United States The Supreme Court of the United States	Dear Chief Justice Stone:
associate justice, U.S. Supreme Court	Justice Stone The Supreme Court of the United States	Dear Justice Stone:
commissioner (federal, state, or local)	The Honorable Joseph (Jane) Stone	Dear Mr. (Ms.) Stone:
delegate, state	The Honorable Joseph (Jane) Stone _____ House of Delegates State Capitol	Dear Mr. (Ms.) Stone:
governor	The Honorable Joseph (Jane) Stone Governor of _____	Dear Governor Stone:
judge, federal	The Honorable Joseph (Jane) Stone Judge of the United States Tax Court	Dear Judge Stone:
judge, state or local	The Honorable Joseph (Jane) Stone Judge of the Superior Court of _____	Dear Judge Stone:

	Form of Address	Salutation
lieutenant governor	The Honorable Joseph (Jane) Stone Lieutenant Governor of _____	Dear Mr. (Ms.) Stone:
mayor	The Honorable Joseph (Jane) Stone Mayor of _____	Dear Mayor Stone:
Postmaster General	The Honorable Joseph (Jane) Stone Postmaster General of the United States	Dear Mr. (Ms.) Stone:
President, U.S.	The President The White House	Dear President Stone:
former President, U.S.	The Honorable Joseph Stone	Dear Mr. Stone:
representative, state	The Honorable Joseph (Jane) Stone House of Representatives State Capitol	Dear Mr. (Ms.) Stone:
representative, U.S.	The Honorable Joseph (Jane) Stone United States House of Representatives	Dear Mr. (Ms.) Stone:
secretary of state, state	The Honorable Joseph (Jane) Stone Secretary of State State Capitol	Dear Secretary Stone:
senator, state	The Honorable Joseph (Jane) Stone The State Senate State Capitol	Dear Senator Stone:
senator, U.S.	The Honorable Joseph (Jane) Stone United States Senate	Dear Senator Stone:

Speaker, U.S. House of Representatives	The Honorable Joseph (Jane) Stone Speaker of the House of Representatives	Dear Speaker Stone:
Vice President, U.S.	The Vice President Executive Office Building	Dear Vice President Stone:

Professions

attorney	Mr. Joseph (Jane) Stone Attorney at Law *or* Joseph (Jane) Stone, Esq.	Dear Mr. (Ms.) Stone:
chiropractor	Joseph (Jane) Stone, D.C. (office) *or* Dr. Joseph (Jane) Stone (residence)	Dear Dr. Stone:
dentist	Joseph (Jane) Stone, D.D.S. (office) *or* Dr. Joseph (Jane) Stone (residence)	Dear Dr. Stone:
physician	Joseph (Jane) Stone, M.D. (office) *or* Dr. Joseph (Jane) Stone (residence)	Dear Dr. Stone:
veterinarian	Joseph (Jane) Stone, D.V.M. (office) *or* Dr. Joseph (Jane) Stone (residence)	Dear Dr. Stone:

	Form of Address	Salutation
Military		
admiral vice admiral rear admiral	Full rank, full name, abbreviation of service branch	Dear Admiral Stone:
airman first class airman airman basic	Full rank, full name, abbreviation of service branch	Dear Airman Stone:
cadet (air force, army)	Cadet Joseph (Jane) Stone United States Air Force Academy United States Military Academy	Dear Cadet Stone: *or* Dear Mr. (Ms.) Stone:
captain, (air force, army, coast guard, marine corps, navy)	Full rank, full name, abbreviation of service branch	Dear Captain Stone:
chief petty officer (coast guard, navy)	Full rank, full name, abbreviation of service branch	Dear Mr. (Ms.) Stone: *or* Dear Chief Stone:
chief warrant officer, warrant officer (air force, army, marine corps, navy)	Full rank, full name, abbreviation of service branch	Dear Mr. (Ms.) Stone:

Rank	Envelope	Salutation
colonel, lieutenant colonel (air force, army, marine corps)	Full rank, full name, abbreviation of service branch	Dear Colonel Stone:
commander (coast guard, navy)	Full rank, full name, abbreviation of service branch	Dear Commander Stone:
commodore (navy)	Full rank, full name, abbreviation of service branch	Dear Commodore Stone:
corporal (army), lance corporal (marine corps)	Full rank, full name, abbreviation of service branch	Dear Corporal Stone:
ensign (coast guard, navy)	Full rank, full name, abbreviation of service branch	Dear Mr. (Ms.) Stone: *or* Dear Ensign Stone:
first lieutenant, second lieutenant (air force, army, marine corps)	Full rank, full name, abbreviation of service branch	Dear Lieutenant Stone:
general, lieutenant general, major general, brigadier general (air force, army, marine corps)	Full rank, full name, abbreviation of service branch	Dear General Stone:
lieutenant commander, lieutenant, lieutenant (jg) (coast guard, navy)	Full rank, full name, abbreviation of service branch	Dear Mr. (Ms.) Stone: *or* Dear Lieutenant Stone:

359

	Form of Address	Salutation
major (air force, army, marine corps)	Full rank, full name, abbreviation of service branch	Dear Major Stone:
midshipman	Midshipman Joseph (Jane) Stone United States Coast Guard Academy United States Naval Academy	Dear Midshipman Stone:
petty officer (coast guard, navy)	Full rank, full name, abbreviation of service branch	Dear Mr. (Ms.) Stone:
private first class, private (air force, army, marine corps)	Full rank, full name, abbreviation of service branch	Dear Private Stone:
seaman, seaman apprentice, seaman recruit (coast guard, navy)	Full rank, full name, abbreviation of service branch	Dear Seaman Stone:
master sergeant (air force, army, marine corps)	Full rank, full name, abbreviation of service branch	Dear Sergeant Stone:
	Note: Other compound titles in enlisted ranks are not shown here. They all follow forms indicated for this example.	
specialist (army)	Full rank, full name, abbreviation of service branch	Dear Specialist Stone:

The Résumé

A résumé is a short description of your history in work and at school. Many white-collar jobs require a résumé from any prospective employee. At times, your résumé will be mailed to a prospective employer. What the résumé reveals about you may determine whether or not you are actually interviewed for a job.

The résumé should be neatly typed. If you are not a good typist, there are services that will retype the material you have written. Spelling and grammar should be correct. It is advisable to have someone else read over what you have written before you send it out. Once you are satisfied that what you have written is in good order, you will want to have copies made. Copies should be made on good quality paper. There are many small shops that reproduce résumés by photo offset or xerography. It is not in your best interest to send out copies of your résumé on the gray or pink slippery paper available in many library duplicating machines.

Format

Résumés have a fairly standard format. At the very top, give your name, address, and telephone number. Many people include their age and marital status, although it is not necessary to include them. You must judge whether your age and marital status will assist you in your job search or work against you.

The next item in the résumé is a brief paragraph that may be labeled "Objectives." In the paragraph, you indicate what job you are looking for and your major qualifications for such a job. Or you may simply use this paragraph to state your basic strengths and the nature of your past work.

Following this is the record of your work experience. This record is the main part of the résumé (except if you are looking for your first full-time job). Your work experience is listed with your most recent job first. The job before that is listed next, and so on with your first job listed last:

> 1977 to present
> 1973 to 1977
> 1970 to 1973

Usually, you give your title for each job and the name of the company (and division when relevant). Sometimes you may not want to reveal the name of your current employer in your résumé. Then you may write a descriptive phrase, such as "independent engineering consultant firm."

Résumés are generally kept to one page. If you have worked for a very long time at a variety of different jobs, it may be necessary to prepare a two-page résumé.

After the record of your work experience, list your schooling, any degrees, relevant noncredit courses, hobbies, honors, and affiliations that you consider worth including. For example, physical fitness is an asset: if you jog, swim, play tennis or golf, or engage in any other fitness activity, it may be worth noting. If you belong to professional societies, you should definitely list them. If you belong to social, civic, or volunteer organizations, list them only if you believe your membership in them is an asset. Do list any awards or honors you have received whether or not they are job-related. Such honors indicate that you are esteemed by others.

Looking for your first job

If you are looking for your first full-time job, you must review your work history somewhat differently. If you have held some sort of part-time or summer job or worked at volunteer jobs, these should be included. If you have participated in school extracurricular activities, these are worth mentioning. Your school record is also an indication of your ability and seriousness of purpose.

In seeking a first job, you must state your field of knowledge, that you are reliable, and that you can work well with others.

Whether you are looking for your first job or your fourth job, the time span from the end of schooling to the present should be accounted for on your résumé. You may be sure that a gap of a year or two will be noticed. If you have taken off a year and traveled around the world, say so. If you have attempted unsuccessfully to start your own business, say so. It is far better than allowing a prospective employer to wonder what you were doing with your time.

Below are two sample résumés. The first is for a person looking for a first job. The second résumé is for a person who has held several jobs. The résumé indicates that each job has involved more responsibility and skills than the previous job.

```
Leslie White
987 East Road
Elmwood, New Jersey 03103
987-6543
```

<u>Objective</u>

```
To find an entry-level job in sales
with a large international company.
Would like to utilize my knowledge
of French.
```

<u>Work</u> <u>experience</u>

Summers 1978, 1977

```
Group leader in a European teen-travel
summer trip. We traveled on bicycles
and by boat. Many of the arrangements
had been made in advance, but I often
had to make substitute arrangements
because of unforeseen events.
```

Summer 1976

Spent three months in France working as a volunteer on a farm. Did so to improve my spoken French.

Part-time employment 1977, 1978, 1979

Salesperson, college bookstore during school year.

School record

1979   B.A. magna cum laude with honors in French Literature and Language. Minor in History. Princeton University.

1975   Elmwood High School, class salutatorian. Honors in language and science.

Extracurricular activities

Member of soccer team in high school and college.
Contributor to school magazine in college.
President of French Club in high school.

Speak and write French fluently.
Have working knowledge of Spanish.

Courtney Black
123 Lincoln Street
Deerfield, Illinois 60015
789-3456

Objectives

To find a job that would utilize a
broad range of my managerial and business skills and offer the potential for
advancement in a large company.

Record of work experience

1977 to present Public Relations
Director for a small manufacturing
company

Am responsible for creating and maintaining a favorable public image by
preparing and disseminating news releases, arranging press conferences,
contests, conferences, and other
activities that keep the company in the
public eye. Supervise a staff of six
and work with various other departments: art, advertising, production,
etc. Maintain close working relations
with various people in the media and
local government.

1973 to 1977   Publicity Writer for the Widget Company

Wrote copy for publicity releases and other public-relations material. Know paper, printing, art styles. Many of my releases appeared in trade journals and local newspapers. Two-person office made for more responsibility than a publicity writer normally encounters.

1970 to 1973   Copy editor for Deerfield Gazette

Corrected copy and did proofreading for the local paper. Did some rewrite and occasional reporting.

Educational background

M.B.A. University of Illinois, 1976. Took night courses for master's degree.

B.A. University of Illinois, 1970. Major in Journalism. Received award for Most Promising Student.

Extracurricular: Worked on college newspaper; member of swim team.

<u>Affiliations</u> <u>and</u> <u>hobbies</u>

Member of Illinois Society of Publicity
Writers
Vice President of Alumni Association,
University of Illinois

Hobbies include swimming, tennis, and
directing amateur theater productions.

The cover letter

A résumé that will be mailed to a prospective employer should be accompanied by a cover letter. The cover letter should be straightforward and brief; it should not be a repetition of all the information contained in the résumé. You should state the specific position you are interested in, briefly discuss your experience, and refer the reader to the enclosed résumé. At the end of the letter you may wish to indicate that you will telephone the prospective employer for an interview.

You will, of course, have to write a separate cover letter for each specific position you want to apply for. The cover letter, like the résumé, should be neatly typed and quality paper should be used. Remember that the cover letter serves as your introduction to a prospective employer and that first impressions are very important. Be sure that the spelling and grammar are correct and that you have spelled all names and addresses properly.

Dear Sirs:

I am applying for the position of assistant sales manager, advertised in Sunday's Boston Globe. I have held a number of selling jobs and am currently working in the sales department of a large manufacturing company.

The enclosed résumé will furnish additional information on my background. I will telephone you next week for an interview. Thank you for your consideration.

Sincerely,

Ellen Kovalcik

Ms. Ellen Kovalcik

Business Letters

The formats of the following four letters are typical of those used in business correspondence, although other variations certainly exist. For example, in the sample executive letter the date could have been centered on the page instead of aligned with the right-hand margin.

Most letters are single-spaced, with double spacing between paragraphs. In the full block and modified block formats the first line of each paragraph aligns with the left-hand margin. In the modified semiblock and executive formats the first line is indented five to ten spaces.

When stationery without a printed letterhead is used, the mailing address of the sender is typed in two lines, centered, at the top of the page:

9988 Beacon Street
New York, New York 12345

Full Block

1 15 Lines
2 4, 6, or 8 Lines
3 Double Spaces
4 4 Lines
5 Copy notation
6 Enclosure notation
7 Identifying Initials

8 Writer's Name and Title
9 Complimentary Close
10 Body of Letter
11 Salutation
12 Inside Address
13 Date

Full Block

Houghton Mifflin Company

Two Park Street, Boston, Massachusetts 02107   Reference Division
(617) 725-5000   Cable HOUGHTON

13   April 3, 19--

12   Ms. Jennifer Stone
Vice President, Corporate Plans
CBA Corporation
43 Hunting Towers Suite 100
Jonesville, ST 98765

11   Dear Ms. Stone:

10   This is the Block Letter, all elements of which are aligned tight with the left margin. Spacing between letter parts is indicated by the key lines. Individual paragraphs in the message are single-spaced internally. Double-spacing separates each of the paragraphs.

If the letter exceeds one page, a continuation sheet may be used. The heading begins six lines from the top edge of the page. The heading includes the name of the addressee, the date, and the page number, blocked and aligned tight with the left margin as shown below:

Ms. Stone
Page 2
April 3, 19--

The message continues four lines below the heading. At least three message lines must be carried over to the continuation sheet: the complimentary close and the signature block should never stand alone there.

The writer's corporate title is shown under the typewritten signature. Typist's initials, enclosure notations, and carbon copy recipients are typewritten tight with the left margin and are spaced as shown by the key lines.

9   Sincerely yours,

John B. Brown

8   John B. Brown
Director of Marketing

7   JBB: ahs
6   enclosures (2)

cc: S.A. Langhorne

5

Atlanta · Dallas / Geneva, Illinois · Hopewell · New Jersey · Palo Alto · London

371

Modified Block

Modified Block

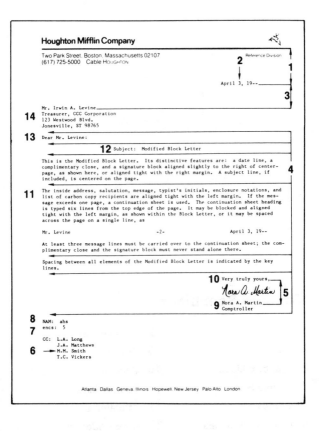

Houghton Mifflin Company

Two Park Street, Boston, Massachusetts 02107
(617) 725-5000   Cable HOUGHTON

Reference Division

2

1

April 3, 19--

3

Mr. Irwin A. Levine
14 Treasurer, CCC Corporation
123 Westwood Blvd.
Jonesville, ST 98765

13 Dear Mr. Levine:

12 Subject: Modified Block Letter

This is the Modified Block Letter. Its distinctive features are: a date line, a complimentary close, and a signature block aligned slightly to the right of center-page, as shown here, or aligned tight with the right margin. A subject line, if included, is centered on the page.

4

11 The inside address, salutation, message, typist's initials, enclosure notations, and list of carbon copy recipients are aligned tight with the left margin. If the message exceeds one page, a continuation sheet is used. The continuation sheet heading is typed six lines from the top edge of the page. It may be blocked and aligned tight with the left margin, as shown within the Block Letter, or it may be spaced across the page on a single line, as

Mr. Levine   -2-   April 3, 19--

At least three message lines must be carried over to the continuation sheet; the complimentary close and the signature block must never stand alone there.

Spacing between all elements of the Modified Block Letter is indicated by the key lines.

10 Very truly yours,

Nora A. Martin **5**

9 Nora A. Martin
Comptroller

8 NAM: ahs
7 encs: 5

CC: L.A. Long
     J.A. Matthews
6 ►M.M. Smith
     T.C. Vickers

Atlanta Dallas Geneva, Illinois Hopewell, New Jersey Palo Alto London

Modified Semiblock

1	15 Lines	**8**	Complimentary Close
2	Date	**9**	Body of Letter
3	4, 6, or 8 Lines	**10**	Salutation
4	Double Spaces	**11**	Subject Line
5	4 Lines	**12**	Attention Line
6	Identifying Initials	**13**	Inside Address
7	Writer's Name and Title		

Modified Semiblock

Houghton Mifflin Company

Two Park Street, Boston, Massachusetts 02107
(617) 725-5000   Cable HOUGHTON

Reference Division

2

1

April 3, 19--

3

3L Typesetters, Inc.
13 123 Industrial Park Road
Jonesville, ST 98765

12 Attention: John Hodges

11 Subject: Modified Semiblock Letter

10 Gentlemen:

        This is an example of the Modified Semiblock Letter. Its date line, com-
plimentary close, and signature block may be typed slightly to the right of center-page
or they may be positioned tight with the right margin, as shown here. The inside
address, salutation, and typist's initials are placed flush with the left margin. An
attention line, if used, is placed flush left. A subject line, if used, is centered
on the page.

9   Individual paragraphs of the Modified Semiblock Letter may be indented by
five or ten character spaces. Carried over lines are aligned tight with the left margin. Double spacing separates the single-spaced paragraphs.

        If the letter exceeds one page, a continuation sheet is used. At least three
message lines should be carried over to the continuation sheet: at no time should the   **4**
complimentary close and the signature block stand alone there.

        Continuation sheet headings in this letter style are typewritten across the
top of the page, six lines from the edge, as shown in the Modified Block facsimile.
The message continues four lines below the heading.

        If a postscript is added to the letter, it too is indented by five to ten
character spaces so as to align with the message paragraphs.

                                                    8 Sincerely,

                                                    Lee Matthews   **5**

                                                    7 Lee Matthews
                                                    Editor

LM: ahs

6
        It is not necessary to introduce a postscript with the abbreviation P.S.,
but the writer should initial the postscript, as shown here.

                                                    LM.

Atlanta Dallas Geneva Illinois Hopewell New Jersey Palo Alto London

Executive

Executive

2

1

April 3, 19--

3

13 Dear Mr. Fitzpatrick:

This is the Executive Letter. In this styling, the inside
address appears from two to five lines below the last line of the
signature block, depending on the length of the message. It is aligned tight with the left margin.

12   The date line appears flush with the right margin. The paragraphs are indented from five to ten character spaces, and lines that
are carried over are aligned flush left. Paragraphs are single-spaced
internally. Double spacing separates one paragraph from another.

The complimentary close is aligned under the date, tight with
the right margin. A typewritten signature block is unnecessary if the
writer's name and title are already included in the printed corporate
letterhead.   **4**

If the typist's initials and other notations are included,
they appear two lines beneath the last line of the inside address.

11 Sincerely,

5

10 Michael A. Robb
Director

6

John X. Fitzpatrick, Esq.
9 Fitzpatrick, Swanson, and Norton
Two Court Street
Jonesville, ST 98765

8 MAR: ahs

Enclosure

7

Atlanta Dallas Geneva, Illinois Hopewell New Jersey Palo Alto London

Minutes of Meetings

Format

Minutes are a brief and official record of the meeting of a group. They are prepared either by a recording secretary or by a specially designated member of the group.

Depending upon the group or the nature of the meeting, minutes may be formal or informal. Many organizations have preferred formats for minutes, and certain kinds of meetings, such as directors' or stockholders' meetings, have specific required formats. Regardless of the format, the following information is always included.

1. Name of the group.
2. Type of meeting: regular, special, etc.
3. Date, time, and place.
4. Names of those present and absent.
5. Name of presiding officer and recording secretary.
6. Proceedings:
   a. Presentation, amendments (if necessary), and approval of previous minutes.
   b. Unfinished business.
   c. New business.
7. Date of next meeting.
8. Hour of adjournment.
9. Signature of secretary.

Style

In preparing minutes you should keep the exact wording of resolutions and motions passed and the names of the proposers. Reports that are appended to the minutes or kept separate may be summarized. Frequently you will find it helpful to summarize the discussion.

It is important to remember that in addition to informing absent members of what took place at a meeting, minutes are an official record that may subsequently be referred to for a variety of purposes. Therefore they must be written cogently and accurately. Even though minutes present only the crucial points of a meeting, the recorder should take full notes to ensure that nothing has been missed. It is very helpful if copies of reports or other material to be presented at the meeting can be obtained beforehand.

Whether minutes are written up in a formal or informal format, care should be taken to ensure clarity and accessibility. The following style points may be used as general guidelines.

1. Minutes may be either single- or double-spaced. Good-sized margins should be provided when single-spacing minutes.
2. Pages should be numbered consecutively.
3. The substance of the minutes should be presented in a direct manner. The object is to relate what was discussed, what was decided, and what was left undecided as clearly as possible.

If the minutes are long and complex, various devices such as headings, subheadings, paragraph headings, and underscoring may be used. Paragraphs or sections may be numbered according to the numbered items on an agenda. Short meetings involving small groups or limited subjects lend themselves to a concise treatment similar to an outline. It is more common today, however, for minutes to be written in narrative form. In the latter case the person preparing the minutes must be especially careful that summarized information is complete enough to convey what transpired. Above all, it is important that the significant points of a meeting stand out and can be easily located.

Minutes should always be written in objective language. All personal opinions and biases should be excluded.

Index

Various kinds of meetings will require an index of important subjects discussed and actions taken. The index is kept in the form of a card index, with one subject to a card. References are listed chronologically and give the page number of the appropriate minutes.

Agenda

An agenda lists all the specific procedures to be covered at a meeting. The agenda may be formal, including such items as "Reading the minutes of the previous meeting'' and ''Adjournment.'' Or it may simply be an informal list of general topics to be discussed.

When preparing an agenda, you must ask every person invited to the meeting if he or she has something to be included. All items should be numbered and double- or tripled-spaced to leave room for notes.

Papers and Reports

Planning and research

A paper or report may be undertaken as a school assignment, a job assignment, a professional opportunity (giving a paper or publishing an article), or for other reasons.

At times, a very specific topic is assigned to you. At other times, you may choose any subject that interests you. Often, you are asked to look into a general subject area and choose a specific topic within it.

Certain techniques will be useful to you in preparing papers on any subject. These techniques can be applied to most subjects and will be suitable for a wide variety of source materials.

Basic research procedures

There is a great deal of work to be done before you begin to write. A good way to begin is to formulate a tentative title (which may or may not be the final title of your paper). The tentative theme may be too broad or too narrow. It may be a topic that you do not have the facilities to research. The title is merely a first statement of the general area of your research.

By definition, all research papers are based on some kind of data. All research papers also require that the writer collect, organize, present, and evaluate the data. Some papers rely very heavily on other people's evaluations. Other papers rely more heavily on the writer's own evaluations. In either case, it is not enough simply to reproduce sources.

The source materials

Before you commit yourself to a topic, consider the materials you will need: books, magazine articles, newspaper clippings, maps, recordings, sheet music, statistics, informants, etc. Begin to examine the library and make preliminary inquiries into other sources. Can you find what you need? If not, you will have to look farther afield, or you may have to restate your topic.

Breaking down the topic

At this point, make some preliminary notes for an outline. The outline notes may be revised, expanded, or totally reorganized once your research is under way. The data you encounter may not be what you expect to find, or it may set you thinking in a different line of reasoning. But you need some notes to start you off.

Take one topic as an example:

What will the world's population be in the year 2000?
Reasons for asking the question
Predictions:
    On what basis are they made?
    Do experts agree?
    Are there areas of general agreement?
    Are there areas of major disagreement?

The unpredictable:

    What events could alter predictions?

    How likely are those events?

    Have events altered past predictions?

Your own evaluations based on the source materials.

As you begin to read, you may want to shift your outline to stress a particular aspect of the topic:

    Shifts in the ratio of older people

    Relation of population growth to earth's resources

    Differences in population trends in developed and
       developing nations

Planning the work

It is best to begin by reading a general book or article about your topic. You may be fortunate enough to find an article that provides a good overall picture of the subject.

Once you have found a background source, further research may be structured in several ways. Different aspects of a topic may be studied one after another. More general material may be examined before more specific material. Material that is easier to understand may be examined before more difficult material, or data may be examined at random.

Practical considerations often impose a sequence of study. For example, research that requires travel must be planned for carefully. Sometimes it is necessary to wait for a reserved book or an inter-library loan. Time must be allotted realistically. Some extra time should always be allowed for the unexpected.

Taking notes

As you work, you will need to keep notes of what you learn. It is advisable to equip yourself with two kinds of index cards (either two sizes or two colors). One set of cards will be used to record your sources. Each card will represent a different source. The second set of cards will be used to take notes of specific information gained from a source. These cards will contain much of the substance of your paper. They will record quotes, opinions, analyses, and other data. They may also contain your own opinions of what you encounter.

In addition to the cards, some of your "notes" may be photocopies of library materials that you will need for reference. Copying machines help you duplicate charts, tables, statistics, as well as long quotations that you may want to use or consult.

Source cards

An index card should be made out for every source you consult. You may not quote every book and article, or even refer to each specifically, but you will probably want to include each in your bibliography.

Source cards will provide the data for bibliographies and footnotes. You can record your own general comments about each source on the card. And, because you have the full data on the source card, you will not need to repeat the full information on each information card.

For a *book,* include the following
- author's full name
- full title and subtitle
- publisher
- city of publication
- most recent copyright date
- edition (if there are several)
- editor, translator, or reviser (if any)
- number of pages

Most of this information will be found on the title page and the reverse of the title page (copyright page). Use the information as you find it. Use the publisher's name as it appears on that book. Indicate only the first city listed.

For a *magazine or newspaper article,* include:
- name of author (if any)
- title of the article
- name of magazine or newspaper
- the date
- volume and issue numbers
- the pages on which the article is found

Also keep cards for maps, sketches, works of art, recordings, filmstrips, and any other material you use. Make notes of the relevant numbers, the location (such as "city hall"), title (if any), and anything else that would enable you or someone else to find that same item again.

Mark the source of any material you photocopy.

Information cards

Most of your notes will record information or opinions you encounter. You may find yourself making a considerable number of information cards from one source and very few cards from another. Some notes will record specific statements, others will summarize ideas. Still others will contain brief quotations (*in quotation marks*). All cards should show the author's name and the page number (or numbers) from which the data was taken. If you are using more than one book or article by the same author, the title may substitute for the author's name. You have the full information for all these sources on your source cards.

Much of what you learned in your research will not be taken in notes. You will be forming ideas about the topic and the manner in which you intend to pursue it. Before you reach the end of your research, you should be able to prepare an outline that will show the final plan of the paper you will write.

Outlines

A substantial paper or report needs a good outline. A well-written paper is based on a well-balanced outline. In the finished product, the framework may be obvious or hidden, but it must be there.

A good outline has a structure of major divisions and subdivisions.

I. Roman numerals (I., II., III., etc.) mark off the major divisions of ideas in the paper.

   A. Capital letters (A., B., C., etc.) are used to subdivide ideas within each Roman numeral group.

      1. Arabic numerals (1., 2., 3., etc.) subdivide the ideas within each capital letter group.

         a. Lower-case letters (a., b., c., etc.) form the subgroups within the arabic numeral divisions.

It is not necessary to subdivide each topic. No topic, however, should have an **A.** subhead without also having a **B.** subhead. Similarly, if there is a **1.**, there must be a **2.**; if there is an **a.**, there must be a **b.** In other words, there should be at least two subdivisions within a category.

The subdivisions within an outline should be balanced. All **I** topics should be as important as **II** and **III** topics. Within each further division, there should also be balance.

Let us examine some possible outlines for the subject "What will the world's population be in the year 2000?" Note that in each example below, the title and the basic point of the outline in the paragraph following the title have been restated to suit the particular subject eventually chosen.

Outline 1

PLANNING FOR AN OLDER POPULATION

All evidence indicates that the proportion of old people to young people in society is increasing. The shift will require new planning for the future.

I. Evidence of the shift
- A. The declining birthrate
- B. The changing death rate
- C. Population profiles for the future
  1. Profiles based on current rates
  2. Profiles based on various predictions for the future
     a. same birthrate, lower death rate
     b. lower birthrate, same death rate
     c. lower birth and death rates

II. Implications of the population shift
- A. For work and retirement patterns
  1. Current patterns
  2. Prospective patterns
- B. For government planning
  1. Government income
  2. Government services
  3. Need for public institutions
- C. For people planning careers
- D. For industries

III. Planning for the future
- A. Fitting current data into planning schemes
- B. Monitoring future changes

IV. Steps to begin to take now

The outline above was written in phrases. The same outline can be written out in full sentences. It is often advisable to do so. Here, for example, is a fuller version of section I.

Outline 2

PLANNING FOR AN OLDER POPULATION

All evidence indicates that the proportion of old people to young people in society is increasing. The shift will require new planning for the future.

I. Evidence of the shift in the ratio of older people in the population is available in our present statistics.
  A. The birthrate is declining. Fewer children are born to the average woman.
  B. The death rate is decreasing. More people are reaching a greater age.
  C. From present statistics we can provide a profile of future population ratios. All profiles will suggest an older population.
    1. We can project the profiles by assuming the same birthrate and a lower death rate.
    2. We can assume a lower birthrate and the same death rate.
    3. We can assume both lower birth and death rates based on current trends.

The outline in sentence form is much clearer than

the phrasal outline. A sentence outline can often help to clarify thinking about a subject. It will reveal the strengths and weaknesses of the structure better than a phrasal outline will.

Below is an example of another outline (and a different title) based on similar subject matter.

Outline 3

IS THE WORLD'S POPULATION OUTGROWING
ITS RESOURCES?

The potential for population growth seems to be infinite. The world's population is doubling in shorter periods of time. The potential for developing the world's resources seems to be finite. Some people claim that we are rapidly approaching our population limits. Others claim that the crisis will not occur.

I. A historical look reveals the accelerating rate of population growth, food production, and energy growth and consumption.
   A. Patterns and rates of population growth have varied in specific periods of the past.
   B. Food production has increased in the past, but not always in step with population growth.
   C. Our need for energy has increased and our sources for energy have decreased.

II. Experts do not agree on the prospects for the future.

A. Pessimists argue that we are overpopulating the world and cannot forever expect to provide the resources for the people.
   1. They project growth charts that indicate evergreater numbers of people.
   2. They cite statistics that indicate limits to our capacity to feed people.
   3. They indicate that we are demanding more and more energy and are unable to continue to provide energy in the amount required for an unlimited time.
B. Optimists argue that although there is a theoretical limit to the number of people the world can support, we are not in danger of reaching that limit.
   1. They cite evidence of a leveling-off of population growth—with a possible zero population growth at some time in the future.
   2. They believe that we have not tapped all our food-production facilities and that we have the capacity to provide far more food than we now provide.
   3. They believe that there are new sources of energy that can provide us with an infinite energy supply.
C. There are areas of general agreement among virtually all experts.

1. It is theoretically possible to overpopulate the world.
2. Present food-growing techniques will not serve a greatly increased population.
3. Present energy technology cannot serve our future needs.

III. Whether you believe the optimists or the pessimists, prospects for the future are most hopeful if the rate of population growth slows and the resource potential is expanded.
   A. Several charts are provided to indicate possible future population patterns.
   B. Various new food-producing systems have been successful or unsuccessful. Reasons are examined.
   C. It is too early to evaluate new sources of energy.

Outline 3 differs from outline 2 in many respects. Outline 3 is subdivided to the same extent as outline 2, and the items in outline 3 are balanced to an unusual degree.

An outline will take various shapes depending on the nature of the data and the way the writer assembles the data. By the time the outline is prepared, the writer should know that the data is available. Sometimes the outline will reveal the need for further data in a particular area.

Relation of information cards to outline

Each writer has a distinct style of relating the information cards to the outline. Some people prepare the outline itself by arranging the cards to create a pattern. Other people develop a mental image of an outline as the research progresses. Then they arrange the cards to suit the outline.

Whatever system is used, at some point the cards will have to be organized to fit the outline. It is advisable to make notes of the subtopic on an upper corner of each card.

A finished paper should never read like an assortment of cards. The data on the cards will be used indirectly in some instances and directly in other instances. Sometimes a card will be no more than a way of reminding you to include an idea. Some cards may be irrelevant to the final topic. The notes may have been made before a final outline was drafted. Do not hesitate to eliminate irrelevant information. It is important for a writer to develop a sense of what is relevant and what is not.

Formats

Style points

A clean and inviting appearance is one of the most important considerations when putting a piece of writing into final form, whether you are composing an original paper based on your own research or organizing and styling a report based on another person's work. All job applicants know the importance of first impressions and hence the need to present a neat appearance when first meeting a prospective employer. Similarly, a cleanly typed and styled paper will encourage a reader to investigate it.

What will the final piece look like? Papers and reports can be written in either a formal or informal format. A formal paper, as we shall see, has a complex structure. An informal paper, on the other hand, may be comprised of only a short text with a title. At its simplest it may take the form of a business letter. But regardless of the format used, the following stylistic points should be observed.

1. All papers and reports need a cover or title page giving the title, the name of the writer, the date, and the name of the class or organization to which the project is being submitted.
2. All pages should be numbered in the same position, either centered at the top or on the upper-right corner.
3. All margins should be uniform. And they should not be skimpy.
4. Any charts, graphs, or similar material should be numbered. A standard style for the title and legend of figures should be maintained.

5. The paper or report should be double-spaced. Any quotation of five lines or more should be single-spaced and indented. Quotation marks should not be used for these. Legends may also be single-spaced.
6. Most papers and reports are typed on standard 8½″ by 11″ white paper. Certain organizations or kinds of projects require the use of preruled or otherwise nonstandard paper. In any case an original copy should always be typed on high-quality paper.

Organization is the second important consideration when planning the final format of a paper or report. A good appearance will encourage someone to begin reading your work, but only clarity of presentation and substance will get that person to read the piece through to the end and to consider it seriously.

Headings

The first decision you must make is whether a paper or report will benefit from the use of headings. A relatively brief or uncomplicated paper will usually require no headings. If well-planned, the framework should be apparent because the finished work has a logical and natural sequence of thought. A long or complicated paper, however, usually requires headings to distinguish among many topics and subtopics. If you are writing a paper or report from an outline, the outline itself will provide the headings and subheadings. If you are working from raw data or a rough outline, you will have to formulate headings. Headings should be brief and informative. Use a single word or a phrase instead of a complete sentence.

Let's say you are writing a paper titled "Planning for an Older Population." If you were working from outline 1, the paper might have the following headings:

EVIDENCE OF THE SHIFT TO AN OLDER POPULATION

The Declining Birthrate
The Changing Death Rate

IMPLICATIONS OF THE POPULATION SHIFT

For Work and Retirement Patterns
Current patterns
Prospective patterns
For Government Planning
Government income
Government services

Note that the gradation in importance of the headings is conveyed by the different styles in which they are printed. Each category of heading should be treated identically. If the first main heading is typed in capital letters and underlined, all successive main headings should be typed in capital letters and underlined.

The formal report

A formal paper or report is made up of different parts, each having a distinct purpose. (Many organizations have a preferred format; if so this will simplify your task.) What follows is the general format of a formal report; it is intended only as a guide and its various sections are adaptable to the needs of a specific project. However, a formal report always includes sections 1, 4, and 5.

1. Title Page and/or Cover
2. Introduction/Preface or Letter of Transmittal
3. Abstract or Summary
4. Table of Contents
   List of Tables and Illustrations
5. Text
   a. Introduction
   b. Discussion
   c. Conclusions and/or Recommendations
6. Appendix
7. Bibliography
8. Index

Title Page. This page contains the title of the paper, the name of the writer (and his or her position, if applicable), the name and address of the department or company (if the paper is written as a job assignment) or the name of the class (if the paper is written as a school project), and the date.

Cover. An informal paper often dispenses with a full title page and instead has a cover giving the title, the writer's name, and sometimes the name of the company or class to which it is submitted. A formal paper may have both a title page and a cover.

Introduction/Preface or Letter of Transmittal. An introduction or preface is a short statement of the subject, purpose, and scope of the paper along with any necessary information about its writer or background about its preparation. A letter of transmittal is more formal than, and is used in place of, an introduction. It is typed on regular business letterhead. In addition to giving some or all of the information contained in an introduction, it is directed specifically to the authorization or request for the paper.

Any acknowledgments, as of contributors, assistants, or sources that are not mentioned elsewhere, should appear in a separate paragraph at the end of the introduction or letter of transmittal.

Abstract or Summary. This is a brief synopsis, normally in one or two paragraphs, of the problem dealt with in the paper, the methodology used in examining it, and the conclusions reached. Once found almost exclusively in technical studies, the abstract is now widely used in academic and business papers. Its condensed form makes it useful in research and as accessible reference material; hence it has become one of the most important parts of a formal paper or report.

Table of Contents. This lists the titles of the chapters or principal sections of the paper (and their numbers, if any are used), the subheadings or subtopics within each chapter or section, the appendix, bibliography, and index, and the page number on which each begins.

Since the actual text of any paper always begins on page 1, all pages preceding the text (including the table of contents) are numbered in Roman numerals and should be so listed in the contents table if you choose to include them. Everything listed in the table of contents should be entered in the exact order in which it appears in the finished work.

The heading of the page, always centered, is *Contents* (*Table of* is now considered extraneous). The table itself begins an inch or two below the heading and is set up in outline form. Chapters, sections, etc., are placed on the left side of the page and page numbers on the right. You may use a string of periods as a leader to connect the left-hand entry to the page number if you wish. In addition, many people use the subheadings *Chapter* and *Page* on top of the left- and right-hand columns respectively.

List of Tables and Illustrations. Many papers make extensive use of tables and illustrations (all illustrations are individually referred to in text as *figures*). These lists follow the table of contents and have the headings *Tables* and *Illustrations*. If the contents page is set with column subheadings, these lists should conform to style, using *Table* and *Figure* on the left and *Page* on the right.

Text. The text of a paper or report should be a logically organized and clearly written presentation. An introduction states the purpose and scope of the project, the methodology used, any pertinent background information, and a brief statement of the conclusions drawn. The discussion is a detailed study of the subject, presented as briefly and succinctly as possible. The final section of the text presents a full explanation of the conclusions and/or recommendations produced by the study.

Appendix. All supplementary materials, such as maps, charts, or graphs, that provide background to or amplification of the topic are listed in the appendix. If there are two or more appendixes, they should be distinguished by letters (capitals) or numbers (Arabic or Roman, though the latter should be used only if they are not used to refer to chapters or sections). A glossary of pertinent terms or list of abbreviations may be placed in the appendix or in a separate section immediately following.

Bibliography. A paper or report that makes use of material from outside sources (including such things as unpublished articles or reports and speeches) requires a bibliography citing those sources (see p. 407).

Index. An index is used primarily in a long and involved work. It lists in alphabetical order all the main topics covered in the paper or report and can usually be put together by rearranging the table of contents. Certain works, however, require a detailed index that goes beyond the contents page listings and can only be drawn from the text itself. This can be a difficult task and there is a specific method to follow (see p. 409).

Writing the paper

It is not necessary to be a great writer to produce a good paper or report. It is necessary to have a good grasp of the major ideas, good information, and a good outline. By the time you are ready to write, you should be familiar with any new words or terms used in the field, and you should be capable of explaining them.

The most difficult part to write is the first paragraph. It should set the stage for what follows. A first paragraph may raise an interesting question that you will answer or attempt to answer later in the paper. It may, instead, propose an idea that will be examined. It may argue a cause, state a conclusion, or do any of a number of other things. At times, a first paragraph may begin with a quotation that will serve as a theme for agreement or disagreement. Above all, the first paragraph should be interesting and should be related to the rest of the paper.

Keep your writing as simple as possible. Use unusual long words when they are the most appropriate words, but do not try to introduce learned words just to sound learned. If the subject you are dealing with has its own vocabulary, do use the appropriate vocabulary. Try to avoid sentences that must be read and reread to arrive at their meaning. Often such sentences can be broken down to their components and rewritten with greater clarity.

There should be a logical flow from sentence to

sentence and paragraph to paragraph. One idea will flow into the next, and your writing will be persuasive. Often when a flow of ideas is lacking, it is because the writer has not absorbed the material well and is simply recording one note after another.

A logic should also exist from section to section of a work. Transition sentences or paragraphs prepare the way for the introduction of new subject matter.

Many people believe that clear writing is related to clear thinking. If you are having a great deal of trouble putting your thoughts into writing, re-examine your thinking. Are you confident of your ideas and your data? Can other conclusions be drawn from your work? If so, how will you deal with them? If you are not confident of your material, do you have enough time to do some more research? If not, can you redefine and limit your topic to material with which you are comfortable?

The preparation of any written work offers an opportunity for the writer to examine new topics, learn new research procedures, and sharpen writing skills. Some papers may be more successful than others, but over the years a person should gain confidence and ability in preparing them.

Preparing footnotes

Footnotes are an important element in any paper or report because they can convey many kinds of information. They must, however, be used judiciously; an absence of any or an overabundance can ruin the finished work.

Footnotes are used for specific purposes:

1. To give the source of quotations, charts, tables, graphs, statistics that you copy as found.
2. To give the source of ideas, arguments, facts, or other data that you present in your own words or diagrams.
3. To give the source of something that is not gleaned from general research.
4. To substantiate your own arguments.
5. To offer comments that are not part of the main idea.

Reference footnotes have a particular style. They begin with a number (typed half space above the line) and are followed by the remaining data. The first reference to a book or article is usually given in full. Further references are given in short form. Below are some examples of footnotes:

First mention of a book
[1] John Wain, *Samuel Johnson* (New York: The Viking Press, 1974), p. 183.

Further references to the same book:
[2] Wain, p. 187.

Two books by same author(s)

[3] Carl Bernstein and Bob Woodward, *All the President's Men* (New York: Simon and Schuster, 1974), p. 71.

Further references:

[4] Bernstein and Wood, *President's Men,* p. 92.

[5] Bob Woodward and Carl Bernstein, *The Final Days* (New York: Simon and Schuster, 1976), p. 77.

Further references:

[6] Woodward and Bernstein, *Final Days,* p. 283.

(Note that even though the authors have listed their names in reverse order on the second book, it is advisable to repeat the title in further references to avoid confusion.)

Footnote for a book with an editor, but no author

[7] Fred L. Israel, ed., *1897 Sears Roebuck Catalog* (New York: Chelsea House, 1968), p. 149.

For an article in an anthology

[8] John T. Hitchock, "Fieldwork in Ghurka Country," in *Being an Anthropologist,* ed. George D. Spindler (New York: Holt, Rinehart and Winston, 1970), pp. 164–165.

Further references:

[9] Hitchcock, p. 173.

For a signed magazine article

[10] Edwin S. Dethlefsen and Kenneth Jensen, "Social

Commentary from the Cemetery," *Natural History,* June–July 1977, p. 34.

Further references:
[11] Dethlefsen and Jensen, p. 37.

For an unsigned magazine article
[12] "Estrogen Therapy: The Dangerous Road to Shangri-La," *Consumer Reports,* Nov. 1976, p. 642.

Further references:
[13] "Estrogen Therapy," p. 644.

For a signed encyclopedia article
[14] Philip James, "Orchestration," *Encyclopedia International,* 1972, Vol. 13, pp. 464–466.

For a famous play
[15] *Much Ado about Nothing,* III, iii, 53–55.

The styles of footnotes used to add commentary or asides may vary. One example would be:
[16] The *Oxford English Dictionary* gives an obsolete meaning for *population* as "devastation, laying waste." Many who fear the effects of overpopulation might tend to support this definition.
(Note: the *Oxford English Dictionary* is a standard general reference. Unlike other references cited, it would not normally appear in a bibliography.)

Footnotes should be typed single-space at the bottom of the page or they can be listed at the end of each section or at the end of the text itself. If placed on the page, footnotes should be typed single-space with a double space between them if there are two or more. Notes are separated from the text by a short line. You must be careful when typing to leave enough room at the bottom to fit in all the footnotes on the page. Notes placed at the end of a section have the centered heading "Footnotes" or simply "Notes." If all the notes are placed at the end of the text you will need to provide the appropriate chapter or section headings.

The works listed in the footnotes, as well as other works that might not be quoted directly, are listed in the bibliography.

Preparing a bibliography

Strictly speaking, a bibliography is a list of books or printed articles, but it may also include material other than printed matter (interviews, graphic works, filmstrips, etc.).

Items in a bibliography follow a particular format. Note that the format is *not* the same as the format for footnotes.

1. *Author's name* is given last name first. If there is more than one author, all the authors after the first are listed first name first.

All books by one author are listed before the books in which that author collaborated with another.

A period follows the author's name.

2. *Full titles are given and underlined* if they are titles of books. Titles of stories, poems, and articles are given in quotation marks. A period follows the title.

3. City of publication, followed by a colon and the publisher (as shown on the book used) are given, followed by the copyright date.

4. For articles, stories, and poems, the pages on which they appear are given.

What do you list in a bibliography? Certainly, you list all books or articles that have been footnoted. Often you list other books or articles that proved useful as general background but not as a source of specific footnotes. Do not list books that were consulted but did not prove helpful.

Sample bibliography:

BIBLIOGRAPHY

Carson, Rachel. *The Sea Around Us*. New York: The New American Library, 1961.

———. *Silent Spring*. Boston: Houghton Mifflin Company, 1962.

Hamilton, Roger. "Can We Harness the Wind?" *National Geographic,* December, 1975.

Hitchcock, John T., "Fieldwork in Ghurka Country." In *Being an Anthropologist,* ed. George D. Spindler. New York: Holt, Rinehart and Winston, 1970, pp. 164–193.

Kahn, Herman. *Thinking about the Unthinkable.* New York: Horizon Press, 1962.

_____ and Anthony J. Wiener. *The Year 2000.* New York: Macmillan Company, 1967.

Ternes, Alan, ed. *Ants, Indians, and Little Dinosaurs.* New York: Charles Scribner's Sons, 1975.

Note: If you list two books by one writer, the name may be replaced by a dash for the second reference.

A guide to MLA documentation style

In 1984, the Modern Language Association (MLA) introduced a new style of documenting sources in research papers. MLA style has three main features:

1. A section entitled "Works Cited" at the end of the paper. This must be a thorough and accurate list of the sources of the words, ideas and evidence presented in the text because it is the only place your reader will find complete bibliographic references.

2. Brief parenthetical references within the text that document material borrowed from another

source and direct your readers to the full citation in the list of works cited.

3. Sparing use of footnotes or endnotes to present commentary or explanation or bibliographical notes containing several source citations.

Preparing the list of works cited

To prepare the list of works cited, follow these general guidelines:

1. Paginate the Works Cited section as a continuation of your text.
2. Double-space within and between entries.
3. Begin the first line of an entry at the left margin, and indent successive lines five spaces.
4. List entries in alphabetical order according to the last name of the author.
5. If you are listing more than one work by the same author, alphabetize his or her works according to title. In place of the author's name in the second and following entries, type three hyphens and a period.
6. Underline the titles of independent works, such as books, plays, and films. Use quotation marks around the titles of shorter works, such as poems, sections of a larger work, or unpublished works.
7. Whenever possible, use shortened forms for the publisher's name (Houghton instead of Houghton Mifflin Co.)

8. Separate author, title, and publication information with a period followed by two spaces.
9. Use a colon to separate the volume number and the year of a periodical from the page numbers.

Sample entries:

Two or more books by the same author

Hirsch, E. D., Jr. *Cultural Literacy: What Every American Needs to Know.* Boston: Houghton, 1987.

_____. *The Philosophy of Composition.* Chicago: U of Chicago P, 1977.

An article from a monthly or bimonthly periodical

Edsall, Thomas Byrne. "The Return of Inequality." *Atlantic* June 1988: 86–94.

Documenting sources

Document sources within the text as follows:

1. Cite the author's last name and the page number(s) of the source in parentheses at the end of the sentence but before the final period; or
2. Use the author's last name in your sentence, and place only the page number(s) of the source in parentheses at the end of the sentence but before the final period; or
3. Give the author's last name in your sentence when you are citing the *entire* work rather than a

specific section or passage, and omit any parenthetical reference.

4. Place a parenthetical reference *within* your sentence, as close as possible to the part of the sentence it documents. Place it at the end of the clause after closing quotation marks but *before* the punctuation.

5. When a reference documents a long quotation set off from the text, place it at the end of the passage quoted but *after* the final period.

Sample entry:

> One historian argues that since the invention of television "our politics, religion, news, athletics, education and commerce have been transformed into congenial adjuncts of show business, largely without protest or even much popular notice" (Postman 3–4).

The citation looks like this:

Works Cited

Postman, Neil. *Amusing Ourselves to Death: Public Discourse in the Age of Show Business.* New York: Penguin-Viking, 1985.

Using notes

In MLA style, notes (preferably endnotes) are used:

1. To give additional commentary on information in the text.
2. To list several sources or to refer readers to additional sources. A note is signaled with a superscript numeral typed at the appropriate place in the text, such as the end of the sentence. The note itself, identified by a matching number followed by a space, appears at the end of the text (endnote) or at the bottom of the page (footnote).

Additional information, including detailed examples, can be found in *MLA Handbook for Writers of Research Papers* by Joseph Gibaldi and Walter S. Achert (New York: The Modern Language Association of America, 1988).

Preparing an index

An index is a list of all significant topics covered in a paper, report, book, article, etc. It is made from the page proofs of a printed work or the final copy of a typed work to ensure that all page numbers are final. The following procedure is used in compiling an index.

Working with the text, underline all items to be indexed; these include chapter or section headings and subheadings, important ideas and theories, and the names of events, places, people, things, etc.

The second step is to transfer the information to 3″

by 5″ cards. Write the subject on the top left, followed by a comma and the appropriate page number or numbers. Use a separate card for each item, including cross-references.

Next arrange the cards alphabetically by subject. During this step you should remove all insignificant items. An overlong index containing trivial entries will be of little use to the reader.

Finally, type the entries double-spaced in a list in either a single- or double-column format. The latter style is preferable and the entries in most indexes should be brief enough to accommodate it.

A number of points should be kept in mind. Entries should be as brief and specific as possible, usually a single word or a phrase. Always index according to the most important word in a phrase.

address to, forms of, 348–360

Avoid if possible a string of page references following a single entry. In such a situation you will usually be able to develop subentries from the text to indicate what aspect of the entry is dealt with at each reference.

For cross-references use the words "See" or "See also." The former is a straight cross-reference and does not have page numbers, which are always entered at the primary index entry. Page numbers are entered when "See also" is used since the cross-reference is to additional information at another entry.

Proofreading

At one time or another everyone has done some simple proofreading, such as reading over a letter to see that everything is correct or checking over a list to see that nothing has been omitted. Strict proofreading involves marking corrections in copy with textual symbols and marginal notations. Knowing how to use proofreaders' marks is helpful if you are a student proofing a theme to be typed or an office worker proofing the final copy of a report, financial statement, etc., before or after it is typed or printed by a compositor.

The act of proofreading involves checking a typed or printed piece of copy against the original manuscript. While there is no single preferred method used in proofreading, there are basic guidelines.

1. Take as much time as you need to ensure accuracy. Most copy to be proofread, especially material that comes from a compositor, has very few mistakes. It is as easy to miss errors in clean copy as it is in dirty copy.
2. Read the copy through to the end once to understand its meaning; then forget about meaning. While some people appreciate suggestions, for example, how wording could be improved, the proofreader's primary responsibility is seeing that everything that is supposed to be in the text is in and that the material is correctly spelled, spaced, etc.

It is a good idea to read through the copy a number of times, checking for different things on each pass (i.e., spelling and punctuation, spacing and alignment). Read the copy three or four characters at a time, saying each letter, punctuation mark, and word space aloud. Remember that a misplaced comma is as crucial an error as a misspelled word. Complicated material, such as intricate tables and charts, is best proofread by two people, one reading from the original while the other checks the copy.

3. Take nothing for granted. Spelling and punctuation errors get by the proofreader who does not check every single word or mark that he or she is unsure about. Remember that even the original copy can contain spelling errors. Important pieces of copy should receive a second proofreading by another proofreader.

What follows is a chart containing the proofreaders' marks and a sample of marked copy.

PROOFREADERS' MARKS

Instruction	Mark in Margin	Mark in Type	Instruction	Mark in Margin	Mark in Type
Delete	(delete)	the ~~good~~ word	colon		The following words∧ skim the
Insert indicated material	good	the∧word	semicolon	∧;	Scan the words∧ the words.
Let it stand	stet	the good word	apostrophe	∨	John's words
Make capital	cap	the word	quotation marks	∀/∀/	the word word
Make lower case	lc	The Word	parentheses	(/)	The word word is in parentheses.
Set in small capitals	sc	See word.	brackets	[/]	He read from the Word the Bible.
Set in italic type	ital	The word is word.	en dash	-N-/	1964 1972
Set in roman type	rom	the (word)	em dash	-M-/	The dictionary how often it is needed belongs in every home.
Set in boldface type	bf	the entry word	Start paragraph	¶	"Where is it?" "It's on the shelf."
Set in lightface type	lf	the entry (word)	Move left	⊏	⊏ the word
Transpose	tr	the (wo/rd)	Move right	⊐	the word
Close up space	◠	the wo rd	Align	‖	‖ the word / the word
Delete and close up space	◠ (with marks)	the word	Wrong font	wf	the word
Spell out	sp	(2) words	Broken type	✕	the word
Insert space	#	the word			
period	⊙				
comma	∧				
hyphen	=				

Sample copy

It is the proofreader's job to ensure that all
typed or printed material is properly spaced and
aligned and contains grammatical, typographical, or
spelling errors. Mark all corrections in a color that
is clearly distinguished that from of the copy. Each
correction requires a symbol in the text and a corresponding explanation in the margin next to the line
in which it is found. if there are 2 or more corrections in one line, write them in the margin the proper order and separate them with a slanting line. Material to be inserted is written in the margin and its
place is indicated by a caret. If you make you more an
improper correction, and these things do happen do
not erase it, put a series of periods below what you
have mistakenly crossed out in the text and write stet
(which means "Let it stand" in the margin.

¶ Always remember to take your time. The proofreader has
only one goal, total accuracy. Never assume or guess that
something is right. Check every word whose spelling you
are unsure of in your copy of The American Heritage Dictionary. ital

418

The Library

The card catalog

The card catalog is your best tool for finding books in the library. In some libraries, the card catalog may also help you locate records, filmstrips, microfilms, microfiches, etc. In other libraries, these materials may have their own reference systems. But books will be listed in the card catalog.

What exactly is a card catalog? A card catalog is an index of books, arranged alphabetically in a set of file drawers usually with 3″ x 5″ cards. Each file drawer is usually labeled to show what portion of the alphabet it contains. The cards list the information about the books: author, title, subject or subjects covered in the book. Some cards give cross-references to other cards. A few cards are information cards: they do not direct you to a particular book, but tell you where to find cards for items that may be hard to locate.

No matter where a book is situated in the library, the card will direct you to it. Although the cards are listed alphabetically, the books are not arranged alphabetically on the shelves. Libraries in the United States usually organize their books by one of two systems: the Dewey Decimal System, or the Library of Congress System. Both systems classify books into the major fields of knowledge, and will be explained in the section "Organization of the Library." Thus, mathematics books will be in one section, history books in another, and so on. Within each broad area of knowledge there are subdivisions. While these systems create an orderly arrangement for the library, without the card catalog it would be very difficult for the average individual to find the required books. The card catalog is an efficient way of directing people to the books they want. Cards are added to the catalog for new books as the books are acquired; cards are eliminated for books that are discarded. Material on the cards can help a person decide if that book will be helpful.

Organization of the cards

The cards in the card catalog are alphabetized word by word. That means that all the cards beginning, for example, with "New" will be placed before the cards beginning with "News" or "Newton." Thus the order will be:

> New astronomy theories
> New Jersey
> New mathematics
> New ports
> New theories of science
> New York
> Newark
> Newport
> News

News gathering
Newton, Isaac
Newtonian physics
Newts

The word-by-word method of alphabetizing differs from the method used by dictionaries. In dictionaries, each word or phrase is alphabetized as if it were written as one word. In a dictionary system, "Newark" would come before "New Jersey" and "New York."

Also, in a card catalog, all abbreviations are listed as if they were spelled out. Thus, "Mt." would be listed as if spelled "mount" and "St." would be listed as if spelled "saint." "Mc" and "M'" would be listed as if spelled "Mac." Articles (a, an, the) are not considered if they appear at the beginning of a title. (*The House of Seven Gables* would be alphabetized at *House,* not at *The.*)

If there are books *by* a person and *about* that same person, all the books *by* that author would be listed before all the books *about* the author.

In situations that are very complicated, an information card in the drawer will often clarify matters. For example, there are many kings named Henry from many countries. There are also people whose last names are Henry. How do you figure out which comes first? An information card will usually explain the order used in the catalog.

What do the cards tell you?

So far, we have investigated how the cards are arranged in the catalog. But the cards are designed to direct you to the books themselves. To find the books, you need to understand what can be learned from the cards.

In the first place, a card in the catalog tells you that the book you want is in the library's collection. The card will not tell you if someone else has the book out on loan, and in many libraries, will not indicate whether the book is at the bindery for repairs. The card will let you know whether the book may be borrowed or must be used in the library, in which case the card is stamped "Reference." In some cases, the most recent edition of a book is a reference book, but an older edition of the same book may be taken out on loan. Then there are usually two cards in the catalog. One is stamped "Reference," the other is not. Or the word "Reference" is inked out on the older card.

Other items that may be learned from a catalog card are: the author's full name, date of birth, date of death, title and subtitle of book, copyright date of the book, number of pages, and publisher. You can learn whether the book has illustrations, a bibliography, an introduction by someone other than the author. Some cards will give the date when a book was first published if the book is a new edition or revision. At the bottom of the card, there are notations that indicate where other cards may be found in the catalog for that same book. These notations can be helpful if you want to pursue the subject matter in other books.

The most important thing that you can learn from the card is the book's *call number,* which will direct you to the shelf on which the book can be found. The call number may look like this: 828.609 (B) if the book is classified by the Dewey Decimal System, or like this: PR3533.w33 if the book is classified by the Library of Congress system. Some books may have no call number. Works of fiction—especially contemporary fiction—are often arranged by author's last name in a separate fiction section in a library. Some catalog cards may have *Fic.* or *F.* in the corner where one would normally find the call number. Other libraries place nothing at all on the fiction cards.

Biographies may be treated as a separate category in some libraries. The call number on a biography book may simply be a *B* (for biography) followed by the first initial of the last name of the person about whom the book is written. Thus, a biography *about* Sigmund Freud would have B-F where the call number would normally appear. A biography *by* Sigmund Freud *about* Woodrow Wilson would have B-W for the call number.

Before we pursue the question of library organization, let us consider some sample catalog cards.

Author cards

Librarians consider the author card to be the basic catalog card. Most books have authors. Sometimes the author is one individual. Sometimes several people, a committee, foundation, magazine, or even the U.S. Government may be the "author" of a book.

The author card lists the author's name, last name first. On the line below, it lists the title of the book. If there are ten books in the library by one author, there will be ten author cards, one for each book. Those cards will be listed alphabetically by their titles.

For example, if you wanted to find books written by Herman Kahn, you would look up "Kahn, Herman" and find:

```
Kahn, Herman
    Thinking about the unthinkable.  Horizon
Press [c1962]  254 p.




            Includes bibliographical references.


1. Atomic warfare          2. U.S.--For. rel.
I Title
```

After that card, you might find:

The first book, *Thinking About the Unthinkable,* was written in 1962 by Herman Kahn. It has 254 pages and bibliographical references. Other catalog cards may be found at: Atomic warfare, U.S.-Foreign relations, and *Thinking About the Unthinkable.*

Most important of all, the card tells you that the book will be found on the shelf with other books having the number 355K. (The K is for Kahn).

The second book by Herman Kahn has a different number: 301.2–K. It falls into a different subject area. It was written by Herman Kahn and other people. Its copyright date is 1967. The book has 431 pages and is illustrated. Other catalog cards for the same book may be found at: Twentieth century, forecasts, Hudson Institute, and *(The) Year 2000.*

Some authors do not write under their own names. The library may list the book at the pseudonym or at the real name. The card catalog will clarify the name and the spelling that the library uses.

```
Twain, Mark
     see
Clemens, Samuel Langhorne
```

All the catalog cards for Mark Twain will be found under "Clemens." And you will find, when you look at the Clemens cards, that not all the fiction by Mark Twain is to be found in the fiction section. Some will be found in the American Literature section. The call number will direct you to the correct section.

Not all writers who use pseudonyms are listed at their real names. When you look up an author, look under the name that you are familiar with. The card catalog will inform you whether the author is listed by his or her pseudonym or real name.

The United States government and its branches may be the "author" of a book. If you try to look up "Library of Congress" in the card catalog, a cross-reference card will tell you to look under "U.S. Library of Congress." There you will find books with "U.S. Library of Congress" as the official author. Following all the author cards, you will find books *about* the Library of Congress. Some of the books about the Library of Congress may have been compiled by the U.S. Library of Congress staff. Others may have been written by individuals.

Title cards

Suppose that you know the title of a book, but don't know who wrote it. The card catalog can help you find it. Titles are also listed in the card catalog in alphabetical order.

The title card gives the title above the author's name. The title is usually typed in. Then the author's name is given, and the title is repeated again. A title card is really the basic author card with the title shown at the top.

If you wanted to find a book named *My Antonia,* you would look under *My.*

```
    My Antonia

Cather, Willa Sibert

    My Antonia.  Houghton Mifflin Co.

Boston.      371 p.
```

There is no call number on this card because it is a work of fiction and will be found in the fiction section under Cather.

Sometimes several short novels are bound into one volume. The volume may have the title of one of the short novels. How do you find the other short novels? Try the card catalog. For example, if you wanted to find *Neighbour Rosicky,* look up *Neighbour*:

```
    Neighbour Rosicky

Cather, Willa Sibert

    Neighbour Rosicky (In Obscure destinies.)
```

The short novel *Neighbour Rosicky* may be found in the volume *Obscure Destinies.* Although the card catalog may help you find short novels, it will usually *not* help you find short stories, poems, plays, and essays. To find these you need reference books. (See the next section, "Basic Reference Materials.")

The main thing to remember when looking for a title card is to ignore the article at the beginning of the title. Look for *A Tale of Two Cities* at "Tale," not at "A." Look for *The Uses of Enchantment* at "Uses" not at "The."

Suppose you are not sure if the name by which you know a book is an author's name or the title. For example, if you wanted to find *The Guinness Book of World Records,* look it up under *Guinness.*

```
                                        Reference
Guinness book of world records. Sterling
   Pub. Co. 19--     illus. ports

   Title varies: The Guinness book of

superlatives.


   1. Curiosities.     (1) Title: The Guinness
book of superlatives
```

The authors' names are omitted from this card, but
a card for an older edition reveals that the authors
were Norris McWhirter and Ross McWhirter.

Some books—such as reference books—have no
official author, since they are compiled by groups of
people. When they are published, these books can be
located by their titles.

Subject cards

Most researchers find that the subject cards are the
most useful cards in the catalog. Often there are some
cards that refer you to books that cover the broad
subject and other cards that refer to books on subdivisions of the subject. There may also be an information card that leads you to related topics.

Suppose that you are doing some research on costumes. Perhaps you must design and make costumes for a play that takes place in eighteenth-century England. You look up the subject COSTUME in the card catalog. Note that the subject card is the basic author card with the subject printed (or typed) in capitals at the top of the card.

```
COSTUME

Evans, Mary     1890-          391-E
    Costume through the ages.  Philadelphia,
Lippincott (c 1950)   360 p. illus. ports.


    "Revised edition."
    Includes bibliographies.


1. Costume    2. Costume - Hist.    I Title
```

The first book you see is *Costume Through the Ages* by Mary Evans. It has illustrations and portraits, and it is a revised edition. That suggests that it was sufficiently interesting to bring out a revised edition. It also has bibliographies. But since the copyright date is 1950, any books listed in the bibliographies will have been printed before 1950.

Other books are listed under the general subject COSTUME. There is also a cross-reference card:

```
COSTUME

    see also

CHURCH VESTMENTS
CLOTHING AND DRESS
FASHION
UNIFORMS
```

These other subjects may or may not be useful in your research. You make a note of the subjects that may help.

After the general subject COSTUME are books on particular aspects of the general subject. For example:

COSTUME—GREAT BRITAIN
COSTUME, THEATRICAL

Both of these subcategories will be helpful in the particular research you are doing, and you note the books listed under each one.

For example, this card may appear:

```
COSTUME, THEATRICAL

  Voland, Virginia              792.42-V
    Designing women; the art and practice of
  theatrical costume design.  Garden City,
  Doubleday (c 1966) 197 p.
```

The book seems to be one that may help you actually make the costumes once you have decided what the costumes are to look like. You make a note of it.

The card catalog can lead you to books, but it cannot help you decide if the books are what you need. To know if a book is useful, you must examine it.

Organization of the library

Today there are two organizational systems that are widely used in the United States: the Dewey Decimal System and the Library of Congress System. When you enter a library see if the books have Dewey Decimal System call numbers (e.g. 792.42) or Library of Congress call numbers (e.g. PN 1993.5). Note that the Dewey Decimal System call numbers begin with Arabic numerals. The Library of Congress call numbers begin with letters.

The call numbers stand for certain categories. The categories in the Dewey Decimal System differ from the categories in the Library of Congress system.

Dewey Decimal System

000	Generalities—bibliographies, encyclopedias, libraries, etc.
100	Philosophy and related disciplines
200	Religion
300	Social science—statistics, political science, economics, law, education, etc.
400	Language—linguistics, other languages
500	Pure sciences—mathematics, astronomy, physics, chemistry, earth science, biological science, botany, zoology, etc.
600	Technology—medicine, engineering, agriculture, domestic science, business, etc.
700	The arts—architecture, sculpture, drawing, painting, photography, music, recreational arts
800	Literature and rhetoric—American and English literature, literature from other languages
900	General geography, history, etc.

Each category is subdivided further (401, 426, 492, etc.) and decimal numbers may be added to make further distinctions (426.12, 792.42, etc.). On the shelf, all the books are arranged in numerical order. Books without the decimal are arranged before books with the decimal (792, 792.12, 792.42, etc.)

Library of Congress System

A	General works
B	Philosophy and religion
C	History and auxiliary sciences
D	History and topography (except America)
E & F	America
G	Geography and anthropology
H	Social sciences
J	Political sciences
K	Law
L	Education
M	Music
N	Fine arts
P	Language and literature
Q	Science
R	Medicine
S	Agriculture
T	Technology
U	Military science
V	Naval science
Z	Bibliography and library science

Note that the letters I, O, W, X, and Y are not included. If further categories become necessary, they may some day be used.

Categories in the Library of Congress System are further subdivided with a second letter, then a numeral of one to four digits, then a decimal followed by a numeral or a letter and a numeral. Sometimes there is a further subdivision of categories introduced by a second decimal.

On the shelf, books are arranged alphabetically by letter categories (P, PN, PS, etc.). Within each of the letter categories, books are arranged in numerical order from 1 to 9999 (PN1, PN86, PN1993, PN1993.5, PN1994, PN6110, etc.)

Library reference sources

After you have searched through the card catalog, you have not yet exhausted the resources of the library. Most libraries have reference sections—separate rooms or areas—containing books that are often consulted as references. Some items may very clearly be reference books: encyclopedias, dictionaries, almanacs, atlases, etc. Other items may not fit as obviously into the category of reference books: anthologies, books of documents, etc. In addition, some valuable reference material may be found not in the reference section but in the general collection.

There are two kinds of library reference sources.

One kind supplies the required information—you look in the book and find what you want to know. The other kind directs you to the required information in another book, magazine, newspaper, etc. Both kinds are needed for most reference projects. Read the introductions to the reference books carefully. Each book organizes material in its own way. Each has its own abbrevations and cross-references.

Indexes to newspapers and periodicals

An index is a guide to direct you to material on a subject or by an author. Using an index involves two processes. The first is finding out whether and where an article has been published. The second process is sometimes more difficult—finding a copy of the required newspaper or magazine. Large libraries may have bound volumes of periodicals and microfilm or microfiche copies of newspapers.

Most magazines have their own yearly indexes. Once a year, they prepare an alphabetical list of the articles that have appeared over that year.

Readers' Guide to Periodical Literature—directs you to articles in the most widely read magazines in the United States. Regular supplements are available to bring you up to date. *Access*—directs you to some periodicals not indexed in *Readers' Guide*. There are also indexes to direct you to more specialized journals in particular fields. A short list of examples includes:

Agricultural Index
Applied Science and Technology Index
Art Index
Business Periodicals Index
Cumulative Book Index
Education Index
Humanities Index
Index to Legal Periodicals
Music Index
Reader's Guide to Periodical Literature
Social Science Index
Ulrich's International Periodical Index (Lists the names of periodicals in many languages. It does not index specific articles.)

Very few newspapers are indexed. It may be possible to find information on world or national events in one of the following newspaper indexes:

Index to the Christian Science Monitor
The New York Times Index
The Times Index, London
The Newspaper Index (indexes a few large American newspapers)

If your library has the material to which the indexes refer, it is probably on microfilm or microfiches.

Local newspapers vary greatly in their manner of filing material about old stories and in their willingness to let people not on staff use the files.

Indexes to material shorter than book length

Short works are difficult to locate. They generally come in anthologies. The anthology title does not necessarily indicate what specific works are contained therein. If you want to find a poem, short story, play, or essay, you may find the relevant anthology or anthologies by using an index.

For poetry

Granger's Index to Poetry
Poems are listed by author, first line, title, and subject.

For short stories

Short Story Index
Short stories are indexed by author, title, and subject. Some periodicals are included, as well as anthologies.

For essays

Essay and General Literature Index
Essays and literary criticism are indexed by author and
   subject.

For plays

Ottemiller's Index to Plays in Collections, 1900–1975
   Indexes plays by author and title.
Play Index (by year)

Bibliographies

Indirectly, you can locate many bibliographies through the card catalog. When you find a book on a subject you are investigating, that book may have a bibliography. No bibliography in a book will be more up-to-date than that book.

> *Bibliography of Bibliographies* Lists many bibliographies.
>
> *Bibliographic Index* Also a bibliography of bibliographies.
>
> *Subject Guide to Books in Print* List of American books still in print. The list is arranged by subject and may prove useful as a means of finding titles of books on a particular subject.
>
> *Cumulative Books Index* Lists English-language books, by subject, author, and title.

There are also many special-subject lists of books. A few examples are:

> *The Reader's Advisor*
> *Sources of Information in the Social Sciences*
> *Harvard Guide to American History*
> *Science and Engineering Reference Sources*

Guides to finding books

It is unreasonable to expect any library to carry all the books on every subject. You may have compiled a good bibliography, but then you may not find the books in your library. What do you do?

1. Find out if your library participates in an interlibrary loan program. If so, there may be a catalog of the books available on loan from another library.

2. Look it up in *Books in Print*. You will find out if it can be purchased by you or by the library.
3. Try *Paperbound Books in Print*. If you have to buy the books yourself, you may find paperbacks more economical.
4. *Guide to U.S. Government Publications* will provide a list of books available from the U.S. Government Printing Office.

Beyond the Library

The good researcher knows enough to go beyond the library for many kinds of research. Here are some other sources of information:

Other kinds of libraries

Company libraries or reference rooms are more likely than a large library to have material on subjects of particular interest to that company's work. If your company does not have at least a reference shelf, it should begin to develop one. At times, you may be able to arrange to use other companies' libraries.

Museum libraries may have highly specialized materials that are helpful. Even a small museum may have a library that is complete in the field of that museum's specialization.

Private libraries may be general or specialized. They may belong to business associations or unions or professional groups. Terms of use differ from one private library to another.

College and university libraries are often for the specific use of faculty and students. Sometimes, however, arrangements can be made by firms or individuals to use the libraries on a regular or temporary basis.

Specialized collections of maps, costumes, recordings, pictures, etc., may be available in your area.

Government and public institutions

Try the offices of the city, town, county, or state government. There are many maps, records, and often special information bulletins available.

Government agencies of all levels have a wealth of information. It is up to you to locate the agency and call or write for the information you need.

Chambers of commerce are often glad to supply material and answer questions about their area. They will often direct you to other people or organizations who can supply what they cannot supply.

The federal government's Government Printing Office publishes a large number of pamphlets and books on a tremendous variety of subjects. You can get their Subject Bibliography price list (describing all the Office's publications) or a price list on a specific subject by writing to:

Superintendent of Documents
Government Printing Office
Washington, DC 20402

The following publications are sources of information about the federal government:

Congressional Record. A daily record of the activities of Congress, including indexes giving the names, subjects, and history of all bills.

Federal Register. A daily record of the activities of executive branch departments and agencies such as the Food and Drug Administration and Internal

Revenue Service, including regulations, policy proposals, and public comments.

Official Congressional Directory. Published by the Government Printing Office, a list of the names and addresses of everyone connected with the federal government, maps of Congressional Districts, and short biographies of members of Congress (published annually).

Official Register of the U.S. Government. A list, by agency, of the name, title, salary, and address of all supervisory and administrative personnel of the federal government (published annually).

Private companies and agencies

Private companies can supply annual reports—a source of a great deal of economic information. Some libraries have collections of annual reports, but you can also obtain them by writing to the companies.

Private companies are often willing to supply other information about the industry or industries at large. Large companies often have pamphlets available about basic industrial techniques or products. Some of the material must be evaluated because the companies are trying to maintain a good public image and may not be presenting opposing views.

Private organizations often exist for the purpose of encouraging or discouraging certain practices. They are willing to supply information presenting their point of view. Again, this material must be carefully evaluated because it is often one-sided.

Private agencies and business organizations may have printed information available. For example, the New York Stock Exchange has a great deal of material on the operations of the stock market. Often, such agencies and organizations will answer questions, as well.

Trade magazines

Most industries have trade magazines that service that industry. Trade magazines have useful articles. They usually put out yearly directories of the companies in that industry, and they may have indexes on the articles published over the year. They may also put out specialized handbooks of interest only to that trade. Most of these trade magazines would not be in a small public library. They may be available on the shelves of businesses in that field. And often back copies can be obtained from the publisher.

Occasionally staff of trade magazines will answer questions or direct you to people who can answer them.

Interviews

Do not ignore the possibility of interviewing people. Some informants may be more reliable than others. You will have to evaluate the information by checking it against what you have learned from other sources.

Guide to Basic Reference Works

Encyclopedias

Encyclopedias provide good background material. They are a fine place to begin research on many topics. Often, an encyclopedia provides a short bibliography as well.

There are two kinds of encyclopedias—general and special purpose. Either kind may be organized alphabetically or by subject.

General encyclopedias

Collier's Encyclopedia
Compton's Encyclopedia and Fact Index
Encyclopaedia Britannica
Encyclopedia Americana
Lincoln Library of Essential Information
New Columbia Encyclopedia—a good one-volume reference work
Random House Encyclopedia (one volume)
World Book Encyclopedia

Special-purpose encyclopedias

When it comes to special-purpose reference books, it can be hard to draw the line between encyclopedias and dictionaries. Both should be consulted (see the next section) if both exist in a special field. Here are some examples of special-purpose encyclopedias:

*Encyclopedia of Computer Science and
    Engineering*
Encyclopedia of Education
The Encyclopedia of Mammals
The Encyclopedia of Philosophy
The Encyclopedia of Sports
*The International Cyclopedia of Music and
    Musicians*
International Encyclopedia of the Social Sciences
*McGraw-Hill Encyclopedia of Science and
    Technology*
*The Oxford Companion to World Sports and
    Games*
Walker's Mammals of the World

Dictionaries and word books

Dictionaries contain information such as definitions, pronunciations, synonyms, and word histories.

General dictionaries
Good general-purpose dictionaries are available with the following titles:

*The American Heritage Dictionary, Second
    College Edition*
The Random House College Dictionary
Webster's New World Dictionary of the American Language
Webster's Ninth New Collegiate Dictionary

Note: Any dictionary may use the name *Webster.*

Word books

For *slang,* you may want to consult a specialized dictionary such as:

> *Dictionary of American Slang* by Harold Wentworth and Stuart Berg Flexner
> *A Dictionary of Slang and Unconventional English* by Eric Partridge

For *pronunciations:*

> *A Pronouncing Dictionary of American English* by John S. Kenyon and Thomas A. Knott

For *synonyms:*

> *The Random House Thesaurus: College Edition*
> *Roget's II: The New Thesaurus*
> *Webster's Collegiate Thesaurus*
> *Webster's New Dictionary of Synonyms*
> *Webster's New World Thesaurus*

For *word division and spelling:*

> *The Legal Word Book, Second Edition*
> *The Medical & Health Sciences Word Book, Second Edition*
> *The Word Book III*

For *word backgrounds and historical usages:*

> *A Dictionary of American English on Historical Principles* by Craigie and Hulbert
>
> *A Dictionary of Americanisms on Historical Principles* by M. M. Mathews
>
> *An Etymological Dictionary of the English Language* by Walter William Skeat
>
> *Morris Dictionary of Word and Phrase Origins* by William Morris and Mary Morris
>
> *Origins* (for etymologies) by Eric Partridge
>
> *The Oxford English Dictionary* (often called the OED)

Also *concordances* to the Bible, to Shakespeare, and to other works will help you find specific uses of the words within the works. A concordance is a book that lists *all* the words used in a particular book and indicates exactly where each word is used each time it is used.

Special-purpose dictionaries

Note that it is often hard to draw the line between encyclopedias and dictionaries when it comes to special-purpose items. A few examples of special-purpose dictionaries are:

> *American Heritage Dictionary of Science*
> *The American Political Dictionary*
> *Black's Law Dictionary*

A Comprehensive Dictionary of Psychological and Psychoanalytic Terms

Concise Chemical and Technical Dictionary

Dictionary of American History

Dictionary of Architectural Science

Dictionary of the Bible

A Dictionary of Classical Antiquities

A Dictionary of Comparative Religion

Dictionary of Education

A Dictionary of the Social Sciences

Dorland's Illustrated Medical Dictionary

The Harvard Dictionary of Music

McGraw-Hill Dictionary of Scientific and Technical terms

The New Grove's Dictionary of Music and Musicians

Stedman's Medical Dictionary

Webster's New World Dictionary of Computer Terms

Webster's Sports Dictionary

English usage

There are many books available on grammar and writing. Among the best are:

The Careful Writer by Theodore M. Bernstein

A Dictionary of Contemporary American Usage by Bergen Evans and Cornelia Evans

A Dictionary of Modern English Usage by H. W. Fowler

The Elements of Style by Strunk and White

Harper Dictionary of Contemporary Usage by William Morris and Mary Morris

Modern American Usage by Wilson Follet

Webster's Dictionary of English Usage

Editing and printing

For information on editing, copy-editing, preparing manuscripts, etc.:

The Chicago Manual of Style from The University of Chicago Press

The New York Times Manual of Style and Usage from Times Books

Style Manual of the United States Government Printing Office

Words into Type from Prentice-Hall

Almanacs and yearbooks

For the most recent facts, figures, and general information, almanacs and yearbooks are excellent.

Almanacs

Information Please Almanac

Statesman's Year-Book

The World Almanac and Book of Facts

Yearbooks

Several encyclopedias put out yearbooks to update the information in the encyclopedia and to add new data. There are also yearbooks put out for many different industries or fields of interest.

Biography books

For brief, condensed facts and dates about people there are many reference books. If you are not sure about the correct biography book to look at, try:

Biography Almanac
Biography and Genealogy Master Index
Biography Index

Some of the more popular biographical reference books are:

Chambers Biographical Dictionary
Current Biography
Dictionary of American Biography
Dictionary of National Biography (for English history)
The International Who's Who (living people)
The McGraw-Hill Encyclopedia of World Biography
Twentieth Century Authors
Webster's Biographical Dictionary
Who's Who (living people)
Who's Who in America

Who's Who in Finance & Industry
Who Was Who in America (dead people)

In addition, there are many specialized *Who's Who* books that are regional, professional, and even ethnic or religious. There are also books of biographies of authors, scientists, etc. For example, *Asimov's Biographical Encyclopedia of Science and Technology.*

Short biographies can also be found in encyclopedias and in dictionaries of specialized fields.

Geography books

There are two basic kinds of geography books: atlases and gazetteers. Atlases may contain maps of the modern world, or of particular historical periods, or of extraterrestrial locations. Gazetteers generally contain facts and figures (population, area, etc.) about places.

Atlases

Goode's World Atlas
Hammond World Atlas
National Geographic Atlas of the World
The New International Atlas
Rand McNally Cosmopolitan World Atlas
The Times Atlas of the World

Some historical atlases are:

Atlas of American History
Atlas of the Classical World

Atlas of World History
Historical Atlas

For nonmap information:

The Columbia Lippincott Gazetteer of the World
Geo-Data: The World Almanac Gazetteer
Political Handbook of the World
The Stateman's Year Book World Gazetteer
Webster's New Geographical Dictionary

Maps

Maps may be obtained from a variety of sources.

The Automobile Association of America makes maps available to members.
National Geographic Magazine prepares both contemporary maps and historical maps.
Rand McNally Co. puts out books of maps and individual maps.
Travel agencies, foreign consulates, chambers of commerce, and other organizations may offer maps.

Business directories

For information about companies, industries, etc.:

Dun & Bradstreet's Million Dollar Directory
Encyclopedia of Business Information Sources, edited by James Woy

Moody's puts out a series of directories on special subjects.

Standard & Poor's Register of Corporations, Directors and Executives

Thomas Register of American Manufacturers— many volumes under headings "Products & Services," "Company Profiles" (with Brand Names Index), "Catalog File."

Many industries put out handbooks. They are often called Red Books, Blue Books, or Year Books. Many are published annually and contain the names and addresses of companies and their main officers. Many trade magazines put out annual directories. Most major companies will provide free copies of their annual reports by written request to the corporate secretary.

Business and secretarial handbooks

For information about office procedures and skills:

Complete Secretary's Handbook by Lillian Doris and Besse May Miller, revised by Mary A. DeVries

The Gregg Reference Manual by William A. Sabin

The Professional Secretary's Handbook from Houghton Mifflin

The Secretary's Handbook by Sarah Augusta Taintor and Kate M. Monro

Standard Handbook for Secretaries by Lois Hutchinson

Webster's New World Secretarial Handbook from Simon & Schuster

Parliamentary procedure

For the rules governing parliamentary procedure:

Barnes & Noble Book of Modern Parliamentary Procedure by Ray E. Keesey

Robert's Rules of Order

Sturgis Standard Code of Parliamentary Procedure by Alice F. Sturgis

Computers and word processors

Books on computers and word processors are appearing on book stores shelves almost as quickly as computers and word processors are appearing in offices and homes throughout the world. Some examples:

The Business Guide to Small Computers by Lawrence Calmus

Computer Dictionary by Charles J. Sippl

Introduction to Word Processing by Hal Glatzer

Small Business Computer Primer by Robert B. McCaleb

Small Business Computing Made Easy: Everything You Need to Know to Get Started With a Computer by Linda Rohrbough

Statistics

Statistics may be found in almanacs, yearbooks, and various other reference books. Some excellent sources are:

Statesman's Year-Book
Statistical Abstract of the United States
Statistical Yearbook United Nations
Statistics Sources

U.S. Bureau of the Census puts out statistics on many subjects.

Document anthologies

If you need to find the text of the Magna Charta or Washington's Farewell Address, look in a book of documents. These go by many names, "documents," "readings," "anthologies," etc. Some examples:

Documents of American History
The World of Mathematics (4 volumes)

Guides to miscellaneous information

Often we need to find out some odd bit of information. There are many books available that provide such information. Among the most useful are:

The Book of Lists
The Dictionary of Cultural Literacy
Famous First Facts by Joseph N. Kane
Guinness Book of World Records
The People's Almanac (three independent
volumes)

Guides to audiovisual material

There are an increasing number of books available that will lead you to filmstrips, records, tapes, and films of various speeds. Ask your librarian to help you locate these.

Books of quotations

Some books offer well-known quotations:

Contemporary Quotations by James B. Simpson
(after 1950)
Dictionary of Quotations by Bergen Evans
Familiar Quotations by John Bartlett
Home Book of Quotations by Burton E.
Stevenson
Hoyt's New Cyclopedia of Practical Quotations
The International Thesaurus of Quotations by
Rhoda T. Tripp
The Oxford Dictionary of Quotations

Appendixes

A   Abbreviations

A 1. ammeter. **2.** Also **a, A. 3.** ampere. **4.** area.

a. 1. acceleration. **2.** adjective. **3.** answer. **4.** Also **A. are** (measurement).

A. 1. alto **2.** America; American.

A.A. Associate in Arts.

AAA 1. American Automobile Association. **2.** American Arbitration Association.

A.B. Bachelor of Arts. (Latin *Artium Baccalaureus*).

abbr., abbrev. abbreviation.

abr. 1. abridge. **2.** abridgment.

ac, AC alternating current.

acad. 1. academic. **2.** academy.

acct. account.

ack. 1. acknowledge. **2.** acknowledgment.

acv actual cash value.

A.D. anno Domini (usually small capitals A.D.).

add. 1. addition. **2.** additional. **3.** address. **4.** addendum.

adj. 1. adjacent. **2.** adjective. **3.** adjourned. **4.** adjunct.

ad loc. to (or at) the place (Latin *ad locum*).

admin. administration.

ADP automatic data processing.

adv. 1. adverb. **2.** adverbial.

advt., adv. advertisement.

A.F., AF 1. air force. **2.** audio frequency.

AFL-CIO, A.F.L.-C.I.O. American Federation of Labor and Congress of Industrial Organizations.

agr. 1. agriculture. **2.** agricultural.

agt. 1. agent. **2.** agreement.

AIDS acquired immune deficiency syndrome.

AK Alaska (with Zip Code).

a.k.a. also known as.

AL Alabama (with Zip Code).

Alta. Alberta.

a.m. Also **A.M.** ante meridiem (usually small capitals A.M.).

Am., Amer. 1. America. **2.** American.

AMA American Medical Association.

amt. amount.

anon. anonymous.

ans. answer.

a/o account of.

appt. 1. appoint. **2.** appointed.

approx. 1. approxi-

mate. **2.** approximately.

Apr. April.

AR 1. Also **A/R.** account receivable. **2.** Arkansas (with Zip Code).

ASAP as soon as possible.

ASCII American Standard Code for Information Exchange.

assoc. 1. associate. **2.** Also **assn.** association.

asst. assistant.

attn. attention.

atty., at., att. attorney.

Aug. August.

av., ave. avenue.

avg., av. average.

AZ Arizona (with Zip Code).

b., B. 1. base. **2.** bay. **3.** book. **4.** born.

B. 1. bachelor. **2.** Baumé scale. **3.** British. **4.** Bible.

B.A. Bachelor of Arts.

bact. bacteria.

bal. balance.

bar. 1. barometer. **2.** barometric. **3.** barrel.

B.B.A. Bachelor of Business Administration.

BBB Better Business Bureau.

B.C. 1. before Christ (usually small capitals B.C.). **2.** British Columbia.

bd. 1. board. **2.** bond. **3.** bookbinding. **4.** bound.

bd. ft. board feet.

bdl. bundle.

B/E. 1. bill of entry. **2.** bill of exchange.

bef. before.

bet. between.

bf, bf., b.f. boldface.

B/F *Accounting.* brought forward.

Bib. 1. Bible. **2.** Biblical.

bibliog. 1. bibliographer. **2.** bibliography.

biog. 1. biographer. **2.** biographical. **3.** biography.

biol. 1. biological. **2.** biologist. **3.** biology.

bk. 1. bank. **2.** book.

bkg. banking.

bkpg. bookkeeping.

bkpt. bankrupt.

bl. 1. barrel. **2.** black. **3.** blue.

B/L bill of lading.

bldg. building.

blk. 1. black. **2.** block. **3.** bulk.

blvd. boulevard.

b.o. 1. box office. **2.** branch office. **3.** buyer's option.

bor. borough.

B/P bills payable.

br. 1. branch. **2.** brief. **3.** bronze. **4.** brother. **5.** brown.

B/R bills receivable.

B.S. 1. Bachelor of

Science. **2.** balance sheet. **3.** bill of sale.

bu. 1. Also **bsh.** bushel. **2.** Also **Bur.** bureau.

bull. bulletin.

bus. business.

bx. box.

c 1. carat. **2.** centi-. **3.** cubic.

C 1. Celsius. **2.** centigrade. **3.** coulomb.

c., C. 1. cape. **2.** cent. **3.** century. **4.** Also **chap.** chapter. **5.** Also **ca** circa. **6.** copy. **7.** copyright.

CA California (with Zip Code).

cal. 1. calendar. **2.** caliber. **3.** calorie.

canc. cancel.

C.B.D. cash before delivery.

cc cubic centimeter.

cc. chapters.

c.c., C.C. carbon copy.

c.d. cash discount.

C.D. 1. civil defense. **2.** certificate of deposit. **3.** compact disc.

CDC Center for Disease Control.

Cdr., Cmdr., Comdr. commander.

CDT, C.D.T. Central Daylight Time.

cent. century.

CEO, C.E.O. chief executive officer.

cert. 1. certificate. **2.** certification. **3.** certified.

cf., cp. compare.

c.f.i., C.F.I. cost, freight, and insurance.

cgs, CGS centimeter-gram-second (system of units).

char. charter.

chg. 1. change. **2.** charge.

CIA Central Intelligence Agency.

cit. 1. citation. **2.** cited. **3.** citizen.

C.J. 1. chief justice. **2.** corpus juris.

ck. check.

cl. 1. class. **2.** classification. **3.** clause. **4.** clearance. **5.** Also **clk.** clerk.

cm. centimeter.

cml. commercial.

C/N credit note.

CO Colorado (with Zip Code).

co. 1. Also **Co.** company. **2.** county.

c.o. 1. Also **c/o** care of. **2.** *Accounting.* carried over. **3.** cash order.

COD, C.O.D. 1. cash on delivery. **2.** collect on delivery.

col. 1. collect. **2.** collected. **3.** collector. **4.** college. **5.** collegiate. **6.** color. **7.** column.

COLA cost of living adjustment.

com. 1. commentary. **2.** common. **3.** commune. **4.** community.

Com. 1. commission. **2.** commissioner.

comm. 1. commission. **2.** commissioner. **3.** commerce. **4.** communication.

comp. 1. companion. **2.** comparative. **3.** complete.

con. 1. *Law.* conclusion. **2.** consolidate. **3.** consolidated.

cons. 1. consignment. **2.** construction. **3.** constitution.

Const. 1. constable. **2.** constitution.

cont. 1. contents. **2.** continue. **3.** continued. **4.** control.

contr. contract.

COO, C.O.O. Chief Operating Officer.

coop. cooperative.

corp. corporation.

COS, c.o.s. cash on shipment.

C.P.A. certified public accountant.

cpd. compound.

CPI consumer price index.

CPR cardiopulmonary resuscitation.

CPU central processing unit.

cr. 1. credit. **2.** creek.

CRT cathode ray tube.

CST, C.S.T. Central Standard Time.

CT Connecticut (with Zip Code).

C.T. Central Time.

ct. 1. Also **c., C.,** cent. **2.** court.

ctf. certificate.

ctn. carton.

ctr. center.

cu. Also **c** cubic.

cur. 1. currency. **2.** current.

c.w.o. 1. cash with order. **2.** chief warrant officer.

cwt. hundredweight.

d. 1. day. **2.** deci-.

d. 1. date. **2.** daughter. **3.** died. **4.** Also **D.** dose.

D. 1. December. **2.** democrat; democratic. **3.** doctor (in academic degrees).

D.A. district attorney.

dB decibel.

d.b.a. doing business as.

dbl. double.

dc, DC direct current.

DC District of Columbia (with Zip Code).

D.D.S. Doctor of Dental Science.

DE Delaware (with Zip Code).

deb. debenture.

dec. 1. deceased. **2.** decrease.

Dec. December.

def. 1. definite. **2.** definition.

deg, deg. degree (thermometric).

del. 1. delegate. **2.** delegation. **3.** delete.

Dem. Democrat.

dep. 1. depart. **2.** departure. **3.** deposit. **4.** deputy.

dept. department.

dft. draft.

dia., diam. diameter.

dict. dictionary.

dif., diff. different.

dim. dimension.

dir. director.

disc. discount.

dist. distance.

div. 1. divided. **2.** division. **3.** dividend. **4.** divorced.

DJIA Dow-Jones Industrial Average.

dlvy. delivery.

dn. down.

DNA deoxyribonucleic acid

do. ditto.

DOA dead on arrival.

dol. dollar.

DOS disk operating system.

doz., dz. dozen.

dr. 1. debit. **2.** debtor.

DST, D.S.T. daylight-saving time.

DTs delirium tremens.

dup. duplicate.

D.V.M. Doctor of Veterinary Medicine.

e. 1. electron. **2.** Also **E, e., E.,** east; eastern.

E Earth.

E. 1. Also **e.,** engineer; engineering. **2.** Also **E** English.

ea. each.

econ. 1. economics. **2.** economist. **3.** economy.

ed. 1. edition. **2.** editor.

462

EDP electronic data processing.

EDT, E.D.T. Eastern Daylight Time.

educ., ed. 1. education. **2.** educational.

EEO equal employment opportunity.

e.g. for example (Latin *exempli gratia*).

elec. 1. electric. **2.** electrical. **3.** electricity.

elev. elevation.

enc., encl. 1. enclosed. **2.** enclosure.

eng., engr. Also **e., E.,** engineer.

EPA Environmental Protection Agency.

ESOP employee stock ownership plan.

esp. especially.

Esq. Esquire (title).

est. 1. established. **2.** *Law.* estate. **3.** estimate.

EST, E.S.T. Eastern Standard Time.

E.T. Eastern Time.

et al. and others (Latin *et alii*).

etc. and so forth (Latin *et cetera*).

Eur. 1. Europe. **2.** European.

ex. 1. example. **2.** Also **exch.** exchange. **3.** Also **exam.** examination. **4.** except. **5.** extra.

exc. excellent.

exec. 1. Also **ex.** executive. **2.** executor.

exp. 1. expenses. **2.**

export. **3.** express. **4.** experiment.

f. 1. Also **f, F., F** female. **2.** Also **F.** folio.

F Fahrenheit.

F.B. freight bill.

FBI, F.B.I. Federal Bureau of Investigation.

FCC Federal Communications Commission.

FDA Food and Drug Administration.

Feb. February.

fed. 1. federal. **2.** federated. **3.** federation.

FHA Federal Housing Administration.

fig. figure.

FL Florida (with Zip Code).

fl oz fluid ounce.

FM, fm frequency modulation.

fn. footnote.

F.O.B., f.o.b. free on board.

fol. 1. folio. **2.** following.

for. foreign.

fpm, f.p.m. feet per minute.

fr. 1. franc. **2.** from. **3.** Also **freq.** frequently.

Fri. Friday.

frt. freight.

ft foot.

FTC Federal Trade Commission.

fut. future.

fwd. forward.

f/x special effects (movies).

FYI for your information.

g 1. gravity. **2.** gram.

GA Georgia (with Zip Code).

gal. gallon.

gd. good.

gds. goods.

gen., genl. general.

geog. 1. geographer. **2.** geographic. **3.** geography.

geol. 1. geologic. **2.** geologist. **3.** geology.

geom. 1. geometric. **2.** geometry.

gloss. glossary.

gm gram.

GNP gross national product.

gov., Gov. governor.

govt., gov. government.

G.P. general practitioner.

gr. 1. grade. **2.** gross. **3.** group.

grad. 1. graduate. **2.** graduated.

gr. wt. gross weight.

GU Guam (with Zip Code).

guar., gtd. guaranteed.

h hour.

h., H. 1. height. **2.** husband.

hdbk. handbook.

hdqrs. headquarters.

hf high frequency.

hf. half.

hgt. height.

HI Hawaii (with Zip Code).

hld. hold.

HMO health maintenance organization.
Hon. 1. Honorable (title). **2.** Also **hon.** honorary.
hor. horizontal.
hosp. hospital.
hp horsepower.
hr hour.
h.s., H.S. high school.
ht height.
HUD (Department of) Housing and Urban Development.
hwy., hgwy. highway.
hyp., hypoth. hypothesis.
Hz hertz.

i. 1. Also **I.** island. **2.** interest.
IA Iowa (with Zip Code).
ib., ibid. in the same place (Latin *ibidem*).
ID Idaho (with Zip Code).
I.D. 1. identification. **2.** intelligence department.
id. the same (Latin *idem*).
i.e. that is (Latin *id est*).
IF, i.f. intermediate frequency.
IL Illinois (with Zip Code).
illus. illustration.
IMF International Monetary Fund.
imp. 1. import. **2.** important.
IN Indiana (with Zip Code).

in. inch.
inc. 1. income. **2.** Also **Inc.** incorporated. **3.** Also **incr.** increase. **4.** incomplete.
ind. 1. independent. **2.** index. **3.** industry.
inf. 1. inferior. **2.** information.
ins. 1. inspector. **2.** insurance.
inst. 1. instant. **2.** institute. **3.** institution. **4.** instrument.
int. 1. interest. **2.** interior. **3.** interval. **4.** international.
intr. *Grammar.* intransitive.
inv. 1. invention. **2.** invoice.
IQ, I.Q. intelligence quotient.
irreg. irregular.
IRS Internal Revenue Service.
is., Is. island.
ISBN International Standard Book Number.
ital. italic.

J joule.
J. 1. journal. **2.** judge. **3.** justice.
J.A. 1. joint account. **2.** judge advocate.
Jan. January.
jct., junc. junction.
J.D. Doctor of Laws (Latin *Jurum Doctor*).
jour. 1. journal. **2.** journalist. **3.** journeyman.

JP, J.P. justice of the peace.
jr., Jr. junior.

k 1. karat. **2.** kilo-.
K 1. kelvin (temperature unit). **2.** Kelvin (temperature scale). **3.** kilobyte.
kc kilocycle.
kg kilogram.
km kilometer.
kn. knot.
KS Kansas (with Zip Code).
kt. karat.
kW kilowatt.
kwh. kilowatt-hour.
KY Kentucky (with Zip Code).

l liter.
l. 1. Also **L.** lake. **2.** left. **3.** length. **4.** line.
LA Louisiana (with Zip Code).
lab. laboratory.
lat. latitude.
Lat. Also **L.** Latin.
lb pound (Latin *libra*).
l.c. lower-case.
L.C. Library of Congress.
L/C letter of credit.
leg., legis. 1. legislation. **2.** legislative. **3.** legislature.
lf 1. *Printing.* lightface. **2.** low frequency.
lg., lge. large.
lib. 1. liberal. **2.** librarian. **3.** library.
liq. liquid.

464

lit. 1. literary. **2.** literature.

LL.B. Bachelor of Laws (Latin *Legum Baccalaureus.*).

LL.D. Doctor of Laws (Latin *Legum Doctor*).

LNG liquefied natural gas.

loc. cit. in the place cited (Latin *loco citato*).

log logarithm.

long. longitude.

L.P.N. licensed practical nurse.

ltd., Ltd. limited.

lv. leave.

m meter.

m. 1. married. **2.** mile. **3.** month.

m., M. 1. male. **2.** medium.

MA Massachusetts (with Zip Code).

M.A. Master of Arts (Latin *Magister Artium*).

man. manual.

Man. Manitoba.

Mar. March.

masc. masculine.

math. 1. mathematical. **2.** mathematician. **3.** mathematics.

max. maximum.

Mb megabyte.

M.B.A. Master of Business Administration.

Mc megacycle.

M.C., m.c. master of ceremonies.

MD Maryland (with Zip Code).

M.D. Doctor of Medicine (Latin *Medicinae Doctor*).

mdse. merchandise.

ME Maine (with Zip Code).

M.E. 1. mechanical engineer. **2.** mechanical engineering. **3.** Middle English.

meas. 1. measurable. **2.** measure.

mech. 1. mechanical. **2.** mechanics. **3.** mechanism.

med. 1. medical. **2.** medieval. **3.** medium.

M.Ed. Master of Education.

mem. 1. member. **2.** memoir. **3.** memorandum. **4.** memorial.

Messrs. 1. Messieurs. **2.** Plural of **Mr.**

mf medium frequency.

mfg. 1. manufacture. **2.** manufactured. **3.** manufacturing.

mfr. 1. manufacture. **2.** manufacturer.

mg milligram.

mgt. management.

MHz megahertz.

MI Michigan (with Zip Code).

mi. 1. mile. **2.** mill (monetary unit).

min. 1. minimum. **2.** minor. **3.** Also **min** minute.

misc. miscellaneous.

mks meter-kilogram-second (system of units).

mkt. market.

mktg. marketing.

ml milliliter.

mm millimeter.

MN 1. magnetic north. **2.** Minnesota (with Zip Code).

MO Missouri (with Zip Code).

mo. month.

m.o., M.O. 1. mail order. **2.** medical officer. **3.** money order.

mod. 1. moderate. **2.** modern.

mol. 1. molecular. **2.** molecule.

mon. monetary.

Mon. Monday.

mpg, m.p.g. miles per gallon.

mph, m.p.h. miles per hour.

Mr. mister.

Mrs. mistress.

ms 1. manuscript. **2.** millisecond.

MS 1. manuscript. **2.** Mississippi (with Zip Code). **3.** multiple sclerosis.

Ms., Ms Title of courtesy for a woman.

MSG monosodium glutamate.

msg. message.

MST, M.S.T. Mountain Standard Time.

MT Montana (with Zip Code).

mt., Mt. 1. mount. **2.** mountain.

m.t., M.T. 1. metric

ton. **2.** Mountain Time.

mtg. 1. meeting. **2.** Also **mtge.** mortgage.

mtn. mountain.

mun. 1. municipal. **2.** municipality.

mus. 1. museum. **2.** music. **3.** musical. **4.** musician.

N Also **n, N., n.** north; northern.

n. 1. net. **2.** noun. **3.** number.

N.A. 1. North America. **2.** not applicable. **3.** not available.

nat. 1. Also **natl.** national. **2.** native. **3.** natural.

naut. nautical.

nav. 1. naval. **2.** navigation.

n.b. note carefully (Latin *nota bene*).

N.B. New Brunswick.

NC 1. North Carolina (with Zip Code). **2.** no charge.

NCO noncommissioned officer.

ND North Dakota (with Zip Code).

NE 1. Nebraska (with Zip Code). **2.** northeast.

N.E. New England.

neg. negative.

Nfld. Newfoundland.

NG, N.G. no good.

NH New Hampshire (with Zip Code).

NJ New Jersey (with Zip Code).

nm, n.m. nautical mile.

NM New Mexico (with Zip Code).

no., No. 1. north. **2.** northern. **3.** number.

nos., Nos. numbers.

Nov. November.

N.P. notary public.

N.S. Nova Scotia.

n.s.f., N.S.F. not sufficient funds.

NV Nevada (with Zip Code).

NW northwest.

n.wt. net weight.

N.W.T. Northwest Territories.

NY New York (with Zip Code).

O O. 1. ocean. **2.** order.

ob. incidentally (Latin *obiter*).

obj. 1. *Grammar.* object; objective. **2.** objection.

obs. 1. obscure. **2.** observation. **3.** Also **Obs.** observatory. **4.** obsolete.

o/c overcharge.

occ. occupation.

Oct. October.

O.D. 1. Doctor of Optometry. **2.** Also **o/d** overdraft. **3.** overdrawn.

OH Ohio (with Zip Code).

OK Oklahoma (with Zip Code).

Ont. Ontario.

op. cit. in the work cited (Latin *opere citato*).

opp. opposite.

opt. 1. optimum. **2.** optional.

OR Oregon (with Zip Code).

org. 1. organic. **2.** organization. **3.** organized.

o.s., o/s out of stock.

oz, oz. ounce.

p. 1. page. **2.** participle. **3.** per. **4.** pint. **5.** population. **6.** Also **P.** president. **7.** past.

PA 1. Pennsylvania (with Zip Code). **2.** public-address system.

P.A. 1. Also **P/A** power of attorney. **2.** press agent. **3.** prosecuting attorney.

Pac. Pacific.

P & L profit and loss.

par. 1. paragraph. **2.** parallel. **3.** parenthesis. **4.** parish.

pat. patent.

payt., pt. payment.

P.B. 1. passbook. **2.** prayer book.

PC personal computer.

p.c. Also **pct.** per cent.

p/c, P/C 1. Also **p.c.** petty cash. **2.** prices current.

pct. per cent.

pd. paid.

p.d., P.D. per diem.

P.E.I. Prince Edward Island.

per. 1. period. **2.** person.

perf. perfect.

pf. preferred.

Pfc, Pfc. private first class.

pg. page.

phar., Phar., pharm., Pharm., 1. pharmaceutical. 2. pharmacist. 3. pharmacy.

phi., philos. 1. philosopher. 2. philosophical. 3. philosophy.

pk. 1. pack. 2. park. 3. peak. 4. Also **pk** peck.

pkg., pkge. package.

pl. 1. Also **Pl.** place. 2. plural.

plf. plaintiff.

pm., prem. premium.

p.m. 1. post mortem. 2. Also **P.M.** postmortem examination. 3. Also **P.M.** post meridiem (usually small capitals P.M.).

P.M. 1. past master. 2. Also **PM** postmaster. 3. prime minister. 4. provost marshal.

P.M.G. postmaster general.

p.n., P/N promissory note.

P.O. 1. Personnel Officer. 2. Also **p.o.** petty officer; post office. 3. postal order.

P.O.E. port of entry.

poet. 1. poetic. 2. poetical. 3. poetry.

pop. 1. popular. 2. population.

pos. 1. position. 2. positive.

poss. 1. possession. 2. possessive. 3. possible. 4. possibly.

POW, P.O.W. prisoner of war.

pp. 1. pages. 2. past participle.

p.p., P.P. 1. parcel post. 2. parish priest. 3. past participle. 4. postpaid.

ppd. 1. postpaid. 2. prepaid.

PR 1. Also **P.R.** public relations. 2. Puerto Rico (with Zip Code).

pr. 1. pair. 2. present. 3. price. 4. printing. 5. pronoun.

Pr. 1. priest. 2. prince.

prec. preceding.

pref. 1. preface. 2. prefatory. 3. preference. 4. preferred. 5. prefix.

prep. 1. preparation. 2. preparatory. 3. prepare. 4. preposition.

pres. 1. present (time). 2. Also **Pres.** president.

prim. 1. primary. 2. primitive.

prin. 1. principal. 2. principle.

prob. 1. probable. 2. probably. 3. problem.

proc. 1. proceedings. 2. process.

prod. 1. produced. 2. product.

prof., Prof. professor.

pron. 1. pronominal. 2. pronoun. 3. pronounced. 4. pronunciation.

prop. 1. proper. 2. properly. 3. property. 4. proposition. 5. proprietary. 6. proprietor.

pro tem., p.t. for the time being; temporarily (Latin *pro tempore*).

prov. province.

P.S. 1. Police Sergeant. 2. Also **p.s.** postscript. 3. public school.

psi, p.s.i. pounds per square inch.

PST, P.S.T. Pacific Standard Time.

pt. 1. part. 2. pint. 3. point. 4. port.

P.T. 1. Pacific Time. 2. physical therapy.

PTA, P.T.A. Parent-Teachers Association.

ptg. printing.

pub. 1. public. 2. publication. 3. published. 4. publisher.

PVC polyvinyl chloride.

pvt. Also **Pvt.** private.

pwr. power.

q. 1. Also **qt** quart. 2. Also **qu., ques.** question.

Q.E.D. which was to be demonstrated (Latin *quod erat demonstrandum*).

qr., q. 1. quarter. **2.** quarterly.

qt. 1. Also **qty.** quantity. **2.** Also **qt.** quart.

quad. 1. quadrangle. **2.** quadrant. **3.** quadrilateral.

Que. Quebec.

quot. quotation.

r, R 1. radius. **2.** *Electricity.* resistance.

r. 1. Also **R.** railroad; railway. **2.** range. **3.** rare. **4.** retired. **5.** Also **R.** right. **6.** Also **R.** river. **7.** Also **R.** road. **8.** rod (unit of length). **9.** Also **R.** rouble.

R. 1. rabbi. **2.** rector. **3.** Republican (party). **4.** royal.

RAM random access memory.

R & D research and development.

R and R rest and recreation.

RD rural delivery.

rd. 1. road. **2.** round.

R.E., RE real estate.

rec. 1. receipt. **2.** recipe. **3.** record. **4.** recording. **5.** recreation.

recd., rec'd. received.

ref. 1. reference. **2.** referred. **3.** refining. **4.** reformation. **5.** reformed. **6.** refunding.

reg. 1. Also **Regt.** regent. **2.** regiment. **3.** region. **4.** Also **regd.** register; registered. **5.** registrar. **6.** registry. **7.** regular. **8.** regularly. **9.** regulation. **10.** regulator.

rel. 1. relating. **2.** released. **3.** religion.

rep. 1. repair. **2.** Also **rpt.** report. **3.** reporter. **4.** Also **Rep.** representative. **5.** -reprint. **6.** Also **Rep.** republic. **7.** repetition.

Rep. Republican (party).

repr. representing.

req. 1. require. **2.** required. **3.** requisition.

res. 1. research. **2.** residence. **3.** resolution.

ret. 1. retired. **2.** return.

rev. 1. revenue. **2.** reverse. **3.** reversed. **4.** review. **5.** reviewed. **6.** revise. **7.** revision. **8.** Also **Rev.** revolution. **9.** revolving.

RF radio frequency.

RFD, R.F.D. rural free delivery.

RI Rhode Island (with Zip Code).

rm. 1. ream. **2.** room.

ROM read only memory.

ROTC Reserve Officers' Training Corps.

rpm, r.p.m. revolutions per minute.

R.R. 1. Also **RR** railroad. **2.** Also **Rt. Rev.** Right Reverend (title). **3.** rural route.

r.s.v.p., R.S.V.P. please reply.

rte. route.

Rx prescription.

s 1. second. **2.** Also **S, s., S.** south; southern. **3.** stere.

s. 1. son. **2.** substantive. **3.** shilling. **4.** singular. **5.** small. **6.** surplus.

S. 1. Saturday. **2.** school. **3.** sea. **4.** September. **5.** Sunday.

S.A. 1. South Africa. **2.** South America.

S.A.S.E. self-addressed stamped envelope.

S.B. Bachelor of Science.

Sask. Saskatchewan.

Sat. Saturday.

SC 1. Security Council (United Nations). **2.** South Carolina (with Zip Code).

sc. 1. scene. **2.** scruple (weight). **3.** namely (Latin *scilicet*).

s.c., sc *Printing.* small capitals.

S.C. Supreme Court.

sch. school.

sci. 1. Also **sc.** science. **2.** scientific.

468

SD South Dakota (with Zip Code).

S.D. special delivery.

SE 1. southeast. 2. southeastern. 3. stock exchange.

SEC Securities and Exchange Commission.

sec. 1. Also **secy.** secretary. 2. sector. 3. second.

sen., Sen. 1. senate. 2. senator. 3. Also **sr.** senior.

Sept. September.

seq. 1. sequel. 2. the following (Latin *sequens*).

ser. 1. serial. 2. series. 3. sermon.

serv. service.

sgd. signed.

sgt. sergeant.

sh. 1. Also **shr.** share (capital stock). 2. sheet. 3. shilling.

shpt. shipment.

shr. share.

shtg. shortage.

sig. 1. signal. 2. signature.

sing. singular.

sm. small.

soc. 1. socialist. 2. society.

so. 1. south. 2. southern.

s.o. 1. seller's option. 2. strikeout.

soln., sol. solution.

SOP standard operating procedure.

soph. sophomore.

SOS 1. international distress signal. 2.

Any call or signal for help.

sp. 1. special. 2. species. 3. spelling. 4. specific.

spec. 1. special. 2. specification.

specs. specifications.

Sr. 1. senior (after surname). 2. sister (religious).

SRO, S.R.O. standing room only.

ST standard time.

st. 1. stanza. 2. state. 3. Also **St.** statute. 4. stet. 5. stitch. 6. stone. 7. Also **St.** street. 8. strophe. 9. start.

St. 1. saint. 2. strait.

sta. 1. station. 2. stationary.

std. standard.

stk. stock.

sub. 1. Also **subs.** subscription. 2. Also **subst.** substitute. 3. suburb. 4. suburban.

subj. 1. subject. 2. subjective. 3. subjunctive.

suf., suff. 1. sufficient. 2. suffix.

Sun. Sunday.

sup. 1. above (Latin *supra*). 2. Also **super.** superior. 3. *Grammar.* Also **superl.** superlative. 4. supplement. 5. supply.

supt., Supt. Also **super.** superintendent.

surg. 1. surgeon. 2. surgery. 3. surgical.

svgs. savings.

SW southwest.

sym. 1. symbol. 2. symphony.

syn. 1. synonymous. 2. synonym. 3. synonymy.

synd. syndicate.

t 1. ton. 2. troy.

T temperature.

t. 1. teaspoon. 2. *Grammar.* tense. 3. Also **T.** time. 4. *Grammar.* transitive. 5. Also **T.** town.

T. 1. tablespoon. 2. Also **ter.** territory. 3. Testament. 4. transit. 5. Tuesday.

T&E travel and entertainment.

t.b. trial balance.

tbs., tbsp. tablespoon.

tech. technical.

technol. 1. technological. 2. technology.

tel. 1. telegram. 2. telegraph. 3. telephone.

temp. 1. in the time of (Latin *tempore*). 2. temperature. 3. temporary.

test. testimony.

Thurs., Th. Thursday.

tkt. ticket.

TM trademark.

TN Tennessee (with Zip Code).

tn. 1. town. 2. train. 3. ton.

tnpk. turnpike.

trans. 1. transaction. **2.** *Grammar,* transitive. **3.** translated. **4.** translation. **5.** translator. **6.** Also **transp.** transportation.

treas. 1. Also **tr.** treasurer. **2.** treasury.

Tues. Tuesday.

TV television.

twp. township.

TX Texas (with Zip Code).

U. 1. university. **2.** Also **u.** upper.

UFO unidentified flying object.

uhf, UHF ultra high frequency.

U.K. United Kingdom.

UL Underwriters' Laboratory.

UN United Nations.

unan. unanimous.

univ. 1. universal. **2.** Also **Univ.** university.

USA, U.S.A. 1. United States Army. **2.** United States of America.

U.S.S.R. Union of Soviet Socialist Republics.

usu. usually.

UT Utah (with Zip Code).

V 1. *Physics.* velocity. **2.** *Electricity.* volt. **3.** volume. **4.** victory.

v. 1. verb. **2.** verse. **3.** version. **4.** Also **vs.** versus. **5.** vide. **6.**

voice. **7.** volume (book). **8.** vowel.

V. 1. Also **v.** vice (in titles). **2.** Also **vil.** village.

VA 1. Also **V.A.** Veterans' Administration. **2.** Virginia (with Zip Code).

var. 1. variable. **2.** variant. **3.** variation. **4.** variety. **5.** various.

VAT value added tax.

VDT visual display terminal.

vel. velocity.

vhf, VHF very high frequency.

VI Virgin Islands (with Zip Code).

VIP *Informal.* very important person.

viz. namely (Latin *videlicet*).

vol. 1. volume. **2.** volunteer.

V.P. Vice President.

vs. versus.

VT Vermont (with Zip Code).

v.v. vice versa.

W 1. *Electricity.* watt. **2.** *Physics.* Also **w** work. **3.** Also **w, w., W.,** west; western.

w. 1. week. **2.** width. **3.** wife. **4.** with. **5.** weight.

W. Wednesday.

WA Washington (with Zip Code).

Wed. Wednesday.

wh. white.

whse., whs. warehouse.

whsle. wholesale.

WI Wisconsin (with Zip Code).

w.i. when issued (financial stock).

wk. 1. weak. **2.** week. **3.** work.

wkly. weekly.

w/o without.

w.o.c. without compensation.

wt. weight.

WV West Virginia (with Zip Code).

WY Wyoming (with Zip Code).

x by.

x, X 1. power of magnification. **2.** unknown.

x. ex.

XL extra large.

Xmas *Informal.* Christmas.

y ordinate.

y. year.

yd yard (measurement).

YMCA Young Men's Christian Assocation.

yr. 1. year. **2.** younger. **3.** your.

Y.T. Yukon Territory.

YWCA Young Women's Christian Association.

Z 1. atomic number. **2.** *Electricity.* impedance.

z. 1. zero. **2.** zone.

zool. 1. zoological. **2.** zoology.

B WEIGHTS AND MEASURES

Length

U.S. Customary Unit	U.S. Equivalents	Metric Equivalents
inch	0.083 foot	2.54 centimeters
foot	1/3 yard. 12 inches	0.3048 meter
yard	3 feet. 36 inches	0.9144 meter
rod	5½ yards. 16½ feet	5.0292 meters
mile (statute, land)	1,760 yards. 5,280 feet	1.609 kilometers
mile (nautical international)	1.151 statute miles	1.852 kilometers

Area

U.S. Customary Unit	U.S. Equivalents	Metric Equivalents
square inch	0.007 square foot	6.4516 square centimeters
square foot	144 square inches	929.030 square centimeters
square yard	1,296 square inches. 9 square feet	0.836 square meter
acre	43,560 square feet. 4,840 square yards	4,047 square meters
square mile	640 acres	2.590 square kilometers

Volume or Capacity

U.S. Customary Unit	U.S. Equivalents	Metric Equivalents
cubic inch	0.00058 cubic foot	16.387 cubic centimeters
cubic foot	1,728 cubic inches	0.028 cubic meter
cubic yard	27 cubic feet	0.765 cubic meter

U.S. Customary Liquid Measure	U.S. Equivalents	Metric Equivalents
fluid ounce	8 fluid drams. 1.804 cubic inches	29.573 milliliters
pint	16 fluid ounces. 28.875 cubic inches	0.473 liter
quart	2 pints. 57.75 cubic inches	0.946 liter
gallon	4 quarts. 231 cubic inches	3.785 liters
barrel	varies from 31 to 42 gallons, established by law or usage	

U.S. Customary Dry Measure	U.S. Equivalents	Metric Equivalents
pint	½ quart. 33.6 cubic inches	0.551 liter
quart	2 pints. 67.2 cubic inches	1.101 liters
peck	8 quarts. 537.605 cubic inches	8.810 liters
bushel	4 pecks. 2,150.42 cubic inches	35.238 liters

British Imperial Liquid and Dry Measure	U.S. Customary Equivalents	Metric Equivalents
fluid ounce	0.961 U.S. fluid ounce. 1.734 cubic inches	28.412 milliliters
pint	1.032 U.S. dry pints. 1.201 U.S. liquid pints. 34.678 cubic inches	568.26 milliliters
quart	1.032 U.S. dry quarts. 1.201 U.S. liquid quarts. 69.354 cubic inches	1.136 liters

	1.201 U.S. gallons. 277.420 cubic inches	4.546 liters
gallon		
peck	554.84 cubic inches	0.009 cubic meter
bushel	1.032 U.S. bushels. 2,219 36 cubic inches	0.036 cubic meter

Weight

U.S. Customary Unit (Avoirdupois)	U.S. Equivalents	Metric Equivalents
grain	0.036 dram. 0.002285 ounce	64.79891 milligrams
dram	27.344 grains. 0.0625 ounce	1.772 grams
ounce	16 drams. 437.5 grains	28.350 grams
pound	16 ounces. 7,000 grains	453.59237 grams
ton (short)	2,000 pounds	0.907 metric ton (1,000 kilograms)
ton (long)	1.12 short tons. 2,240 pounds	1.016 metric tons

Apothecary Weight Unit	U.S. Customary Equivalents	Metric Equivalents
scruple	20 grains	1.296 grams
dram	60 grains	3.888 grams
ounce	480 grains. 1.097 avoirdupois ounces	31.103 grams
pound	5,760 grains. 0.823 avoirdupois pound	373.242 grams

C GUIDE TO THE METRIC SYSTEM

Length

Unit	Number of Meters	Approximate U.S. Equivalent
myriameter	10,000	6.2 miles
kilometer	1,000	0.62 mile
hectometer	100	109.36 yards
dekameter	10	32.81 feet
meter	1	39.37 inches
decimeter	0.1	3.94 inches
centimeter	0.01	0.39 inch
millimeter	0.001	0.04 inch

Area

Unit	Number of Square Meters	Approximate U.S. Equivalent
square kilometer	1,000,000	0.3861 square mile
hectare	10,000	2.47 acres
are	100	119.60 square yards
centare	1	10.76 square feet
square centimeter	0.0001	0.155 square inch

Volume

Unit	Number of Cubic Meters	Approximate U.S. Equivalent
dekastere	10	13.10 cubic yards
stere	1	1.31 cubic yards
decistere	0.10	3.53 cubic feet
cubic centimeter	0.000001	0.061 cubic inch

Capacity

Unit	Number of Cubic Liters	Approximate U.S. Equivalents Dry	Liquid
kiloliter	1,000	1.31 cubic yards	
hectoliter	100	3.53 cubic feet	2.84 bushels

dekaliter	10	0.35 cubic foot	1.14 pecks	2.64 gallons
liter	1	61.02 cubic inches	0.908 quart	1.057 quarts
deciliter	0.10	6.1 cubic inches	0.18 pint	0.21 pint
centiliter	0.01	0.6 cubic inch		0.338 fluidounce
milliliter	0.001	0.06 cubic inch		0.27 fluidram

Mass and Weight

Unit	Number of Grams	Approximate U.S. Equivalent
metric ton	1,000,000	1.1 tons
quintal	100,000	220.46 pounds
kilogram	1,000	2.2046 pounds
hectogram	100	3.527 ounces
dekagram	10	0.353 ounce
gram	1	0.035 ounce
decigram	0.10	1.543 grains
centigram	0.01	0.154 grain
milligram	0.001	0.015 grain

D   METRIC CONVERSION CHART — APPROXIMATIONS

When You Know	Multiply By	To Find
Length		
millimeters	0.04	inches
centimeters	0.4	inches
meters	3.3	feet
meters	1.1	yards
kilometers	0.6	miles
Area		
square centimeters	0.16	square inches
square meters	1.2	square yards
square kilometers	0.4	square miles
hectares (10,000m²)	2.5	acres
Mass and Weight		
grams	0.035	ounce
kilograms	2.2	pounds
tons (1000kg)	1.1	short tons

When You Know	Multiply By	To Find
Volume		
milliliters	0.03	fluid ounces
liters	2.1	pints
liters	1.06	quarts
liters	0.26	gallons
cubic meters	35	cubic feet
cubic meters	1.3	cubic yards
Temperature (exact)		
Celsius temp.	9/5, +32	Fahrenheit temp.
Fahrenheit temp.	−32, 5/9 x remainder	Celsius temp.

When You Know	Multiply By	To Find
Length		
inches	2.5	centimeters
feet	30	centimeters
yards	0.9	meters
miles	1.6	kilometers
Area		
square inches	6.5	square centimeters
square feet	0.09	square meters
square yards	0.8	square meters
square miles	2.6	square kilometers
acres	0.4	hectares
Mass and Weight		
ounces	28	grams
pounds	0.45	kilograms
short tons (2000 lb)	0.9	tons
Volume		
fluid ounces	30	milliliters
pints	0.47	liters
quarts	0.95	liters
gallons	3.8	liters
cubic feet	0.03	cubic meters
cubic yards	0.76	cubic meters

E   SYMBOLS AND SIGNS

The following symbols and signs are among those most commonly used by printers. The designations are also those most commonly used, and do not exhaust the meanings that may be attached to the symbols.

+ plus
− minus
± plus or minus
∓ minus or plus
× multiplied by
÷ divided by
= equal to
≠ or ≠ not equal to
≈ or ≈ nearly equal to
≡ identical with
≢ not identical with
⇔ equivalent
∼ difference
≅ congruent to
> greater than
≯ not greater than
< less than
≮ not less than
≧ or ≥ greater than or equal to
≦ or ≤ less than or equal to
| | absolute value
∪ logical sum or union
∩ logical product or intersection
⊂ is contained in
ε is a member of; permittivity; mean error
: is to; ratio
:: as; proportion
≐ approaches

[ ] brackets
| | braces
° degree
′ minute
″ second
△ increment
ω angular frequency; solid angle
Ω ohm
μΩ microhm
MΩ megohm
Φ magnetic flux
Ψ dielectric flux; electrostatic flux
ρ resistivity
Λ equivalent conductivity
ℛ reluctance
→ direction of flow
⇌ electric current
◯ benzene ring
→ yields
⇌ reversible reaction
↓ precipitate
↑ gas
‰ salinity
⊙ or ☼ sun
● or ● new moon
☽ first quarter
○ or ✪ full moon
☾ last quarter
☿ Mercury

● rain
* snow
⊠ snow on ground
← floating ice crystals
▲ hail
△ sleet
∨ frostwork
⊔ hoarfrost
≡ fog
∞ haze; dust haze
⊤ thunder
< sheet lightning
◐ solar corona
⊕ solar halo
◸ thunderstorm
\ direction
○ or ⊙ or ① annual
⊙⊙ or ② biennial
♃ perennial
♂ or ♂ male
♀ female
□ male (in charts)
○ female (in charts)
℞ take (from Latin *Recipe*)
ĀĀ or Ā or āā of each (doctor's prescription)
℔ pound
℥ ounce
ʒ dram

477

→	approaches limit of
∝	varies as
‖	parallel
⊥	perpendicular
∠	angle
∟	right angle
△	triangle
□	square
▭	rectangle
▱	parallelogram
○	circle
⌒	arc of circle
⊥	equilateral
≜	equiangular
√	radical; root; square root
∛	cube root
∜	fourth root
Σ	sum
! or ∟	factorial product
∞	infinity
∫	integral
ƒ	function
∂ or δ	differential; variation
π	pi
∴	therefore
∵	because
‾	vinculum (above letter)
( )	parentheses

♀	Venus
⊖ or ⊕	Earth
♂	Mars
♃	Jupiter
♄	Saturn
♅	Uranus
♆	Neptune
♇	Pluto
♈	Aries
♉	Taurus
♊	Gemini
♋	Cancer
♌	Leo
♍	Virgo
♎	Libra
♏	Scorpius
♐	Sagittarius
♑	Capricornus
♒	Aquarius
♓	Pisces
☌	conjunction
☍	opposition
△	trine
□	quadrature
✶	sextile
☊	dragon's head, ascending node
☋	dragon's tail, descending node

℈	scruple
℥	fluid ounce
ƒ℈	fluid dram
♍	minim
& or &	and; ampersand
℔	per
#	number
/	virgule; slash; solidus; shilling
©	copyright
%	per cent
℅	care of
℀	account of
@	at
*	asterisk
†	dagger
‡	double dagger
§	section
☞	index
´	acute
`	grave
˜	tilde
^	circumflex
¯	macron
˘	breve
¨	dieresis
¸	cedilla
∧	caret

F   ROMAN NUMERALS

I	1	VII	7
II	2	VIII	8
III	3	IX	9
IV	4	X	10
V	5	XI	11
VI	6	XII	12

XIII	13	L	50
XIV	14	LX	60
XV	15	XC	90
XVI	16	XCIX or IC	99
XVII	17	C	100
XVIII	18	CI	101
XIX	19	CC	200
XX	20	CD	400
XXI	21	D	500
XXIX	29	DC	600
XXX	30	CM	900
XL	40	M	1,000
XLIX or IL	49	MCMXC	1990

G NATIONAL HOLIDAYS

New Year's Day	January 1
Martin Luther King, Jr.'s Birthday	January 15, observed on 3rd Monday in January
Washington's Birthday	February 22, observed on 3rd Monday in February
Memorial Day	May 30, observed on last Monday in May
Independence Day	July 4
Labor Day	1st Monday in September
Columbus Day	October 12, observed on 2nd Monday in October
Veterans Day	November 11
Thanksgiving Day	4th Thursday in November
Christmas Day	December 25

When a holiday falls on Sunday, the following Monday is observed; when on Saturday, the previous Friday (but not by postal employees).

H CURRENCY TABLE

Basic Unit or Subdivision	Country	Basic Unit	Subdivision
afghani	Afghanistan		100 puls
agora	Israel	shekel	100 agorot
at	Laos	kip	100 at
austral	Argentina		100 centavos
avo	Macao	pataca	100 avos
baht	Thailand		100 satang
baiza	Oman	riyal-omani	1000 baiza
balboa	Panama		100 centesimos
ban	Romania	leu	100 bani
birr	Ethiopia		100 cents
bolivar	Venezuela		100 centimos
boliviano	Bolivia		100 centavos
butut	Gambia	dalasi	100 bututs
cedi	Ghana		100 pesewas
cent	Australia	dollar	100 cents
	Bahamas	dollar	100 cents
	Barbados	dollar	100 cents
	Belize	dollar	100 cents
	Brunei	dollar	100 cents
	Canada	dollar	100 cents
	Cayman Islands	dollar	100 cents
	Taiwan	yuan	100 cents
	Dominica	dollar	100 cents
	Ethiopia	birr	100 cents
	Fiji	dollar	100 cents
	Grenada	dollar	100 cents
	Guyana	dollar	100 cents
	Hong Kong	dollar	100 cents
	Kenya	shilling	100 cents
	Liberia	dollar	100 cents
	Malta	pound	100 cents
	Mauritius	rupee	100 cents
	Nauru	dollar	100 cents
	Netherlands	guilder	100 cents
	Netherlands Antilles	guilder	100 cents
	New Zealand	dollar	100 cents
	Saint Lucia	dollar	100 cents
	Saint Vincent and the Grenadines	dollar	100 cents
	Seychelles	rupee	100 cents
	Sierra Leone	leone	100 cents
	Singapore	dollar	100 cents
	Solomon Islands	dollar	100 cents
	Somalia	schilling	100 cents
	South Africa	rand	100 cents
	Sri Lanka	rupee	100 cents
	Surinam	guilder	100 cents

Basic Unit or Subdivision	Country	Basic Unit	Subdivision
	Swaziland	lilangeni	100 cents
		rand	100 cents
	Tanzania	shilling	100 cents
	Trinidad and Tobago	dollar	100 cents
	Uganda	shilling	100 cents
	United States	dollar	100 cents
	Western Samoa	tala	100 cents
	Zimbabwe	dollar	100 cents
centavo	Argentina	austral	100 centavos
	Bolivia	boliviano	100 centavos
	Brazil	cruzado	100 centavos
	Cape Verde	escudo	100 centavos
	Chile	peso	100 centavos
	Colombia	peso	100 centavos
	Cuba	peso	100 centavos
	Dominican Republic	peso	100 centavos
	Ecuador	sucre	100 centavos
	El Salvador	colon	100 centavos
	Guatemala	quetzal	100 centavos
	Guinea-Bissau	peso	100 centavos
	Honduras	lempira	100 centavos
	Mexico	peso	100 centavos
	Nicaragua	cordoba	100 centavos
	Philippines	peso	100 centavos
	Portugal	escudo	100 centavos
centesimo	Italy	lira	100 centesimi
	Panama	balboa	100 centesimos
	San Marino	lira	100 centesimi
	Uruguay	peso	100 centesimos
	Vatican City	lira	100 centesimi
centime	Algeria	dinar	100 centimes
	Andorra	franc	100 centimes
	Belgium	franc	100 centimes
	Benin	franc	100 centimes
	Burkina Fasso	franc	100 centimes
	Burundi	franc	100 centimes
	Cameroon	franc	100 centimes
	Central African Republic	franc	100 centimes
	Chad	franc	100 centimes
	Comoros	franc	100 centimes
	Congo	franc	100 centimes
	Djibouti	franc	100 centimes
	Equatorial Guinea	franc	100 centimes
	France	franc	100 centimes
	Gabon	franc	100 centimes
	Guinea	franc	100 centimes
	Haiti	gourde	100 centimes
	Ivory Coast	franc	100 centimes
	Liechtenstein	franc	100 centimes
	Luxembourg	franc	100 centimes
	Madagascar	franc	100 centimes
	Mali	franc	100 centimes

Basic Unit or Subdivision	Country	Basic Unit	Subdivision
	Monaco	franc	100 centimes
	Morocco	dirham	100 centimes
	Niger	franc	100 centimes
	Rwanda	franc	100 centimes
	Senegal	franc	100 centimes
	Switzerland	franc	100 centimes
	Togo	franc	100 centimes
	Vanuatu	vatu	100 centimes
centimo	Andorra	peseta	100 centimos
	Costa Rica	colon	100 centimos
	Equatorial Guinea	ekpwele	100 centimos
	Paraguay	guarani	100 centimos
	Peru	inti	100 centimos
	São Tomé and Principe	dobra	100 centimos
	Spain	peseta	100 centimos
	Venezuela	bolivar	100 centimos
chetrum	Bhutan	ngultrum	100 chetrums
chon	North Korea	won	100 chon
	South Korea	won	100 chon
colon	Costa Rica		
	El Salvador		100 centavos
cordoba	Nicaragua		100 centavos
crown	Czechoslovakia		100 halers
cruzado	Brazil		100 centavos
dalasi	Gambia		100 bututs
deutsche mark	West Germany		100 pfennigs
dinar	Algeria		100 centimes
	Bahrain		1000 fils
	Iran	rial	100 dinars
	Iraq		1000 fils
	Jordan		1000 fils
	Kuwait		1000 fils
	Libya		1000 dirhams
	Southern Yemen		1000 fils
	Tunisia		1000 milliemes
	Yugoslavia		100 para
dirham	Morocco		100 centimes
	Qatar	riyal	100 dirhams
	United Arab Emirates		100 fils
dobra	São Tomé and Principe		100 centimos
dollar	Australia		100 cents
	Bahamas		100 cents
	Barbados		100 cents
	Brunei		100 cents
	Canada		100 cents
	Cayman Islands		100 cents
	Dominica		100 cents
	Fiji		100 cents
	Grenada		100 cents
	Guyana		100 cents
	Hong Kong		100 cents

Basic Unit or Subdivision	Country	Basic Unit	Subdivision
	Jamaica		100 cents
	Liberia		100 cents
	Nauru		100 cents
	New Zealand		100 cents
	Saint Lucia		100 cents
	Saint Vincent and the Grenadines		100 cents
	Singapore		100 cents
	Solomon Islands		100 cents
	Trinidad and Tobago		100 cents
	United States		100 cents
	Zimbabwe		100 cents
dong	Vietnam		10 hao
drachma	Greece		100 lepta
escudo	Cape Verde		100 centavos
	Portugal		100 centavos
eyrir	Iceland	krona	100 aurar
fils	Bahrain	dinar	1000 fils
	Iraq	dinar	1000 fils
	Jordan	dinar	1000 fils
	Kuwait	dinar	1000 fils
	Southern Yemen	dinar	1000 fils
	United Arab Emirates	dinar	100 fils
	Yemen	riyal	100 fils
fillér	Hungary	forint	100 fillér
forint	Hungary		100 fillér
franc	Andorra		100 centimes
	Belgium		100 centimes
	Benin		100 centimes
	Burkina Fasso		100 centimes
	Burundi		100 centimes
	Cameroon		100 centimes
	Central African Republic		100 centimes
	Chad		100 centimes
	Comoros		100 centimes
	Congo		100 centimes
	Djibouti		100 centimes
	Equatorial Guinea		100 centimes
	France		100 centimes
	Gabon		100 centimes
	Guinea		100 centimes
	Ivory Coast		100 centimes
	Liechtenstein		100 centimes
	Luxembourg		100 centimes
	Madagascar		100 centimes
	Mali		100 centimes
	Monaco		100 centimes
	Niger		100 centimes
	Rwanda		100 centimes
	Senegal		100 centimes
	Switzerland		100 centimes
	Togo		100 centimes

Basic Unit or Subdivision	Country	Basic Unit	Subdivision
gourde	Haiti		100 centimes
groschen	Austria	schilling	100 groschen
grosz	Poland	zloty	100 groszy
guarani	Paraguay		100 centimos
guilder	Netherlands		100 cents
	Netherlands Antilles		100 cents
	Suriname		100 cents
haler	Czechoslovakia	crown	100 halers
hao	Vietnam	dong	10 hao
inti	Peru		100 centimos
jiao	China	renmimbi	10 jiao
khoum	Mauritania	ouguiya	5 khoums
kina	Papua New Guinea		100 toea
kip	Laos		100 at
kobo	Nigeria	naira	100 kobo
kopeck	U.S.S.R.	rouble	100 kopecks
krona	Iceland		100 aurar
	Sweden		100 öre
krone	Norway		100 öre
kroner	Denmark		100 öre
kuru	Turkey	pound	100 kurus
kwacha	Malawi		100 tambala
	Zambia		100 ngwee
kwanza	Angola		100 lwei
kyat	Burma		100 pyas
laree	Maldives	rufiyaa	100 larees
lek	Albania		100 quintar
lempira	Honduras		100 centavos
leone	Sierra Leone		100 cents
lepton	Greece	drachma	100 lepta
leu	Romania		100 bani
lev	Bulgaria		100 stotinki
likuta	Zaire	zaire	100 makuta
lilangeni	Swaziland		100 cents
lira	Italy		100 centesimi
	San Marino		100 centesimi
	Vatican City		100 centesimi
lisente	Lesotho	loti	100 lisente
loti	Lesotho		100 lisente
lwei	Angola	kwanza	100 lwei
mark	East Germany		100 pennigs
markka	Finland		100 penni
mil	Cyprus	pound	1000 mils
millieme	Tunisia	dinar	1000 milliemes
mongo	Mongolia	tugrik	100 mongo
naira	Nigeria		100 kobo
ngultrum	Bhutan		100 chetrums
ngwee	Zambia	kwacha	100 ngwee
öre	Denmark	kroner	100 öre
	Norway	krone	100 öre
	Sweden	krona	100 öre
ouguiya	Mauritania		5 khoums

Basic Unit or Subdivision	Country	Basic Unit	Subdivision
pa'anga	Tonga		100 seniti
paisa	Bangladesh	taka	100 paisas
	India	rupee	100 paise
	Nepal	rupee	100 paisas
	Pakistan	rupee	100 paisas
para	Yugoslavia	dinar	100 para
pataca	Macao		100 avos
penni	Finland	markka	100 penni
penny	Ireland	pound	100 pence
	United Kingdom	pound	100 pence
peseta	Andorra		100 centimos
	Spain		100 centimos
pesewa	Ghana	cedi	100 pesewas
peso			
	Chile		100 centavos
	Colombia		100 centavos
	Cuba		100 centavos
	Dominican Republic		100 centavos
	Guinea-Bissau		100 centavos
	Mexico		100 centavos
	Philippines		100 centavos
	Uruguay		100 centesimos
pfennig	East Germany	mark	100 pfennigs
	West Germany	deutsche mark	100 pfennigs
piaster	Egypt	pound	100 piasters
	Lebanon	pound	100 piasters
	Sudan	pound	100 piasters
	Syria	pound	100 piasters
pound	Cyprus		100 cents
	Egypt		100 piasters
	Ireland		100 pence
	Israel		100 agorot
	Lebanon		100 piasters
	Malta		100 cents
	Sudan		100 piasters
	Syria		100 piasters
	Turkey		100 kurus
	United Kingdom		100 pence
pul	Afghanistan	afghani	100 puls
pya	Burma	kyat	100 pyas
quetzal	Guatemala		100 centavos
quintar	Albania	lek	100 quintar
qurush	Saudi Arabia	riyal	20 qurush
rand	South Africa		100 cents
	Swaziland		100 cents
renminbi	China		10 jiao
rial	Iran		100 dinars
riel	Cambodia		100 sen
riyal	Qatar		100 dirhams
	Saudi Arabia		20 qurush
	Yemen		100 fils

Basic Unit or Subdivision	Country	Basic Unit	Subdivision
riyal-omani	Oman		1000 baiza
rouble	U.S.S.R.		100 kopecks
rufiyaa	Maldives		100 larees
rupee	India		100 paise
	Mauritius		100 cents
	Nepal		100 paisas
	Pakistan		100 paisas
	Seychelles		100 cents
	Sri Lanka		100 cents
rupiah	Indonesia		100 sen
satang	Thailand	baht	100 satang
schilling	Austria		100 groschen
	Somalia		100 cents
sen	Cambodia	riel	100 sen
	Indonesia	rupiah	100 sen
	Japan	yen	100 sen
	Malaysia	ringgit	100 sen
sene	Western Samoa	tala	100 sene
seniti	Tonga	pa'anga	100 seniti
shekel	Israel		100 agorot
shilling	Kenya		100 cents
	Tanzania		100 cents
	Uganda		100 cents
sol	Peru		100 centavos
stotinki	Bulgaria	lev	100 stotinki
sucre	Ecuador		100 centavos
syli	Guinea		100 cory
taka	Bangladesh		100 paise
tala	Western Samoa		100 sene
tambala	Malawi	kwacha	100 tambala
toea	Papua New Guinea	kina	100 toea
tugrik	Mongolia		100 mongo
vatu	Vanatu		100 centimes
won	North Korea		100 chon
	South Korea		100 chon
yen	Japan		100 sen
yuan	Taiwan		100 cents
zaire	Zaire		100 makuta
zloty	Poland		100 groszy

Index

Alphabetical Key For Quick Reference